EXPLICIT ENGLISH TEACHING

EXPLICIT ENGLISH TEACHING

TOM NEEDHAM

SAGE Publications Ltd
1 Oliver's Yard
55 City Road
London EC1Y 1SP

SAGE Publications Inc.
2455 Teller Road
Thousand Oaks, California 91320

SAGE Publications India Pvt Ltd
B 1/I 1 Mohan Cooperative Industrial Area
Mathura Road
New Delhi 110 044

SAGE Publications Asia-Pacific Pte Ltd
3 Church Street
#10-04 Samsung Hub
Singapore 049483

Library of Congress Control Number: 2022943272

British Library Cataloguing in Publication data

A catalogue record for this book is available from the British Library

Editor: James Clark
Editorial assistant: Diana Alves
Production editor: Sarah Cooke
Marketing manager: Dilhara Attygalle
Cover design: Wendy Scott
Typeset by: TNQ Technologies
Printed in the UK

ISBN 978-1-5297-4167-4
ISBN 978-1-5297-4168-1 (pbk)

At SAGE we take sustainability seriously. Most of our products are printed in the UK using responsibly sourced papers and boards. When we print overseas we ensure sustainable papers are used as measured by the PREPS grading system. We undertake an annual audit to monitor our sustainability.

TABLE OF CONTENTS

ABOUT THE AUTHOR

Tom has been teaching for over fifteen years. He currently teaches English in South London. He has previously taught English in International Schools in Malaysia and Nigeria; EFL in Bangkok and Harrogate, as well as Sociology, Media Studies and all the Humanities in Croydon.

For Vikki, Ruby and Joe.

1

WHAT IS LEARNING?

This chapter will explore

- Two useful definitions of learning
- A model of cognition that teachers can use
- Transfer and the flexibility of knowledge
- Common misconceptions about learning
- Learning as a cognitive process

INTRODUCTION

The aim of this book is to help teachers make evidence informed decisions about teaching English. Teachers want their students to learn as much as possible, and in this first chapter, we will explore what learning means as an outcome as well as a process.

DEFINING LEARNING IS DIFFICULT

Defining learning in a general sense is difficult, and as a result, many psychology textbooks deliberately avoid doing so (Barron et al., 2015). Because learning is such a broad concept, proposed definitions often strain or break under the weight of examples that they are supposed to describe and it is often easy to come up with an instance of learning that is not covered by a general definition (Willingham, 2017a). Those definitions that succeed in being inclusive often become so generalised and vague as to be effectively meaningless. Instead of a general overarching definition, we often see definitions that exist in relation to specific theories, disciplines or goals (Willingham, 2017a). In a recent survey (Barron et al., 2015) of different disciplines where learning is of interest, including psychology, cognitive psychology, neuroscience and behavioural ecology, over 50 different definitions are listed, each tailored to their respective field of study.

Even within one domain – in our case education or more specifically classroom teaching – many would argue that the complexity and breadth of the concept means that attempting to define it is a futile pursuit, a mere language game or academic distraction that will result in nothing of practical use for teachers or students. However, a definition of learning can be useful for teachers if it helps them to make decisions and choices that result in desirable outcomes or goals. But this is where we run into another problem. Much of the debate and argument that surrounds education is borne from the fact that people cannot agree upon the goals of education: schools strive to achieve multiple, sometimes conflicting goals, and different contexts value some more than others. Are exam results the most important thing? Is student happiness the main goal? Is socialisation of paramount importance? What about developing background knowledge? Is it better knowing a lot about a little or a little about a lot? Can we teach transferable skills? What about character education? These are just some of the questions that people disagree about and while this continual debate can be seen as a further hindrance to any attempt to define learning, it is also one of the reasons why working in education is so interesting.

So, if a definition is useful, if it helps teachers to achieve desirable outcomes, then we need to define those outcomes. This book – and the definitions of learning that I will use – is primarily focused upon these goals:

1. Increasing and developing student knowledge and skills
2. Achieving success in examinations and assessments

LEARNING IS A CHANGE IN LONG-TERM MEMORY

The first definition of learning that I will use is taken from *Why Minimal Guidance During Instruction Does Not Work: An Analysis of the Failure of Constructivist, Discovery, Problem-Based, Experiential, and Inquiry-Based Teaching* by Kirchner, Sweller and Clark:

> Learning is 'a change in long-term memory'.

Although this definition has become well-known recently – even being adopted by Ofsted, England's schools inspectorate – I think it is important to analyse why it is useful for teachers. It is certainly not uncontroversial and has been critiqued for a number of reasons. Some claim that it needs to specify the intended or required durability of what is being learned (Willingham, 2017a); others would prefer that it included the ability to 'transfer' learning to new situations. While both of these amendments have merit, Kirschner et al.'s (2006) definition is useful to teachers because of its succinct nature.

A MODEL OF COGNITION

Defining learning as 'a change in long-term memory' makes most sense when placed in the context of a model.

Figure 1.1 shows a diagram of Willingham's simple memory model made by Oliver Caviglioli. The model's strength is its simplicity.

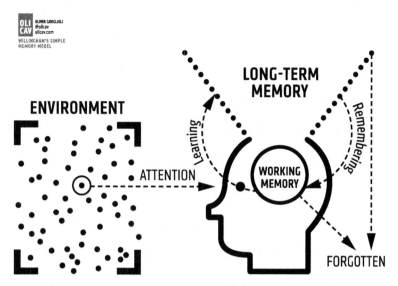

Figure 1.1 Simple memory model

Source: Oliver Caviglioli.

Teachers should be given a simple and concise model of cognition that focuses on empirical generalisations, observations that are sufficiently reliable across individuals and contexts and that seem to capture an important part of the domain (Willingham, 2017b). Some examples of empirical generalisations include observations such as 'practice is crucial to gaining expertise' and 'probing memory improves retention'.

An empirical generalisation, if it is to be of some use to a teacher, has to be directly useful and relevant to classroom practice. As an example, one empirical generalisation is that people can identify 20 or so stimuli in 50 milliseconds but this information is forgotten rapidly in 2 seconds or so (Willingham, 2017b). While this is a reliable finding, one that is included in many cognition textbooks, it is of no real use to teachers: no teacher gives students such a short timeframe to identify material.

Some generalisations are associated with small effects, for example the link between memory and emotional state and that 'memories encoded when one is happy are easier to later retrieve if one feels happy rather than sad'. While there is a link between memory and affective state, the effect is too small to be worthy of teachers' attention (Willingham, 2017b). It goes without saying that this in no way means that we should ignore student happiness.

Teachers don't need an introduction to the broad intellectual trends in the discipline; instead, they need a practical model of cognition that is easy to understand. A model of cognition for teachers will be different to a model for psychologists (Willingham, 2017b).

Willingham (2017b) describes his model of cognition as a 'modal model' because it contains the most frequently occurring aspects from other models, namely, the sensory register, working memory and long-term memory. A useful model should be composed of the shared features of competing models. To an academic, these features may be obvious; to a teacher they are helpful.

While academics may criticise the imprecise usage of simplified, 'folk psychological terms' like referring to 'mental space', Willingham (2017b) points out that this simplification is the strength of the model and the factor that makes it useful for classroom practitioners.

This strength also applies to Kirschner et al.'s (2006) definition that learning 'is a change in long-term memory'. This succinct definition encourages teachers to concentrate on the vital role of memory and retention in learning and, when success is often judged via closed books exams, this can be no bad thing.

But learning isn't as simple as this, is it? If we solely define learning as 'a change in long-term memory', don't we ignore the fact that learning is both a process and an outcome, a verb and a noun? The process of learning itself is clearly far more than mere memorisation and, before we look at a second definition of learning that explicitly recognises this, we need to briefly outline and define two important and connected ideas:

1. **Transfer**

   When we think of learning, we almost always think of it as being more than mere memorisation: the goal of education is often the application of knowledge and skills. Transfer is the ability to apply things that have been learnt in one context to another context. When we teach students in class, we want them to be able to transfer and apply what they have learnt to subsequent lessons, assessments and even different texts or units. Transfer is often seen as a continuum that ranges from near transfer to far transfer, and this continuum represents the level of similarity between the two contexts. If your students had just learnt the word 'domineering' and can successfully answer a question about a character's domineering nature, then their ability to answer a differently worded question on the same topic would be seen as near transfer. If they could then use the word 'domineering' when exploring a different text, then this may be seen as 'far' transfer.

2. **Inflexible to flexible knowledge**

   When you begin learning something, your knowledge is inflexible (Willingham, 2002) and restricted to the context in which you learnt it. If you were teaching the word 'tyrant' to a class for the first time, then their understanding of what it means will be restricted to the examples that you give. If you have taught the word 'tyrant' in conjunction with Animal Farm, then student recall and understanding may be limited to a specific part of that text: students will only be able to recall the word by referring to a character from the novella. At this early stage, it is unlikely that they will be able to transfer this new knowledge to another context. Perhaps they can give a basic definition and refer to the actions of Napoleon but, in the absence of further instruction, their knowledge of the word 'tyrant' will be limited, narrow and inflexible. At this stage, they may not recognise that a character from another book is a 'tyrant'.

The ability to transfer is directly connected to the flexibility of knowledge. If a student can successfully transfer and apply what they have learnt to new contexts, then their knowledge can be said to be flexible. If they cannot, then their knowledge is inflexible.

Let's have a look at an example that demonstrates the relationship between these two ideas:

Imagine you are teaching a unit on Macbeth and in one lesson you teach students the concept of 'hubris'. The lesson is focused on Macbeth's soliloquy in Act 1 scene 7 and his assertion that he has 'only Vaulting ambition, which o'erleaps itself' as a reason to commit the 'horrid deed' of regicide. Initially, students will learn the concept of 'hubris' in conjunction with the original context in which it is taught: they will be able to recognise that 'Vaulting ambition' is an example of his burgeoning hubris. If we ask 'how do you know that Macbeth is hubristic', a student will be able to answer 'because of his vaulting ambition'. This response is shallow and restricted to the example and cues that the teacher has given: the student is making the link between 'hubris' and one line of Macbeth's soliloquy – the student's knowledge here is inflexible and clearly not evidence of a comprehensive understanding of hubris. Unless there is further instruction aimed at deepening and broadening their knowledge of the concept, it is possible that a student would be unable to even answer a differently worded question about hubris. If a teacher asks 'why does Macbeth kill Duncan?', then a student may not see that this is also asking about hubris. If so, the student has failed to transfer their learning because their knowledge is too inflexible.

Although inflexible knowledge is almost always the start point in a sequence of learning, the goal is almost always for students to gain deep and flexible knowledge so that they can transfer and apply it to the widest possible range of contexts and situations. While a student's knowledge of hubris will be initially limited to one specific line of one specific scene in Macbeth, this is clearly not the end goal of our instruction: we want them to be able to recognise and discuss hubris across the play, in other texts and maybe even other domains of knowledge.

Chapters 2 and 3 will explore how teachers can help their students develop flexible knowledge so that it can be transferred to new contexts.

This chapter began by defining learning as 'a change in long-term memory', a succinct definition that, when placed in the context of a simple model of cognition, provides a useful focus for teachers. While the strength of this definition is its brevity, some would see this as its weakness as it fails to delineate either the process of learning or the importance of transfer, the process where a student can apply what they have learnt to a new context.

Here is a second definition that focuses more on the process of learning as well as referring to transfer:

> Learning is when students 'actively make sense of the material so they can build meaningful learning activities to transfer what they have learned to solving new problems'. (Fiorella and Mayer, 2015, p. vii)

This definition is far more detailed than the proposition that 'learning is a change in long-term memory' and the additional requirement of transfer means that many would reject it as being too exacting. As an example, if transfer is a necessary condition of learning, then this would imply that memorising your social security number is not an example of learning (Willingham, 2017a).

If transfer and flexible understanding are important aspects of learning, why is 'a change in long-term memory' still a useful definition of learning? Firstly, it foregrounds the role of memory in learning and although retention is not the totality of either the process or goal of learning, if you cannot remember what you have been taught, then it is difficult to say that you have learnt. Yes, you can say that you learnt something – as in you engaged in a process of learning in the past or that you used to know something – but you can't say that you have learnt it in the sense that you remember and understand it now. Secondly, its breadth allows it to encompass the entire continuum from inflexible to flexible knowledge. Both ends of this continuum have important roles to play in learning, and, while 'flexible knowledge' is the end goal of almost all instructional sequences, 'inflexible knowledge' almost always forms the foundations of understanding. If a definition of learning effectively excludes 'inflexible knowledge' by adding the additional requirement of transfer, then this may have adverse effects: teachers may come to believe that inflexible learning is undesirable or ineffective when it may form an important first step in learning; equally, teachers might focus entirely on writing complete essays in the belief that the best way to improve this ability is to practice writing essays when, counterintuitively, it may be more effective to begin by engaging in restrictive practice activities and building student background knowledge which will initially be inflexible. Under the broad definition of learning as being 'a change in long-term memory', both the rote memorisation of your social security number (inflexible knowledge) and the ability to successfully write a response to an unseen text (flexible knowledge) would be defined as learning.

Let's return to the second definition that learning is when students 'actively make sense of the material so they can build meaningful learning activities to transfer what they have learned to solving new problems' (Fiorella and Mayer, 2015, p. vii).

This definition of learning seems aimed at the end goal of most instructional sequences: flexible knowledge and understanding that allows students to apply what they have learnt. This seems entirely uncontroversial: we want students to be able to flexibly apply their knowledge. When we first learn a concept, our understanding is shallow, especially if it is a concept unrelated to our existing background knowledge. As we begin to make sense of what we have learned, we make connections between the newly learnt concept and our existing knowledge.

As we shall see in Chapter 8, defining a concept is often made that much easier when we use non-examples to help us both rule out misconceptions and, most importantly, set the boundaries of the definition; as a result, here are some common misconceptions about learning.

COMMON MISCONCEPTIONS ABOUT LEARNING

LEARNING WORKS BY ENGAGING IN HANDS-ON ACTIVITY, SO IT IS BETTER FOR YOU TO LEARN BY DOING RATHER THAN BY BEING TOLD

This conception of learning can be seen as being overly concerned with behavioural activity and the nature of the learning tasks that students attempt. It fails to focus 'enough on cognitive activity' (Fiorella and Mayer, 2015, p. 3) as students could be busily engaged in an activity without purposively thinking about the content in a way that helps them make sense of it, a position that is directly analogous to the idea that 'learning happens when you think hard' (Coe, 2013). When teachers focus on the activity rather than what students are thinking about, this often results in classrooms that seem busy and purposive but lack any real cognitive processing.

This line of thinking often involves enquiry- and discovery-based approaches where students are encouraged to engage in authentic, real-world tasks that induce them to behave like experts. In science classes, this can lead classrooms to focus on conducting experiments and testing hypotheses – in other words 'doing science' – as these are the kind of things you would expect scientists to spend their time doing. In an English class, this conception of learning can result in teachers who believe that students should not be told about the common interpretations of a classical text; instead, through a process of minimally guided enquiry, students are expected to generate their own as this is the kind of activity that experts might engage in. Equally, it may result in the mistaken belief that if students are to improve their writing, they should do lots of unguided, extended and original writing as this is what expert writers do. As we shall see in later chapters, expecting novice students to behave like mini-experts and generate knowledge themselves is almost certainly not an optimal instructional approach: the behaviours and methods of professional writers or even students who operate at a more expert level are qualitatively different to those of novices and beginners. Students will not learn science efficiently by pretending to be a junior scientist (Ausubel, 1964), nor will they improve their writing by pretending to be a professional writer.

Instead of focusing on real-world tasks or creating busy activities, a good piece of advice when planning lessons is to always think about what the students will be thinking about. Activities or tasks should be chosen so students can spend as much time as possible thinking as deeply as possible about the content. If seen through the lens of Cognitive Load Theory (which we will explore in Chapter 4), tasks should be easy to explain to students with no irrelevant procedures or activities that can either cause confusion or distract students from thinking about the content that they need to 'actively make sense of'.

LEARNING WORKS BY BUILDING ASSOCIATION, SO YOU SHOULD PRACTICE GIVING THE RIGHT RESPONSE OVER AND OVER

While making associations and links between concepts is clearly a part of the process of learning, using this conception as an overall definition is too prohibitive to as it only really applies to situations where students are expected to give the right response for a given stimulus. This conception is not wrong, it is just too limited. Although there are many instances of learning that are described by associative learning (the social security example mentioned above fits this well), if this conception were to be a catch all definition, it would fail to describe what is the end goal of most instructional sequences: generalised, flexible understanding that can be transferred to similar contexts.

LEARNING IS A SOCIAL ACTIVITY, SO IT IS BETTER FOR YOU TO LEARN WITH OTHERS IN A GROUP THAN TO LEARN ALONE

Schools are social places, and the default setting is usually whole class teaching. Although students can learn in groups, the actual process of learning should primarily be seen as a cognitive activity rather than a social one (Fiorella and Mayer, 2015, p. 4). If we conceive of learning as primarily a social activity, then teachers may focus upon this and see classroom activities that are social, collaborative or group based as being superior methods of learning. While group work can be an effective method, particularly at the latter stages of instruction when students have built up the necessary knowledge base in order to discuss and collaborate meaningfully (Bennett, 2015), it is often very difficult to manage and execute successfully, requiring the creation of both group goals and individual accountability (Slavin, 2010). Not only that but also the potential for social loafing and off-task behaviour makes this approach even more difficult to manage.

LEARNING WORKS BY ADDING INFORMATION TO YOUR MEMORY, SO YOU SHOULD WORK HARD TO FIND AND MEMORISE NEW INFORMATION

Unlike computers, we do not simply and reliably add information that we encounter to our memories (Fiorella and Mayer, 2015, p. 4). Because of this, we need to adopt proven strategies like distributed practice and the testing effect in order to aid us with encoding and retaining information in our long-term memories. While a computer reliably stores information without error as soon as it is asked to, our messy and fallible cognitive processes require the adoption of deliberate and specific learning strategies if we are to retain information. As we shall see in Chapter 4, Cognitive Load Theory highlights the absolute importance of background knowledge, making the important point that 'novices use thinking skills, experts use knowledge' when attempting problems. Background knowledge also has a huge role in reading comprehension (Hirsch, 2003). Memorising or automatising information can give a huge advantage to students. Time tables are good examples here: even simple algebraic problems are made impossible if students do not have reliable and rapid recall of multiplication facts. Learning is clearly more than mere memorisation though. Students need to make sense of what they are learning by making connections, applying what they have learnt and practising.

Table 1.1 summarises the advantages and disadvantages of the two definitions of learning that this chapter has discussed:

Table 1.1   Advantages and disadvantages of the two definitions of learning

Definition of learning	Advantages	Disadvantages
'Learning is a change in long-term memory' (Kirschner et al.)	1. Encourages teachers to focus on memory and retention 2. Encompasses continuum from inflexible to flexible knowledge	1. Does not explicitly mention transfer 2. Reductive nature is seen by some as a problem 3. Focus on memory may cause people to lose focus on understanding
'Learning is actively making sense of the material so they can build meaningful learning activities to transfer what they have learned to solving new problems' (Fiorella and Mayer)	1. Inclusion of transfer encourages teachers to aim for flexible, generalised understanding 2. Focus on process of sense making could encourage meaningful learning	1. Inclusion of transfer may cause teachers to ignore development of background knowledge and focus on solving new problems 2. Does not explicitly mention memory 3. Complexity may be a problem here.

THE PROCESS OF LEARNING

If learning necessarily involves memory but is not solely concerned with memorisation, then what else is involved in the process of learning? We want students to experience a 'change in long-term memory' but how does this change happen? Even if learning materials are clear, logically sequenced and contain powerful and interesting content, then this in itself is no guarantee at all that students will learn the information: for this to happen, they need to engage in a process of sense making.

Asking a student to read a text will not necessarily result in learning: it is how they process the content that matters. Let's take reading a book as an example: text is often the most efficient way of presenting complex, abstract information and a school that asks students to read frequently and widely is clearly doing the right thing. However, reading in order to learn is qualitatively different from reading for pleasure. When we read for pleasure, reading is about escapism, joy, inspiration and imagination and while we may learn much from the experience, often learning is not the primary goal of the activity. For learning to happen, students need to engage in three stages of cognitive processing (Fiorella and Mayer, 2015, p. 7):

- **Stage 1:** *Selecting* **relevant information to attend to**
- **Stage 2:** *Organising* **the material into a coherent cognitive structure in working memory**
- **Stage 3:** *Integrating* **it with relevant prior knowledge activated from long-term memory**

All three stages of cognitive processing are essential to learning and the absence of a particular stage will almost certainly preclude engagement with another. At one level, the stages can be seen as hierarchical as each depends upon the other in a sequence: the process of learning may begin with 'selecting' and proceed towards 'integrating' the new content with prior knowledge in long-term memory.

However, this does not mean that the three stages occur in a strict, fixed sequence as each process will inevitably influence another. For example, your prior knowledge – a concept mentioned in the 'integrating' stage – will directly influence what you pay attention to when dealing with new information, thereby having an influence over the 'selecting' stage. If, as an expert, you are reading an extract from *Othello*, you are far more likely to notice and select the salient information than someone who is new to the play.

Let's look at each stage in turn.

STAGE 1: SELECTING RELEVANT INFORMATION TO ATTEND TO

Ensuring that students pay attention to what is being taught is a fundamental aspect of teaching and learning: if students don't pay attention, then no learning will happen at all.

As Samuel Johnson pointed out: 'The true art of memory is the art of attention. If the mind is employed on the past or the future, the book will be held before the eyes in vain.'

The idea of attention is wide ranging. At one level, it is used to refer to general motivation and behaviour and whether a student is engaging – in a general sense – with the lesson. At another, it refers to the precise interaction between teacher, content and learner and whether the learner is focusing on the exact things that the teacher intends.

WHAT HAPPENS IF STUDENTS FAIL TO 'SELECT' THE RELEVANT INFORMATION?

If students fail to 'select' the relevant information, then this will effectively preclude them from engaging in the second two stages of cognitive processing: you cannot organise information into a coherent cognitive structure in working memory or integrate it with prior knowledge if you haven't attended to and selected the relevant information in the first place.

If students select the wrong information and use this information within a sense making process, then this will potentially be even worse: unlearning or unpicking misconceptions will often take far longer than learning things for the first time.

WHAT CAN WE DO TO ENSURE THAT STUDENTS SELECT THE RELEVANT INFORMATION?

If we accept that the first stage of learning is crucial and that a failure to select the correct information will hinder or completely prevent learning from happening, then teachers need to ensure that all students-not just high attainers-are able to do so. In Chapters 6, 7 and 8, we will explore explicit and Direct Instruction, frameworks that can help ensure that students are more likely to select the relevant information.

Whether or not a student succeeds in selecting the relevant information will partly depend upon their prior knowledge and students with less prior knowledge will benefit from a more directed and scaffolded approach to their more knowledgeable peers.

Let's look at an example:

Imagine you are reading a two page non-fiction article about nostalgia as preparation for reading the poem *Émigrée* by Carol Rumens. Each student has a copy of the article, the teacher has a visualiser and projector and everyone follow when someone is reading. At the end of the article, there are two text-dependent questions (Lemov et al., 2016, p. 71) that you want students to answer:

a. From the first page, list five psychological benefits of nostalgia
b. From the second page, explain the effects of nostalgia. Your answer should contain at least three effects

Assuming that motivation and behaviour are good and that your class contains students with sufficient prior knowledge, you could merely ask them to read it in silence and then answer the questions, safe in the knowledge that the breadth of their vocabulary and reading proficiency will mean that they will (hopefully) select the information required to answer the questions.

With a class of students who might struggle, you could do something like this:

1. Read the whole text out loud to them, adding annotations (all students do the same on their copy) to explain vocabulary and asking lots of questions to check for understanding.
2. Read the text again, stopping just past where the first psychological benefit can be found.
3. Ask a student to read the question: 'From the first page, list five psychological benefits of nostalgia.'
4. Check that everyone understands the question: add explanatory annotations to 'psychology/benefit/nostalgia.'
5. Put red brackets around the section where the first benefit can be found.
6. Ask all students to reread the bracketed section and underline the benefit.
7. Ask a student for feedback and underline your text under the visualiser.
8. Ask lots of questions about the answer and give further annotations and elaborations about what is being underlined.
9. Ask all students to check that they have the same underlined answer and annotations as you.
10. Repeat steps 2–9 for the next benefit.

By following this step-by-step approach, it is far more likely that all students will 'select' the relevant information than if you had adopted the same approach as the class with higher prior knowledge.

Successfully 'selecting' information is also dependent on being able to discriminate between what is important from what is not (Fiorella and Mayer, 2015, p. 13). When learning a new concept, a student needs to understand its breadth and boundaries in order to fully understand it and this can also be achieved through the careful sequencing and manipulation of examples and non-examples, an approach we will explore in Chapter 8.

The intention of both the step-by-step approach and the manipulation of examples is to explicitly teach students what they need to do in order to successfully select information. Once this has been taught, the instructional support should be faded so that students eventually have to determine what is important and what is not without assistance.

WHAT HAPPENS IF STUDENTS FAIL TO 'ORGANISE THE MATERIAL INTO A COHERENT COGNITIVE STRUCTURE IN WORKING MEMORY'?

If students fail to organise the material in their working memory, then they will be unable to make any sense of it as they will quickly become confused or give up. When this happens, the incoming information will not be processed properly, effectively preventing it from being integrated with the relevant prior knowledge activated from long-term memory.

As teachers, we often forget what it is like to be confused by complex content but being overwhelmed by too much information is a common experience for many students.

Here is an example of something confusing, try reading it:

> In mathematical terms, Derrida's observation relates to the invariance of the Einstein field equation under nonlinear space-time diffeomorphisms (self-mappings of the space-time manifold which are infinitely differentiable but not necessarily analytic). The key point is that this invariance group "acts transitively": this means that any space-time point, if it exists at all, can be transformed into any other. In this way the infinite-dimensional invariance group erodes the distinction between observer and observed; the Pi of Euclid and the G of Newton, formerly thought to be constant and universal, are now perceived in their ineluctable historicity; and the putative observer becomes fatally de-centered, disconnected from any epistemic link to a space-time point that can no longer be defined by geometry alone. (Sokal, 1996)

When reading this, you probably became confused very quickly, perhaps even before the end of the first sentence as there are multiple concepts that are opaque and abstruse. If you did become confused, it was because you could not retrieve these concepts from long-term memory, meaning that you quickly reached the limits of your working memory and became cognitively overloaded.

WHAT CAN WE DO TO ENSURE THAT STUDENTS ORGANISE THE MATERIAL?

Effective teachers will take a number of steps to ensure that students are not overwhelmed by new material. Content should be broken down into manageable chunks and introduced at a rate that does not cause cognitive overload. Teachers should use worked examples and a teaching sequence should progress through a process of backwards fading where initial learning is modelled and scaffolded by the teacher, allowing the student to focus on one or fewer elements of a problem or task and preventing them from becoming confused. We will delve into these ideas more in Chapter 4 when we explore what we can learn from Cognitive Load Theory.

WHAT HAPPENS IF STUDENTS FAIL TO INTEGRATE INFORMATION WITH RELEVANT PRIOR KNOWLEDGE ACTIVATED FROM LONG-TERM MEMORY?

If the new material is not integrated properly into long-term memory, then it is unlikely to be retained by a student. If we accept that 'learning is a change in long-term memory', then a failure to integrate equates to a failure to learn.

WHAT CAN WE DO TO ENSURE THAT STUDENTS INTEGRATE THE MATERIAL?

In order for new information to be successfully integrated into long-term memory, a student needs to already possess relevant prior knowledge to connect it to. To understand complex and abstract ideas, a learner often needs to understand the concepts that underpin them: if these subordinate concepts are not understood, it is likely that the higher order concept will not be fully understood.

As teachers, we should be spending much of our time building student background knowledge and teaching high-utility vocabulary, content and approaches to writing. If prior knowledge is lacking, then we need to teach it!

When teaching abstract ideas, teachers should ensure that they are exemplified through concrete examples.

Let's look at an example:

Imagine you are teaching the concept of 'ignominy' in connection with the jingoistic poem 'Fall In' by Harold Begbie. In order for this to be successful, you will need to be able explain the term using words that the student already understands, thereby beginning the integration with relevant prior knowledge. It can be helpful to start with a definition and example which can then be questioned and annotated (see Table 1.2).

Assuming that students understand the definition, the teacher could then ask questions like:

1. What does shame and humiliation mean?
2. Can you give me an example of something humiliating?
3. What is the difference between public and private?
4. 'Funked' means avoiding something because you're scared. What do the onlookers think the character is scared of?

Table 1.2   Concept of ignominy

Ignominy (n)	Public shame and humiliation
Ignominious (adj)	*Begbie asks 'where will you look when they give you the glance that tells you they know you funked', hinting at ignominy and public criticism.*

5. Why is this seen as ignominious?
6. Why does Begbie ask 'where will you look'?
7. Orally complete these sentences from the start: avoiding going to war would be seen as ignominious because...The poem suggests that cowardice will result in ignominy because...
8. Complete these sentences in your books: when Begbie says 'where will you look', he is hinting at ignominy because... The poem explores the ignominious consequences of cowardice so...

   After this sequence, later lessons could then involve wider questions and practice to broaden student understanding above and beyond the initial context of the poem:
9. Complete these sentences in your books: Liverpool's defeat at Watford was ignominious because...Her mistakes were ignominiously announced to the whole class, so...

The term 'understanding' here refers to creating more meaningful connections between the new item (ignominy) and the student's prior knowledge. The more connections that are made, the greater the depth of understanding.

If we want all students to understand and remember what we teach, then we should be explicitly teaching them the connections between different concepts and this will be one of the foci of the next chapter.

SUMMARY

- Trying to define learning is difficult, and useful definitions will often be based upon the area in which they are to be used.
- When situated within a model of cognition, practical and succinct definitions of learning can be beneficial for teachers.
- Good teaching will always focus on memory and retention.
- While the goal of an instructional sequence is often transferable, flexible knowledge, the start point is often inflexible and shallow knowledge.
- Learning can be perceived as a three-stage process where students select, organise and integrate new information.

REFERENCES

Ausubel, D. P. (1964). Some psychological and educational limitations of learning by discovery. *The Arithmetic Teacher, 11*, 290–302.

Barron, A. B., Hebets, E. A., Cleland, T. A., Fitzpatrick, C. L., Hauber, M. E., & Stevens, J. R. (2015). Embracing multiple definitions of learning. *Trends in Neurosciences, 38*(7), 405–407.

Bennett, T. (Spring 2015). Group work for the good unpacking the research behind one popular classroom strategy. *American Educator*, 32–34.

Coe, R. (2013). *Improving education: A Triumph of hope over experience*. Inaugural lecture of professor Robert Coe, Durham University, 18 June 2013. https://profcoe.net/publications

Fiorella, L., & Mayer, R. (2015). *Learning as a generative activity: Eight learning strategies that promote understanding.* Cambridge: Cambridge University Press.

Hirsch, E. D. (Spring 2003). Reading comprehension requires knowledge – of words and the world. *American Educator, 27,* 16–22.

Kirschner, P. A., Sweller, J., & Clark, R. E. (2006). Why minimal guidance during instruction does not work: An analysis of the failure of constructivist, discovery, problem-based, experiential, and inquiry-based teaching. *Educational Psychologist, 41*(2), 75–86.

Lemov, D., Driggs, C., & Woolway, E. (2016). *Reading reconsidered: A practical guide to rigorous literacy instruction.* San Francisco, CA: Jossey-Bass.

Slavin, R. (2010). Co-operative learning: What makes group work work? OECD (2010) The nature of learning: Using research to inspire practice Chapter 7, 161–178.

Sokal, A. D. (1996). Transgressing the boundaries: Towards a transformative hermeneutics of quantum gravity. *Social Text,* 46–47.

Willingham, D. (Winter 2002). Ask the cognitive scientist: Inflexible knowledge: The first step to expertise. *American Educator, 26,* 31–33.

Willingham, D. (2017a). http://www.danielwillingham.com/daniel-willingham-science-and-education-blog/on-the-definition-of-learning

Willingham, D. (2017b). A mental model of the learner: Teaching the basic science of educational psychology to future teacher. *Mind, Brain and Education, 11*(4).

2

HOW CAN WE HELP STUDENTS UNDERSTAND AND REMEMBER THINGS?

This chapter will explore

- Long-term memory and working memory
- Retrieval strength and storage strength of memories
- The difference between performance and learning
- A definition of understanding
- The difference between deep and shallow processing
- The role of forgetting

INTRODUCTION

We want students to retain and understand what we are teaching them but what do teachers need to know about these two ideas? This chapter will build upon the ideas from Chapter 1 and outline some of the theory that underpins memory and understanding.

THE IMPORTANCE OF MEMORY IN LEARNING

Learning is about so much more than merely committing things to memory, yet memory holds a central and vital position within the process. To ignore the role of memory is to jeopardise student success: if a student struggles to recall the content that they have been taught – whether this be in a lesson or more worryingly, an examination – then this will almost certainly prevent them from achieving. Not only that, but if students cannot remember the content that we teach, then what was the point in teaching it in the first place? At one level, teaching is about successfully imparting and explaining information to the students in front of us; however, successful communication is absolutely no guarantee that students will retain what you have told them or what they experienced in class.

Just because you told a class of students something about Romanticism does not mean that they will remember it. Having a discussion about the homosexual subtext in *The Strange Case of Dr Jekyll and Mr Hyde* may not result in students retaining the ideas that were explored. If a student reads an article about a certain topic, then this doesn't necessarily mean that the important points will be committed to memory.

We have all experienced frustration when confronted by students who cannot remember what we have taught them. 'But we did this last week! But we spent three weeks on this topic! But you seemed to understand it at the time! But your essay that you wrote was brilliant: how can you not recall it now?' In many of these cases, the problem is caused by the fact that lessons and curricula were not planned and taught with any consideration given to the role of memory. Experience does not equate to retention: if we assume that just because a student attended a series of lessons, completed a task or participated in an activity, then they should be able to recall the information at a later date then we are not only deluding ourselves, but we are potentially doing a huge disservice to the students that we teach.

As we shall see in Chapter 8 when we explore Siegfried Engelmann's Direct Instruction, as professional educators, we should hold ourselves responsible for student success or failure instead of blaming the students. If a student cannot remember what we have taught them, then this might be our fault. Thankfully, there are a number of easy to apply techniques that we can use to ensure that students don't forget what we teach them. Effective teachers use specific and often counter-intuitive strategies, planning their lessons and curricula with memory in mind so that students retain and are able to recall the information that they have been taught. Before we look at some of these strategies, we need to outline a few key ideas regarding memory.

Willingham's simple memory model splits the mind into two main areas: working memory and long-term memory (refer back to Figure 1.1 in Chapter 1). As explored in Chapter 1, this is a simplified version of our cognitive architecture, and, while more complex models will contain far more components, interactions and detail, narrowing the focus to these two aspects is a deliberate choice to help classroom teachers (Willingham, 2017). This simplified model sits at the heart of many of the ideas that this book will explore, helping us to answer questions like 'How can we get students to remember what we teach them? What is the importance of prior knowledge? Which instructional choice is best at this point in a sequence of learning?' Effective teachers help students to develop their background knowledge and recall and apply it from their long-term memories while ensuring that the limitations of working memory do not prevent students from succeeding.

As we saw in Chapter 1, although the definition of learning can be seen as 'a change in long-term memory', the process of learning involves three stages, each of which describes the relationship between our teaching, working memory and long-term memory:

- **Stage 1: *Selecting* relevant information to attend to**
- **Stage 2: *Organising* the material into a coherent cognitive structure in working memory**
- **Stage 3: *Integrating* it with relevant prior knowledge activated from long-term memory**

LONG-TERM MEMORY

Your long-term memory is comprised of everything you know, including events from your life, facts and knowledge, beliefs, opinions and skills (Mccrea, 2017). If you know a particular text well, then you will have a detailed mental representation of it in your long-term memory that will contain lots of interconnected information about plot, themes, characters, style and structure. When we talk about understanding – an idea that we will explore in detail later in this chapter – we are talking about how integrated and connected this information is in our minds: if you think you understand *Frankenstein* really well, your long-term memory will be comprised of myriad interconnected ideas and concepts to do with the novel, making up a rich and detailed mental representation of the text; if you don't understand Shelley's novel so well, you might only know a few isolated things about it like the names of a few characters or a cursory knowledge of the plot.

Long-term memory can be seen as a kind of huge storage cupboard although as soon as we start making comparisons with physical storage, the analogy becomes strained. If you take an item out of a storage cupboard and then put it back again in the same state that you found it, the item will remain unchanged: the next time you take it out, it will be the same. This is not the case with memories, however, because they are not immutable and fixed; instead, they are reconstructive (Schacter, 2015). This means that the act of retrieving a memory will modify it. As Professor Robert Bjork has asserted: 'an item can seldom, if ever, be retrieved from memory without modifying the representation of that item in significant ways' (Bjork, 1975). As we shall see later in this chapter, the modifying effect of retrieving memories – if harnessed correctly – can be hugely beneficial to student success, helping them to recall and apply their knowledge efficiently as well as deepening their understanding.

Our long-term memories are huge and their massive capacity is seemingly endless. The potential difficulty that students face with regards to their long term memories is not anything to do with capacity, it is to do with retrieval. To return to the shaky storage cupboard analogy, if I place a bag of rice on the third shelf, then retrieving that rice at a later date will be easy because it will be in the same place and in the same form. If, however, I learn about the socio-psychological phenomenon of 'diffusion of responsibility' in relation to *Lord of the Flies* and demonstrate my learning through writing a successful essay, this doesn't necessarily mean that I will be able to successfully recall this information at a later date. Unlike the bag of rice, which has a fixed physical location and is therefore easy to locate, my knowledge of the boy's emerging savagery in Golding's novel is linked to specific cues which change each time I retrieve the information (Bjork, 1975). These changes are often beneficial, making the information more durable or accessible. Additionally and bizarrely, the memory's accessibility can also decrease as a result of the successful retrieval of similar information (Bjork and Bjork, 1992). To return to the shaky cupboard analogy, this surprising and counter-intuitive idea would be the equivalent of taking a bag of pasta from the shelf and finding that this made it more difficult to find the rice. If you're thinking that this weird relationship between memories – called 'retrieval induced forgetting' where the retrieval of one memory can inhibit the retrieval of another one – seems like a flaw in our cognitive architecture, the reality is that forgetting is an evolutionary adaptive characteristic of our minds and we will touch on this shortly.

WORKING MEMORY

Our working memories act a little like a gateway, allowing sensory data from the environment into our minds and combining it with accessible and relevant information from our long-term memories. The capacity of our working memories is limited and they can only hold and manipulate a few items at once. Some people estimate this to be around four items (Cowan, 2000). Added to this limitation is the fact that it doesn't seem like there is much that can be done in order to expand it or improve it. While there are lots of 'brain training' games and programmes available, all they seem to be able to do is help students get better at the brain training game: the effect does not transfer to other tasks, even if they are really similar (Stojanoski et al., 2018).

The limitation of our working memories is of crucial importance for teachers and students alike. In Chapters 6–8, we will explore how explicit or direct instruction – as well as the far more rigorous Direct Instruction – offers strategies and pedagogical approaches that respect this limitation so as to ensure that learning is both successful and efficient. As we shall see in Chapter 4 when we explore Cognitive Load Theory, the limitation of our working memory must drive how we design instructional materials so that we do not overload our students and make them feel confused.

Think back to the abstruse and complex extract that you read in Chapter 1: unless you knew a lot about the topic, you probably became confused very quickly and this was because you were trying to hold and manipulate multiple novel concepts in your mind at once. Other typical errors or difficulties caused by the limitation of working memory include the inability to follow complex instructions, omitting steps within a multi-step procedure or someone simply giving up because the task at hand seems impenetrable (Didau and Rose, 2016, p. 39). You may well recognise most, if not all, of the problems in the last sentence, particularly when you ask low attaining students to write essays. Engaging in a multi-step, complex piece of writing like an essay requires students to have automatised – and therefore committed to long-term memory – a whole range of separate components, allowing them to concentrate on the planning and crafting of the writing itself. As an example, here are just some of the things that a student needs to be able to use accurately and fluently within an essay response, moving from smaller to larger components:

1. Formation of letters
2. Spelling of words
3. Grammar rules and syntax
4. Vocabulary
5. Knowledge of text
6. Analytical components like embedding evidence and creating multiple interpretations

7. Knowledge of what analysis is meant to be: a comprehensive mental representation of analytical writing
8. Paragraphing and essay structure

If some or all of these things are not secure and easily accessible in long-term memory, meaning that attention – and therefore working memory – has to be directed towards them, then it will not be long before a student becomes confused. As we shall see in Chapter 11, if we are to respect the limitations of our working memories, then we should be practising the components of essay writing initially in isolation before combining them into pieces of extended writing.

RETRIEVAL VS STORAGE

Our memories can be perceived as having two related measurements of strength (UCLA Bjork Learning and Forgetting Lab): retrieval strength and storage strength. The retrieval strength of a memory refers to how easily you can recall it or bring it to mind. The storage strength of a memory is how well you have learnt the information that the memory contains. If you are currently teaching *Hamlet* and have done so for a number of years, it is likely that your knowledge and memory of the text has both high retrieval and storage strength. You know the play in depth, having spent a number of years teaching it, and if asked to, can easily recall a wealth of information about it.

If you have ever left your studying to the last minute and crammed for an exam – and this was my experience when studying for my English A-level as I revised Chaucer's *The Wife of Bath's Prologue* into the wee hours of the morning – then when you took the exam, the memory of the content had high retrieval strength but low storage strength. You might have succeeded in the exam, but you probably can't remember it now.

If you taught *All my Sons* by Arthur Miller for a number of years, but haven't taught it or thought about it since, then it is likely that your memory of the text will have high storage strength but low retrieval strength. You may find it difficult to recall detailed information about the play despite once considering yourself to be an expert on it. However, if you were to read it again, you would probably experience a sense of familiarity with the text: as you are reading it, you may find that you begin to remember subsequent plot details or certain qualities of characters before they are revealed. You would find that you would quickly regain your expertise and reaching a level of proficiency would not take anywhere near as long as it did the first time that you read and taught the play.

Information can also have both low retrieval and low storage strength. If you meet a new student for the first time and they tell you their name, only for you to find that as your conversation ends you cannot recall it, then this is why you had to ask them their name again. In this instance, you never really acquired the information in the first place.

Table 2.1 demonstrates how retrieval and storage strength interact. Although students can pass exams by cramming and revising intensively in the lead up to the test, we want the students to experience the benefits of the top right-hand quadrant of the table: durable knowledge that is easy to recall. Yes, passing exams is of crucial importance to students, but so is the development of well integrated and organised background knowledge.

Table 2.1 How do retrieval and storage strength interact?

	Low storage strength (learned badly)	High storage strength (learned well)
High Retrieval Strength **(Good Performance)**	The text that you crammed before an exam *The Wife of Bath's Prologue* **'Crammed'**	The text that you are currently teaching and have taught for some time *Macbeth* **'Current Mastery'**
	Benefit: Passed the exam	**Benefit:** You know it in depth and can easily recall information from it.
	Detriment: Knowledge is now forgotten so you can't think with it or use it	**Detriment**: It may have taken considerable effort and time to achieve this
	Low storage strength (learned badly)	**High storage strength (learned well)**
Low Retrieval Strength **(Poor Performance)**	When you meet a new student and cannot remember their name **'Forgotten'**	The text that you used to teach but haven't taught for a while *All My Sons* **'Buried'**
	Benefit: If you wanted to learn their name, then there isn't a benefit here!	**Benefit:** 1. If the knowledge is not currently relevant to you, then its inaccessibility will prevent interference with more relevant knowledge. 2. Should you need to, relearning it (meaning you can access it again) will be an accelerated process
	Detriment: 1. You'll need to ask them again	**Detriment:** 1. Knowledge is 'buried'. You know you used to know it but you can't retrieve it now.

Source: Adapted from Yan 'Learning Scientists' (2016) and Kirby (2013).

In Chapter 4, we will explore how experts rely upon broad, detailed and well-organised webs of background knowledge when solving problems, an approach that is entirely dependent upon the vast capacity of long-term memory. Although our working memories are limited and it seems like their capacity is fixed and cannot be improved by instruction, we can harness the vast capacity of our long-term memories to develop in proficiency or expertise. Knowledge acts as a kind of mental Velcro and new information is integrated into our long-term memories by connecting it to existing knowledge (Bjork and Bjork, 1992). As more knowledge and better mental representations are added to our long-term memory, this also creates more capacity for additional knowledge to be added as there is more stuff for new stuff to stick to (Bjork and Bjork, 1992). In fact, if we have better organised and more developed background knowledge, we will find that learning new information is both faster and easier (Shing and Brod, 2016).

PERFORMANCE VS LEARNING

You may be asking yourself why retrieval and storage strength are important ideas for teachers to understand. The answer lies in the crucial distinction between performance and learning (Soderstrom and Bjork, 2015). The distinction can be defined as follows:

> Learning is 'the relatively permanent changes in behaviour or knowledge that support long-term retention and transfer'

> Performance is 'the temporary fluctuations in behaviour or knowledge that can be observed and measured during or immediately after the acquisition process'. (Soderstrom and Bjork, 2015)

The first major difference between these two ideas is that, while performance can be 'observed and measured' during lessons, the same cannot be said for learning. The second major distinction between learning and performance is temporal: learning is 'relatively permanent' but performance is 'temporary'.

Whether a student has learnt something can only be inferred after instruction has taken place and this is one reason why students typically take exams or complete assessment portfolios in order to demonstrate their learning. The fact that we cannot actually observe or measure learning in our lessons should make us stop and think: as teachers we are quite rightly obsessed with evaluating whether students are learning in class. We read their writing and listen to their spoken answers in order to ascertain if they have learnt what we are teaching them and a large part of a teacher's role in the classroom is to constantly make judgements based on student output in order to inform the next steps in that lesson and the lessons that follow. If their responses are good, then they must have learnt what we have taught them, right? If student success rates are high, then surely this means that they are learning, right?

Unfortunately not.

Let's look at an example that clarifies these ideas and places them within a classroom context:

In the middle of a lesson or sequence of lessons on teaching students how to embed quotations within their analytical writing, the fact that lots of students are succeeding at the tasks in front of them is no reliable indicator that they will retain this ability and be able to apply it at a later date. In the lesson, what we are observing is their *performance*. It is perhaps unsurprising that students seem to make rapid gains if you spend a number of lessons on a particular topic or skill. These lessons may be filled with helpful supports like writing frames, vocabulary tables, prompts, cues or model answers, ensuring that students are able to succeed in the tasks that you have asked them to complete, which, in itself, may be no bad thing at all. These approaches can be really effective when teaching students to acquire new knowledge or skills, especially when they are relative novices. However, we are making a huge error if we treat their *performance* in these lessons as evidence of *learning*. If students were asked to recall or apply what you had taught them at a later date, you may find that they are unable to do so.

If you look back to Table 2.1, we can categorise each of the quadrants in terms of *performance* and *learning* and this is because performance and learning are directly linked to retrieval and storage strength (Soderstrom and Bjork, 2015). If students are *performing* well in class, then they are retrieving information successfully: we can say that the retrieval strength is high. If students can still recall what you have taught them at a later date-perhaps in an examination – then they have *learnt* the information: we can say that the storage strength is high.

But hold on, what about the example of cramming *The Wife of Bath's Prologue* the night before my English A-level? For me, this was a successful – albeit risky – approach as I did well in the exam. Isn't this an example of learning as I demonstrated what I knew about the text? No. Because the exam was *'immediately after'* my intense period of revision (a few hours afterwards in this case), I was able to retain the information just long enough to apply it in the test. My responses in the examination were an example of *performance* not *learning*. If I had taken a second test after a longer delay, perhaps a few days or weeks later, I would have found remembering and applying the relevant information very difficult if not impossible and would have probably failed.

HOW CAN WE HELP STUDENTS TO UNDERSTAND THINGS?

DEFINING UNDERSTANDING

What does it actually mean to say that you understand something? Is it the same as saying that you know something? How does it connect to retention and memory?

Although memory and retention are crucial, we ultimately want our students to understand the ideas that we are teaching them. This often means that we want some level of depth and flexibility to their learning. If you think back to Chapter 1, we briefly sketched out two connected ideas: transfer (the ability to apply learning to new contexts) and the continuum from inflexible to flexible knowledge (the gradual change from shallow learning to deeper and more generalised learning). When we first learn something, our knowledge is almost always inflexible in that our ability to apply what we have learnt is restricted to the initial context in which we learnt it. If we engage in effective practice, then we can build our understanding by making our knowledge more accessible, more connected to our existing knowledge and therefore more flexible, meaning we can apply it across a wider range of contexts.

In Chapter 1, we explored a more detailed definition of learning, taken from Fiorella and Mayer (2015): learning is when students 'actively make sense of the material so they can build meaningful learning activities to transfer what they have learned to solving new problems'.

This definition implicitly describes the process of understanding as when students 'make sense' of what we teach them and engage in 'meaningful' learning, then they build understanding. If students can 'transfer what they have learned to solving new problems', then it is fair to say that they have understood what we have taught them.

Connected to Fiorella and Mayer's (2015) definition of learning is the idea that if we want students to understand and make sense of what we teach them, they need to engage in the three stages of learning:

- **Stage 1:** *Selecting* **relevant information to attend to;**
- **Stage 2:** *Organising* **the material into a coherent cognitive structure in working memory;**
- **Stage 3:** *Integrating* **it with relevant prior knowledge activated from long-term memory.**

If a student engages in all three stages, then it is likely that they have understood what we have taught them because their learning has been meaningful (Mayer, 2008, p. 23).

There are three possible outcomes here.

1. Non-learning

Table 2.2   Non-learning

Stage of cognitive processing	Successful?	Description of learning
Selecting	NO	• Poor retention
Organising	NO	• Poor transfer
Integrating	NO	• Minimal or no understanding

If the student doesn't select the correct information, then they won't learn anything. Imagine a student was asked to study *Still I Rise* by Maya Angelou. Even if the student was thinking about all she knows about oppression, resistance and pride, she won't learn anything about the poem if she doesn't read it carefully (Mayer, 2008, p. 22).

If the student was given a retention test that asked them what they could remember about the poem, they would score poorly. Equally, if the student was given a transfer test like an essay task which could be seen as a measure of understanding, they would also score poorly.

2. Non-Understanding

Table 2.3   Non-understanding

Stage of cognitive processing	Successful?	Description of learning
Selecting	YES	• Potentially good retention
Organising	NO	• Inflexible knowledge
Integrating	NO	• Poor transfer
		• Minimal or no understanding

If a student selects the correct information but fails to organise it into a coherent whole in working memory, then they are unlikely to understand it. For example, if a student reads *Still I Rise* and, afterwards, is unable to adequately explain its powerful message, then this may be because they failed to organise the information in Angelou's poem into a coherent whole.

If a student fails to integrate the information in the poem with their existing prior knowledge, then this will also stop them from understanding the poem.

In either of these two cases, we can refer to the learning as 'rote learning'. The student has learnt the information in a nonmeaningful way (Mayer, 2008, p. 23) and it is not integrated with any relevant existing knowledge.

In an article about the difference between inflexible and flexible knowledge, Daniel Willingham (2002) gives the example of a student who has learned the definition of the equator by rote and is able to produce the answer that it is 'A menagerie lion running around the Earth through Africa'. The student has memorised the form, albeit wrongly, of the concept but has not understood it all.

The student who learned *Still I Rise* in this 'rote' fashion may well score well on a retention test; however, they would score poorly on a transfer test like an essay task.

3. Understanding

Table 2.4 Understanding

Stage of cognitive processing	Successful?	Description of learning
Selecting	YES	• Good retention
Organising	YES	• Flexible knowledge: good transfer
Integrating	YES	• Understanding

If a student successfully engages in all three stages of cognitive processing, then it is likely that they have understood the content. A student who understands *Still I Rise* will not only be able to describe the images and ideas in the poem, but they will also have connected them to their existing knowledge. Perhaps, by referring directly to the poem and adding additional interpretation and explanation, they can discuss how Angelou expresses the power of resistance in the face of oppression.

DEPTH

If we want students to engage in meaningful learning, they need to think deeply about the content that we are teaching them. Professor Robert Coe (2013) expresses this idea as 'learning happens when people have to think hard'. The notion of 'depth' is often used as a proxy for rigour or complexity of thought; after all, when given the choice between deep and shallow learning, the former seems inarguably more desirable, carrying connotations of detail, comprehensiveness and academic scholarship. If you look back to Table 2.2, the top right-hand quadrant describes the ultimate goal: deep, durable learning that is easily accessible.

So what is the difference between deep and shallow processing? In The Levels of Processing Model (Craik and Lockhart, 1972), the authors propose that we process information in three ways:

Shallow processing:

1. **Structural processing**

   This is when we process information based upon its appearance.

2. **Phonemic processing**

   This is when we process information based upon its sound.

   Both of these types of processing would result in poor retention.

Deep processing:

3. **Semantic processing**

   This is when we encode the meaning of a concept by *integrating* it with our existing knowledge.

One of the key ideas in The Levels of Processing Model is that if we think deeply about something by engaging in semantic processing, rather than shallow level processing based upon appearance or sound, we will increase the storage strength of the memory that we are encoding. This idea is directly analogous to Professor Daniel Willingham's (2009) assertion that 'memory is the residue of thought'. We remember the things that we think deeply about and this is partly why I can effortlessly recall information about Macbeth, the text that I currently teach. My processing of Macbeth has been on a semantic level, ensuring that I selected, organised and integrated the information effectively and this is why it has both high retrieval and high storage strength. When I meet a new student and embarrassingly forget their name within what seems like seconds, then this is because my processing is phonemic and shallow. In this first interaction, their name has little meaning attributed to it apart from its sound; as our relationship grows, meaning will be slowly added to their name as I learn more about them.

Similarly, the student who defined the equator as 'a menagerie lion' probably only engaged in erroneous, shallow, phonemic processing of the definition and this partly explains their mondegreen.

Let's look at an example from the classroom that clarifies the application of The Levels of Processing Model:

As we shall see in Chapter 5, explicitly teaching vocabulary can be a powerful way of improving the sophistication of student writing. Imagine you want to teach students the word 'disdainful'. If we want students to understand, retain and apply this new word, then we need them to engage in deep processing at a level that extracts meaning from it (Craik and Lockhart, 1972).

Here are some approaches that involve shallow processing:

a. Students learn the spelling of 'disdainful' perhaps as part of a decontextualised list of 'important vocabulary words'.
b. Students memorise the word, its definition and maybe an example sentence. This is done without reference to a specific text.

c. Students answer a simple question that is always the same: 'What does disdainful mean? What word means showing contempt or lack of respect?'
d. Students are never asked to practice using the word in their own writing or in response to a text.

All of these approaches would result in inflexible knowledge that is tied to the cues that students received. If these are the only strategies that were used, you may find that asking students even slightly different questions would result in failure: a student may not be able to successfully answer the questions 'Can you tell me an example of a disdainful character? What kind of things might a disdainful person do?'

Teaching vocabulary is far more effective if the focus is on practice and application. Yes, students need to be able to remember and retain the form, meaning and usage of the word that is being taught, but the ultimate goal should be for students to be able to use the word themselves. Good teaching will develop both retention and understanding. Craik and Lockhart (1972) would point out that by focusing on meaning, students will not only develop their understanding, they will also improve their ability to remember and therefore recall what they are being taught.

When teaching something for the first time, teachers should ensure that students are thinking as deeply as possible about the content. Deep and meaningful processing will involve the successful engagement of all three stages of processing that we explored in Chapter 1: selecting, organising and integrating.

Here is one possible approach that would involve deeper, more meaningful processing:

a. Instead of asking students to learn a word from an arbitrary list, vocabulary should be taught in context.

If we want students to begin thinking about meaning from the outset, then we should teach new words in conjunction with a text that we are studying or with a specific purpose in mind. As an example, you could teach 'disdainful' in conjunction with Percy Bysshe Shelley's *Ozymandias* so that students are better equipped to explore the tyrant's contemptuous and callous nature.

b. After having read the poem, students can be given a simple definition and example sentence that explicitly links the word to the poem, focusing on meaning from the beginning:

Table 2.5 Excerpt from a vocabulary table (see Chapter 5 for a full example)

Disdainful (adj)	The feeling that a person or a thing is worthless or beneath consideration
Disdainfully (adv)	*Its 'wrinkled lip' suggests intense disdain and scorn.*
Disdain (n)	

c. It can be useful to include all relevant forms of the word, helping students to broaden their understanding
d. The teacher could then annotate the definition, providing further explanations or additional information
e. The teacher can then ask a range of questions about the vocabulary explanation and poem to help students extract and develop meaning:

Possible questions:

1. What does it mean to be 'worthless'?
2. How do you know that Ozymandias felt that his subjects were worthless?
3. Finish my sentence: 'Its 'wrinkled lip' suggests intense disdain and scorn because...'
4. Finish my sentence: 'Ozymandias was a disdainful King, so...'

The suggestions above are certainly not exhaustive, instead providing a few examples of how teachers can focus on meaning when teaching new content. The key idea here is that if students engage in 'elaborative rehearsal', the process of analysing information meaningfully by using and manipulating it in some way, then this will aid both understanding and retention.

The approaches that are explained throughout this book are designed with both understanding and retention in mind so that students are more likely to learn rather than perform, remember rather than forget and understand rather than mimic. As we saw earlier, if students don't understand or retain the content that we teach to them, then we cannot really say that they have learned anything.

Before we look at some of the methods that can help students to learn rather than merely perform well, let's take a quick diversion into the role of forgetting.

WHY DON'T WE REMEMBER EVERYTHING AND WHAT IS THE ROLE OF FORGETTING?

If you read, hear, see or experience something, then this in no way guarantees that you will remember it. Our minds do not work like infallible recording devices and merely pointing your eyes or ears towards information will not result in retention. If a smartphone failed to flawlessly record and store the images and sounds that we pointed it towards, we would consider the device to be defective. Our minds, thankfully, do not record and retain all of the sensory data that we are presented with. Imagine remembering everything! Imagine having instant and automatic recall of everything you had ever experienced! While this may seem like some kind of cognitive superpower, giving us a huge advantage in life, if our minds did work like video recording devices and we retained every piece of sensory data that we experienced, this would be hugely detrimental to our everyday lives.

In 2006, Jill Price was diagnosed with 'Highly Superior Autobiographical Memory Syndrome' or HSAMS (Parker et al., 2006) or HSAM. Also known as *hyperthymesia*, her condition means that she can recall most of the days of her life in rich vivid detail, including who she was with, where she was and events from current affairs that fell on those dates. If you are thinking that her amazing memory would be a benefit, then you're wrong. She describes her condition as being 'non-stop, uncontrollable and totally exhausting' because events in the present are constantly triggering memories from her mind. One of the researchers involved with people who have HSAMS explained that 'The overall summary of all of this is that they're bad forgetters' (McRobbie, 2017). We often perceive the process of forgetting as something negative but there are good reasons why we forget things.

Forgetting is an adaptive process (Bjork and Bjork, 1992) that allows us to function effectively in a complex environment. Because our long-term memory capacity is so vast, we need a process that acts as a filter and helps us focus on things that are relevant. Forgetting things that we are unlikely to use in the near future allows us to have relevant memories close to us. To return to the shaky cupboard analogy, it's similar to organising objects in a cupboard: we keep things we use every day in easy-to-reach places, while items we use less frequently are kept at the back and are more difficult to access. This way, we can more efficiently achieve our intended goals by having more relevant memories closer to hand.

If you have ever learnt a foreign language and, after a long period of disuse, have found that you seem to regain proficiency rapidly when you start to use it again-perhaps when you go on holiday – then you have experienced another adaptive function of forgetting. Before the holiday, you may have found it difficult or impossible to recall vocabulary or specific phrases even if, at some point in the past, you considered yourself to be a competent speaker. This is because the retrieval strength of your memories of the language has diminished, meaning that you struggle to remember what you once knew. The storage strength, however, will not have decreased, and this is why you seem to relearn it at such an accelerated rate. This is also an adaptive function as it means that we don't have to expend the same amount of effort as we did when we first learnt the language, allowing our learning to be more efficient (Bjork and Bjork, 1992). If the storage strength decayed concurrently with the retrieval strength, relearning a body of knowledge would be tiresome and long winded. Your inability to recall *le mot juste* means that this knowledge does not interfere with other more relevant knowledge that you have been more recently using (Bjork, 2011).

If I ever teach *All My* Sons again, I could expect to experience a similarly accelerated rate of relearning and to reach a level of expertise far quicker than the first time I taught it.

SUMMARY

- Just because a student has attended lessons, listened and completed their work does not mean that they will retain what they have been taught.
- It can be helpful to think of memory as having two main components: working memory, which is limited in capacity, and long-term memory.
- Performance is different to learning: if a student is performing well in class, we should be wary of using this as a reliable indicator that they have learned what we have taught them.
- Although retention is important, we want students to understand what we teach them. For this to happen, they need to successfully engage in three stages of cognitive processing: select, organise and integrate.

REFERENCES

Bjork, R. A. (1975). Retrieval as a memory modifier: An interpretation of negative recency and related phenomena. In R. L. Solso (Ed.), *Information processing and cognition: The Loyola Symposium* (pp. 123–144).

Bjork, R. A. (2011). On the symbiosis of remembering, forgetting, and learning. In A. S. Benjamin (Ed.), *Successful remembering and successful forgetting: A festschrift in honor of Robert A. Bjork* (pp. 1–22). Psychology Press.

Bjork, R. A., & Bjork, E. L. (1992). A new theory of disuse and old theory of stimulus fluctuation. In A. Healy, S. Kosslyn & R. Shiffrin (Eds.), *From learning processes to cognitive processes: Essays in honor of William K Estes* (*Vol. 2*, 35–67). Hillsdale, NJ: Erlbaum.

Coe, R. (2013). *Improving education: A triumph of hope over experience*. Inaugural lecture of professor Robert Coe, Durham University, 18 June 2013. https://profcoe.net/publications

Cowan, N. (2000). The magical number 4 in short-term memory: A reconsideration of mental storage capacity. *Behavioral and Brain Sciences, 24,* 87–114.

Craik, F. M., & Lockhart, R. S. (1972). Levels of processing: A framework for memory research. *Journal of Verbal Learning and Verbal Behaviour, 11,* 671–684.

Didau, D., & Rose, N. (2016). *What every teacher needs to know about psychology*. London: John Catt.

Fiorella, L., & Mayer, R. (2015). *Learning as a generative activity: Eight learning strategies that promote understanding*. Cambridge: Cambridge University Press.

Kirby, J. (2013). https://pragmaticreform.wordpress.com/2013/11/16/memory/

Mayer, R. (2008). *Learning and instruction* (2nd ed.). Upper Saddle River, NJ: Pearson Merrill Prentice Hall.

Mccrea, P. (2017). *Memorable teaching: Leveraging memory to build deep and durable learning in the classroom*. London: CreateSpace Independent Publishing Platform.

McRobbie, L. R. (2017). Total recall: The people who never forget. *Guardian.* https://www.theguardian.com/science/2017/feb/08/total-recall-the-people-who-never-forget

Parker, E., Cahill, L., & McGaugh, J. L. (2006). A case of unusual autobiographical remembering. *Neurocase, 12,* 35–49.

Schacter, D. L. (2015). Memory: An adaptive constructive process. In D. Nikulin (Ed.), *Memory in recollection of itself.* New York, NY: Oxford University Press.

Shing, Y. L., & Brod, G. (2016). Effects of prior knowledge on memory: Implications for education. *Mind, Brain, and Education, 10*(3), 153–161.

Soderstrom, N. C., & Bjork, R. A. (2015). Learning versus performance: An integrative review. *Perspectives on Psychological Science, 10*(2), 176–179.

Stojanoski, B., Lyons, K. M., Pearce, A., & Owen, A. M. (2018). Targeted training: Converging evidence against the transferable benefits of online brain training on cognitive function. *Neuropyschologia, 117,* 541–550.

UCLA Bjork Learning and Forgetting Lab. https://bjorklab.psych.ucla.edu/research/

Willingham, D. (2002). Ask the cognitive scientist: Inflexible knowledge: The first step to expertise. *American Educator, 26*(4), 31–33.

Willingham, D. (2009). *Why don't students like school?: A cognitive scientist answers questions about how the mind works and what it means for the classroom*. San Francisco, CA: Jossey-Bass.

Willingham, D. (2017). A mental model of the learner: Teaching the basic science of educational psychology to future teacher. *Mind, Brain and Education, 11*(4), 166–175.

Yan, V. (2016). https://www.learningscientists.org/blog/2016/5/10-1

3

REMEMBERING AND UNDERSTANDING IN PRACTICE

: This chapter will explore
:
: • The testing effect
: • Different approaches to retrieval practice
: • How to ensure that retrieval practice is as effective as possible
: • The benefits of retrieval practice

INTRODUCTION

How can we help students to remember and understand what we teach them? Which approaches are our best bets and what needs to be considered in order to ensure that they are as effective as possible? This chapter will delve into the importance of using testing as a learning strategy, explaining the benefits of retrieval practice and demonstrating how it can be used when teaching English.

THE IMPORTANCE OF REVIEW

Ever since the late 19th century when a German Psychologist by the name of Ernest Ebbinghaus pioneered research into human memory, we have known that retention is a battle against time. Ebbinghaus systematically tested his ability to recall nonsense words and found that the larger the gap between initial learning and testing, the more difficult it was to successfully recall the information.

As time progresses, our ability to successfully recall information rapidly decreases. This has huge implications for teaching and curriculum planning. If the rate of forgetting is so rapid, then what can we do to slow it down? How can we get students to remember and retain what we have taught them? We know that experience does not equate to retention and the mere fact that a student has *performed* well in class doesn't mean that they have *learned* what we have taught them.

We can review the information, an approach that will slow the rate of forgetting. But what does 'review' mean? What strategies can we use and encourage our students to use in order to slow the rate of forgetting and succeed in the battle against time?

Unfortunately, many of us treat our memories as if they operate more like computer systems or video recorders and we mistakenly believe that merely exposing ourselves to information will result in retention (Bjork, 2011). As we have already seen, this is not how our minds work. Before we look at some useful strategies for aiding retention, let's look at some approaches that won't work. If you recognise these strategies, then that's because they are surprisingly commonplace among students and teachers alike: people believe that they are effective (Dunlosky, 2013) and, while they can sometimes help students perform well in an exam-particularly after an all-night session of cramming like I did with my A-level-they will not result in long-term retention or understanding.

1. Rereading texts or notes.

    The classic yet flawed method of revision used by students is to merely reread the course materials. A study of 177 U.S. college students (Karpicke et al., 2009) reported that 84% of respondents used this strategy with 55% of them ranking it as their number one approach to studying. This approach often underpins the idea of a revision lesson where a teacher goes back over the content that they had previously taught to students, perhaps in a really similar fashion to the original teaching. While rereading can be helpful if distributed over time, helping to flatten the forgetting curve, there are far more effective methods of review that could be used (Dunlosky, 2013).

2. Highlighting or underlining

    We've all seen students armed to the teeth with arrays of neon highlighter pens, lavishly colouring in their course materials so as to make them more memorable. Perhaps you have asked students to use them or underline information in class when reading a text. As part of an instructional procedure, the underlining of information may help students to engage in the first stage of learning by selecting the information to attend to. If, however, this is all that is done and there is no effort to organise or integrate the information, then it is likely that this will be an ineffective method of learning.

Both of these methods provide students with the 'illusion of competence' (Karpicke et al., 2009), meaning that as they read something multiple times, they will experience an increased familiarity as they seem to recognise the content and read it more fluently than the first time that they did so. This is dangerous for both students and teachers. If a teacher asks their students to reread a passage of text that they had previously studied, in the mistaken belief that this will help them retain the information, then they may well observe their students *performing* with ease. This might cause the teacher to believe that the students are proficient at this particular topic so that they move onto something else even though the students may well not have retained the information. Equally, the teacher may have wasted lesson time using ineffective strategies when they could have used something far more powerful to help their students remember the content that is being taught.

Perhaps the most effective of these strategies is to test our students.

THE TESTING EFFECT

Also known as retrieval practice or low stakes quizzing, the testing effect describes the phenomena where testing enhances retention (Roediger and Karpicke, 2006a). Compared to restudying or rereading material, retrieval practice is more effective at causing a 'change in long-term memory' and is therefore a powerful learning strategy (Rowland, 2014).

Many teachers see testing as something to be avoided (Roediger and Karpicke, 2006b) as it unnecessarily wastes limited classroom time and if you mistakenly believe that the only purpose of testing is to measure what students know, then this concern seems understandable. Added to that, teachers don't enjoy marking tests and students do not enjoy taking them (Roediger and Karpicke, 2006b) so it is perhaps unsurprising – if not disheartening – to find out that its usage as a learning event is not common at all.

Research on the testing effect dates back over 100 years (Karpicke, 2017) although the idea that retrieving information from memory (it used to be referred to as 'recitation') is beneficial for learning has been around for much longer. In 1620, Francis Bacon wrote:

> If you read a piece of text through twenty times, you will not learn it by heart so easily as if you read it ten times while attempting to recite from time to time and consulting the text when your memory fails. (Roediger and Karpicke, 2006b)

It seems as though Bacon could have taught the U.S. college students a thing or two about effective learning techniques.

Because the word 'testing' seems to carry so many negative connotations, bringing to mind pressurised examinations and students riddled with anxiety, I will use 'retrieval practice' to refer to this approach from this point onwards. Retrieval practice involves testing what students know by asking them to recall information from their memories that they have previously learned but this is where the similarity with summative testing ends. Students are not given grades in retrieval practice tasks and teachers rarely mark them.

The simplest approach to retrieval practice involves asking a series of questions about previously learned content – a bit like a quiz. The questions will ask about content that is essential or important for students to know and retain: not because retention is in itself the ultimate aim here – although it is of crucial importance – but because knowledge added to long-term memory can then be used by students to think with and apply in subsequent tasks. In Chapter 1, we discussed how learning can be defined as 'a change in long-term memory' and this was in order to foreground the absolute importance of retention. However, the second definition that we explored was a little more expansive, adding that learning requires students to 'make sense of the material' so that they can 'transfer what they have learned to solving new problems'.

Effective retrieval practice will involve far more than rote memorisation, although, as we saw in Chapter 1, inflexible knowledge may well be the start point of a learning sequence; effective retrieval practice will also help students to develop their understanding and improve their ability to transfer their knowledge to new contexts (Roediger et al., 2011).

As we have seen, our long-term memories seem to have almost limitless capacity and, as we shall see in Chapter 4, people who are considered to have expertise in a particular area have more extensive and better organised background knowledge which they can use to think with. As there doesn't seem to be much we can do in order to improve the working memories of our students (Shipstead et al., 2012), we should be spending a large proportion of our time in class on activities that develop, connect and improve the accessibility our students' background knowledge so that they can develop in expertise.

Retrieval practice, when done effectively, does exactly this: it helps to incrementally build and connect background knowledge in our students' long-term memories, increasing the breadth and depth of their knowledge and understanding. If this knowledge is organised and accessible, then they can rely on it when reading, helping them to make necessary inferences and comprehend the text. Similarly, when students write essays, reports or complete examination tasks, they need to rely upon their background knowledge when writing; after all, it is difficult to write about something you know little about.

SO WHAT IS RETRIEVAL PRACTICE? WHAT DOES IT LOOK LIKE IN THE ENGLISH CLASSROOM?

Before beginning to explain what retrieval practice looks like in the classroom, it is important to recognise that there is one major prerequisite that you need: an explicit curriculum. If you don't explicitly state what it is you want students to remember, then it is difficult to keep track of what you want to retrieve from their memories.

I ask questions orally and students write answers in the backs of their books. Every question that I ask is about content from previous lessons – this is not about eliciting novel information from their heads. They know that they are not permitted to shout out, confer or talk, and this is so that everyone has an opportunity to retrieve the information from their own memories. It is worth explaining to students the rationale behind retrieval practice by briefly going over some of the learning science behind it; after all, retrieval practice is probably the most effective strategy that they can use when studying independently too (Dunlosky, 2013). Students need to know that it is not a 'test' – they cannot fail and I just want them to try their best. I do not take scores or mark the quizzes, the process of retrieval being the purpose here, not the recording of data. With weaker classes or information that is trickier to recall, I give clues, perhaps providing the first couple of letters and writing them under the visualiser:

What term means the 'S' sound:

Sib. . . . .(sibilance)

I often ask 10–20 quick-fire questions although the number of questions is by no means fixed. I do not create quiz sheets or resources or anything else that is potentially time-consuming and may only be used once: the quiz is done on paper under a visualiser, and the questions are based upon content from previous lessons.

FEEDBACK AND FOLLOW-UP QUESTIONS

This is how I give feedback for individual episodes of retrieval practice. I ask individual students for the answer, sometimes choosing and sometimes accepting someone whose hand is up. When the student says the answer, I ask them to explain what the word means, reinforcing the link between definition and meaning. I then write the correct answer down under the visualiser, asking all students to correct their errors or add the answer if they did not know. It is far better that students mark and correct their own answers and this is because of a phenomenon known as 'the hypercorrection effect'. This is the idea that the more confident you are that an incorrect answer is correct, the more likely you are to not repeat that error if you are corrected (Wiliam, 2018). If a student gives an incorrect answer and then receives feedback so that they can correct their error, then this process of self-correction or 'hypercorrection' will improve long-term retention. One possible theory for this potentially counter-intuitive finding is that when you discover that an answer that you were really sure was correct was actually incorrect, the accompanying feeling of surprise means that you devote a heightened sense of attention to it, thereby facilitating the strengthening of the memory (Butterfield and Metcalfe, 2006).

Then, I ask a series of oral follow-up questions connected to the original retrieval practice question and students give spoken responses. The intention here is to deepen their understanding of the initial answer by engaging in a process of elaboration. These follow-up questions help students to integrate the information with their existing knowledge as well as ensuring that they engage in deeper, semantic processing, thereby improving both retention and understanding (Dunlosky, 2013).

Let's look at an example:

Answer to retrieval practice question: 'Sibilance'

Possible oral follow-up questions:

a. What is the adjective of sibilance?

Drawing attention to and practising different forms of the same word can have a noticeable effect on students' interest in word formation, encouraging them to make generalisations as they attempt to nominalise and make other morphological transformations.

b. Tell me a sibilant phrase

c. What is the effect of the sibilance in 'the merciless iced east winds that knives us'

While the first follow-up question focuses on the form of the word, an approach that could be seen as only involving shallow processing as it is centred upon the words appearance, these two questions are very much focused upon meaning and involve deeper, semantic processing. You may recognise the quotation as a line from Wilfred Owen's haunting war poem, *Exposure* and, in this example, 'sibilance' was initially taught in conjunction with it.

Accurate and effortless application of vocabulary is the ultimate aim. Initially, I want them to successfully use a word in the first context that they encounter it and will ask them to apply it to the current text we are studying; later on, I will ask them to apply it to different texts, attempting to achieve near transfer. It seems that, despite the fact that transfer is difficult to achieve, prompting and asking students to repeatedly extend their practice and application to different situations, tasks and units may go some way towards achieving it (Butler, 2010).

> Answer to retrieval practice question: 'Juxtaposition'
> Possible oral follow-up questions:

a. What is the verb?
b. What is the general effect of juxtaposition?
c. How is it different from an oxymoron?

Asking questions about concepts that are minimally different from the original idea allows students to better discriminate between the two. If they understand both the scope and the boundaries of a concept, the potential for confusion and ambiguity will hopefully be minimised.

> Answer to retrieval practice question: 'Polysemic'
> Possible oral follow-up questions:

a. What does the prefix 'poly' mean?

> Suffixes, prefixes and roots are important: morphology allows students to generalise and adapt.

b. Think of another word that starts with the prefix 'poly'
c. If 'poly' means many, which prefixes can mean 'one'?
d. Is 'polysemous' the same as 'ambiguous'?

> Answer to retrieval practice question: 'Venerate'
> Possible oral follow-up questions:

a. Which word is a synonym of 'venerate'?

In this particular example, I am asking them to connect 'venerate' with another similar word that they have previously been taught: 'revere'. This type of question can be used to make deliberate connections to previous content but equally, it can be used to help student integrate the word with their existing knowledge.

b. What is the noun?

c. Why is Macbeth venerated at the start of the play?

d. Give me a sentence using 'venerate'

Let's look at a second example of retrieval practice from a Year 7 unit on Shakespearean rhetoric which exemplifies the range of questions that could be asked. Crucially, all the questions are about content that they have been taught.

1. What rhetorical technique involves three ideas in a row?
   Possible oral follow-up question:

   a. Give me an example of a tricolon from Marc Anthony's speech in Julius Caesar

2. Who wrote Telephone Conversation and what country is he from?

   But isn't this just a pub quiz type question? What is the point in knowing this? At one level, all knowledge is trivial: what one person deems important, another considers trifling. This question asks about a poem from a previous unit and is included here because I want students to remember the name of Wole Soyinka, a Nobel Prize winning writer, as well as the ideas and words within his poem.
   Possible oral follow-up questions:

   a. What was the difference between the two characters in the poem?
   b. What does the poem convey about racism?

   Of course, the aim here is not to learn disconnected, individual facts; instead, the longer term aim is to build up rich, interconnected webs of knowledge (Christodoulou, 2014) – mental representations that are also called schemata which we will explore in more depth in the next chapter.

SURELY A QUIZ CANNOT HELP STUDENTS WRITE ESSAYS?

Despite the body of research that demonstrates the efficacy of retrieval practice (see Karpicke, 2017 for a review of the some of the last decade's progress in this area), there has been a notable concern about how it is being approached and whether or not it really is as effective as its proponents would claim. One line of criticism is that the questions – often closed, recall questions – are nothing like the final performance that students encounter when they take an exam. Merely asking students something along the lines of 'What word means excessive pride or ambition?' is, on its own, not going to help students with their understanding of Macbeth. However, understanding the meaning of 'hubris' (even in this most restrictive question answer example) may well be the necessary, inflexible beginning of their journey towards knowing how Macbeth's hubris is his harmartia.

It is the job of teachers to skilfully transform this inflexible knowledge into flexible understanding.

In *Learning as a Generative Activity* by Fiorella and Mayer (2015), a book that explores eight learning strategies that promote understanding, self-testing (a different name for retrieval practice) is explained as being an effective study strategy. One of the strengths of Learning as a Generative Activity is that the authors are careful to outline the boundary conditions under which a strategy is most effective. In the minds of some teachers, retrieval practice has reached the status of 'universally a good thing' and this is potentially a problem. Like all pedagogical approaches, the decision when and how to apply it requires thought and judgement. If a strategy reaches the status of '100% effective', then the nuance and theory that supports it will be lost as teachers pursue the surface features, unaware that the deep structure of the approach requires more than the mere robotic delivery of a quiz every single lesson.

Fiorella and Mayer (2015, p. 98) point out that, for retrieval practice to be most effective, there are a number of important things that need to be considered:

1. **Learners need to receive corrective feedback following practice testing.**
   This can act as a form of AfL as, when corrections are provided, students are able to plug tiny gaps in their knowledge. With instant corrective feedback, students can also benefit from the *hyper-correction effect*. This is the idea that the more confident students are that their answer is correct, the more likely they are to not repeat the error if they are corrected.

2. **Self-testing is often more effective when questions are free-recall or short answer.**
   Free-recall is also known as a 'brain dump' and involves students writing down everything that they know regarding a specific topic.
   Here are some examples of free recall questions:

   a. Write down everything you know about Hyde in *The Strange Case of Dr Jekyll and Mr Hyde*
   b. Spend 5 minutes writing as much as you can about dystopia in *The Giver*.

3. **Tests should be taken repeatedly.**
   If we are to slow the rate of forgetting and help our students to retain what they have learnt, then we should be regularly and repeatedly testing our students instead of just testing them once. Repeated retrieval practice is far more effective at improving long-term retention than repeated studying, especially when there is a delay between the final assessment and the initial period of study (Roediger and Karpicke, 2006b).
   But how frequently should we test students? What do we need to bear in mind when planning retrieval practice episodes into our curricula?
   For retrieval practice to be most beneficial, students need to be able to successfully recall the content (Karpicke and Bauernschmidt, 2011). However, the greatest boost to long-term retention comes from effortful, difficult retrieval (Bjork and Bjork, 1992).
   Here are some approaches that will involve more effortful retrieval:

   1. Spacing out the initial retrieval episode so that there is a time gap between initial teaching and initial retrieval

2. Using 'free recall' in the initial retrieval episode (Karpicke, 2017)
3. Giving students weaker or lesser cues to aid them (Carpenter and DeLosh, 2006)

All three approaches above are useful if, and only if, they result in successful retrieval. The challenge here is to balance retrieval success with retrieval effort (Karpicke, 2017). If retrieval is too difficult, either because too much time has passed or not enough cues were given in the retrieval task, then students will not be able to retrieve the information successfully, meaning they won't improve their long-term retention. However, if retrieval is too easy, either because not enough time has passed or too many cues were given, then the boost to long-term retention will be small or even non-existent. Professor Robert Bjork explains that 'When something is maximally accessible from memory, little or no learning results from studying or retrieving that something' (Bjork, 2011).

The ideal approach will be to give students the smallest amount of support that results in retrieval success (Karpicke, 2017). Additionally, the time gap between initial teaching and subsequent retrieval episodes should be as long as possible while again ensuring that each retrieval episode is successful (Karpicke and Bauernschmidt, 2011). The sweet spot seems to be successful retrieval just before the content is forgotten.

4. **There should be a close match between practice test items and the final test.**
    A common criticism of retrieval practice is that there is a disconnect between quizzing and final performance. This is particularly apparent with English as our subject is usually assessed via extended writing: there is a stark difference between closed recall questions and essays. Being able to recall that a word beginning with 'At...' means 'relating to or characterized by reversion to something ancient or ancestral' is in no way going to help a student with writing an essay response that explores how the boys in *Lord of the Flies* descend into barbarism and savagery. However, if retrieval practice is being used appropriately, the closed question about 'atavism' would not exist on its own, instead being the beginning of a series of questions or being part of a wider recall activity that allows students to make the necessary links between vocabulary, character and theme. If the retrieval practice is effective, the concept of 'atavism' would not be retrieved in isolation or seen as an end itself. The teacher would carefully situate it within a wider body of knowledge, asking follow-up questions and discussing it in terms of the final test outcome: extended critical interpretation.

A recent paper by Pooja Agarwal (2019) entitled 'Retrieval Practice & Bloom's Taxonomy: Do Students Need Fact Knowledge Before Higher Order Learning?' explored the efficacy of different forms of retrieval practice and came to similar conclusions to those in Learning as a Generative Activity.

Here are some of Agarwal's (2019) key findings with some commentary:

1. **Closed, unconnected 'fact' quizzing will not help students perform well in higher order tasks**
    If retrieval practice means merely asking a series of closed recall questions, then this activity will probably not lead to successful performance on higher order tasks like extended writing.

2. **Higher order quizzing helps students with higher order testing**
   We should ask students retrieval questions that span the higher strata in Bloom's taxonomy.

   While there may be some contention regarding the strict hierarchical nature of the taxonomy (Lemov, 2017), it is a good idea to ask questions that involve a deeper level of processing than mere factual recall.

   I often have an open recall question on the board at the start of a lesson. Because students tend to trickle into the class over a number of minutes, this means that those who arrive the earliest can begin working instantly instead of waiting for all students to get there before we begin a quiz. Also, the tasks are deliberately open ended – I often give them a 5-minute limit – so that low and high attainers can attempt them successfully, the differentiation here being by the depth and complexity of the outcome. I will often follow these open-ended tasks with something that looks more like a quiz.

   Here are some examples of higher order, open recall questions:

   a. Why is Gerald the most sinister character in An Inspector Calls?
   b. Think back to London, how do you know that Blake was a Romantic poet from the content of the poem?
   c. What kind of ruler is Creon in *Antigone*?
   d. Which of Owen's war poems is the most harrowing and why?

All of these questions are asking for higher order cognitive processing, ensuring that there is a closer link between the practice and final test. However, if students are to produce high quality answers to these questions, it is often important to have previously asked them narrower retrieval questions on the required components, initially in isolation, then later asking students to make links between the individual items thereby facilitating the integration of the individual concepts. This process reflects the journey from inflexible to flexible knowledge: well planned and carefully sequenced retrieval tasks can help students move along this continuum. While initial quizzing may be factual and restrictive, later retrieval tasks will look far more like essays or extended writing. If I were to skip straight to asking open-ended retrieval tasks, then students may not be able to retrieve and therefore apply the relevant components, precluding them from producing a high quality response.

Let's look at an example:

Why is Gerald the most sinister character in *An Inspector Calls*?

Assuming a student has attended the lessons where Gerald's character has been taught, then they will be able to answer this question at some level. If, however, this was the first retrieval question that they were asked, then their answer may lack some of the specific components that the question requires. Teaching students the components and ensuring that they can retrieve and apply these before they are asked to attempt a more complex task may well be a more efficient approach to mastering the content than beginning with a higher order complex retrieval task. If students skip straight to the open-ended retrieval task, then their poor performance will necessitate complex and detailed feedback in order to close the gap. Not only will this be time-consuming, but it may also be very difficult or even impossible for students to take on board the feedback because of the myriad omissions and errors that they made. It may be far more efficient to insist that students retrieve and master each component before attempting to combine them into a complex task.

Here is a list of some of the components that I want students to be able to include in their answer:

Vocabulary

- exploitative
- objectify
- infidelity
- unscrupulous
- disparity
- benevolence
- supercilious

Textual References

- 'I suppose it was inevitable'
- 'young and fresh and charming'
- 'made the people find food for her'
- 'I didn't feel about her as she felt about me'
- 'I didn't install her there so that I could make love to her'

  Initial retrieval questions that focus on these components may look like classic closed questions, things like:
- Which word beginning with EX means the take advantage of someone?
- Complete the quotation: 'I suppose it was inev.........'

When feeding back with these initial retrieval questions, the teacher should ask a number of follow-up questions to ensure that students begin, even at this early stage, to engage in higher order thinking, therefore focusing on understanding from the beginning. Although the initial retrieval questions may be closed, these follow-up questions will have mixed formats.

Here is the original, closed, single component retrieval question:
- Which word beginning with EX means the take advantage of someone?
  Here are some possible follow-up questions:
- How does Gerald exploit Eva?
- What is it about Gerald that makes his actions so exploitative?
- What is the most sinister part of his exploitative behaviour?
- Who else exploits Eva?
- How were the lower classes exploited in Edwardian society?

In Chapter 8, we will explore some of the theory behind Direct Instruction. One core idea from DI is that individual components-perhaps vocabulary or sentence structures-are 'firmed' before students are asked to use them in wider applications. The term 'firmed' here refers to accuracy, fluency and retention, and students are often expected to demonstrate these stages of learning by applying a concept in a restricted context before they are asked to combine a concept or skill into something more broad or complex. DI schemes use track planning where many different concepts are being 'firmed', each concept moving along a continuum from inflexible to flexible knowledge and slowly being combined and integrated with others. The idea here is that the atomisation of content allows students to experience consistently high success rates which can be really motivating, particularly for low attaining students. Equally, it allows the teacher to give instant, precise and effective feedback on each of the components. In the initial stages of learning, instant feedback is really important and if used in conjunction with some form of atomisation where components are taught and practiced initially in isolation, then this can help prevent cumulative dysfluency, the idea that if a student has multiple gaps within their knowledge base, then this will effectively prevent them from acquiring or developing more complex skills like essay writing. If students are asked to skip straight to the higher order retrieval question (Why is Gerald the most sinister character in *An Inspector Calls*), then the danger is that they may make so many errors and omissions that effective feedback becomes impossible. Additionally, if students find a task too challenging or seemingly impossible, then this can demotivate them.

3. **If a test item involves higher order processing, then retrieval practice activities should involve 'higher order and mixed quizzing'.**
   Writing essays is a complex task that involves the full range of strata within Bloom's taxonomy, including lots of 'higher order processing'. Using the 2001 revised Bloom's taxonomy, the paper defines 'higher order learning' as being the top three layers of the Bloom's pyramid: 'apply, analyse, evaluate and create'.

   Agarwal (2019) defines 'mixed quizzes' as retrieval practice that involves both factual and higher order questions and posits that 'mixed complexity during initial learning may serve as an effective alternative to the prevalent 'factual knowledge first' standpoint'. Agarwal (2019) also demonstrates that fact quizzing will not, on its own, lead to good outcomes on higher order test items.

   Because almost all examination questions or final assessment tasks in English involve some level of higher order processing, this finding is of crucial importance to teachers.

   The optimum retrieval approach to choose at a point in time will be heavily dependent upon the prior knowledge of the students in front of you. At the beginning of an instructional sequence with novice students, it may be appropriate to ask closed fact questions first so that students can acquire the concept or idea that you are teaching. This does not mean that this is all you should do though. As we have seen with The Levels of Processing Model, teachers should continually be asking students to think hard about the concepts that they acquire so that their understanding gradually moves from being inflexible to flexible, helping them make links between different concepts and integrate them with their prior knowledge as well as asking them to apply, analyse, evaluate what is being taught.

   So what might a mixed quiz look like?

   For students to succeed in extended writing tasks, they need to *select, organise* and *integrate* often complex and abstract information, and then thread it all together into a coherent argument or explanation. To add to the challenge, the assessment task is often delayed past the point of original instruction, meaning that they also need to do this from memory, retrieving and applying the information under pressure and in a limited time frame. Students need to have lightning quick recall as well as the cognitive dexterity to not only recognize which concepts are best deployed to a specific question, but also the ability to transfer their knowledge to questions that, while using novel terminology or phrasing, are essentially asking the same thing as those that they have practiced in class.

Here are some approaches that can help with this challenge:

1. **Listing Stuff**
   Instead of asking a series of unconnected factual questions, students can be asked to group information together in lists.

   While asking for a list of facts is clearly more challenging that merely asking for one adjective, this still does not involve students doing anything more than remembering these words. Agarwal (2019) would point out that this disconnect between retrieval task and final test (in this case an essay) would mean that this quiz would be unlikely to help student performance in their Literature GCSE. However, the initial teacher question would then be followed by a number of other questions that would involve higher order processing, ensuring that the retrieval is mixed, an approach that should improve higher order test performance.

Here are some possible follow-up retrieval questions that involve higher-order questioning:

2. **Because/But/So**
   Teacher: Copy and complete my sentences:

   - Romeo is dejected because...
   - Romeo is melancholic so...

3. **Because/But/So with additional success criteria**
   Teacher: Copy and complete my sentences, making sure you include the additional components

   - Romeo is lovelorn because

   Include:
   - unrequited
   - fickle
   - two pieces of evidence from act 1:2
     The regular inclusion of success criteria like these is a useful way to help students combine components into their responses. If I were to ask the question above, each of the bullet points would have already been taught and retrieved separately beforehand. Unless students have been taught the components here, it is likely that they will not be able to apply them, even in this restrictive activity. As an instructional sequence progresses and students become gradually more competent, two things will slowly change. Firstly, the context of these practice activities will slowly widen: students may start with sentence based practice, then move to paragraphs and then finally attempt full essays. Secondly, these prompts will slowly be removed

as students no longer need to be made explicitly aware of the links between components or what is required by the question. The speed in which these changes happen will be dependent upon the prior knowledge of the students: higher ability classes will move more quickly towards independent and more extended responses and some may be able to skip these restricted, scaffolded stages entirely. For students with lower prior knowledge, these heavily prompted tasks can be invaluable stepping stones on the journey towards independence.

4. **Analytical questioning**
   Teacher: Why is Mr Birling haughty?
5. **Evaluative questioning**
   Teacher: Who is more patronising? Mrs B or Mr B
6. **Extended Quizzing**
   Self-testing that uses a 'free recall' approach (also known as a 'brain dump') can be a really effective method and asking students to write down all the ideas that they know about a subject is clearly more challenging than splitting the information up into lots of different questions. However, if an instructional sequence begins with free recall as the method of retrieval, there are two potential problems. Firstly, students may find the task so difficult that they then become demotivated. Secondly, students may dump what they know onto the page in a haphazard and disorganized fashion, preventing them from thinking about and retaining the connections and links between individual ideas.

Similarly, if we merely ask a series of closed unconnected fact recall questions, this approach on its own will not enhance higher order learning as it will not allow students to see how concepts connect with each other, nor will it help them combine their ideas into schemas. For this to happen, teachers need to make these connections explicit to students and one way of doing this is through 'extended quizzing'.

Let's look at an example:

Figure 3.1 Extended quizzing example

Figure 3.1 shows the answers to a retrieval quiz about Macbeth. These were the questions that were asked in the order that they were posed:

- Complete the quotation 'fair is foul and .... is ....'
- What technique is being used here? 'chi...............'
- Write down two words that describe the witches language

All these questions are connected, and the intention here is to get student to start connecting this information together: asking this sequence of questions makes the links between the individual concepts explicit, allowing students to organize and integrate them, the intention being to not only teach the specific concepts, but to also teach how they fit together in a larger knowledge system. If teachers do not teach these organisational structures and connections, then some students will not make these links. As we shall see in 3, 4 and 5, a core tenet of explicit and direct instruction is that teachers teach everything that students will need and teaching the relationship between concepts is a vital part of this.

Here is a second example:

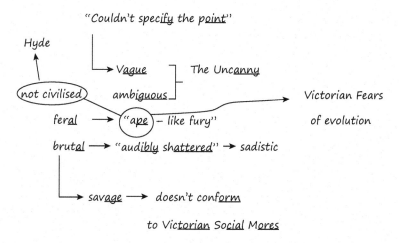

Figure 3.2 Extended quizzing example 2

Figure 3.2 is from a retrieval quiz about Jekyll and Hyde, focusing upon Hyde.

These are the questions that were asked in the initial retrieval quiz in the order that they were posed:

- How does Enfield describe Hyde's repulsiveness? (couldn't specify the point)
- What two words describe his repulsiveness? (vague, ambiguous)
- What psychological concept does this relate to? (The Uncanny)
- Hyde is uncivilised and almost wild, what word can we use to describe this idea? (feral)
- Complete the quotation that demonstrates this attribute (ape-like fury)
- Circle the word that demonstrates that Hyde is animalistic (ape)
- What broader societal unease and fear does this word link to? (Victorian fears of evolution)
- Hyde's violence is extreme, what word can we use to describe it? (brutal)
- Complete the quotation that demonstrates this (audibly shattered)

- Hyde seems to enjoy inflicting pain on people, write down the word we can use for this pleasure (sadistic)
- Write down another word to describe Hyde's attack (savage)
- What does his extreme behaviour suggest? (doesn't conform to Victorian social mores)

While this example has plenty of clues and hints to help students successfully retrieve the information from memory, these are not always required. As an instructional sequence progresses, these hints and clues can be faded out so that students are retrieving the information with less support and higher attaining classes can dispense with this support at a much earlier point.

I would use extended quizzing as an intermediary approach in between classic short answer, closed questions and free recall. Earlier lessons may see extended quizzing; later lessons may see freer recall style retrieval. While extended quizzing sees the teacher creating the links and organising the material into a logical structure, free recall shifts the responsibility to the student as they are asked to recall and organise the information themselves.

With essay writing as the final outcome, Table 3.1 explores the benefits and detriments of different retrieval types:

Table 3.1 Benefits and detriments of different approaches to retrieval practice

Type of retrieval practice	Example question	Benefit	Detriment	How to overcome problem
Restricted, closed lower order question	What word means harmful of evil? ...*sinister*	High success rate; precise corrective feedback can be given	Isolated closed question on its own will not help students if final test involves higher order tasks	Ask follow-up questions or use extending quizzing to help student integrate knowledge and use higher order thinking
Extended Quizzing	See examples above	Explicitly teaches links and relationships between concepts; encourages students to integrate concepts	Initially, success is dependent upon teacher created cues	Fade out cues over time; slowly shift responsibility to student
Free Recall	Write down everything you know about Hyde	Close match between retrieval task and final assessment	Does not teach relationships between concepts	Use extended quizzing before free recall
Higher order questions **early** in an instructional sequence	Why is Gerald the most sinister character?	Will help students if final test involves higher tasks	Student success rate may be low: demotivating for students, difficult to give corrective feedback.	'Firm' up components (vocabulary/ evidence etc) before asking this wider question
Higher order questions **later** in an instructional sequence	Why is Gerald the most sinister character?	Will help students if final test involves higher tasks	If students have not been firmed on components earlier in sequence, success rate may be low	Retrieve and master components before attempting this wider task

TWO IMPORTANT VARIABLES: TIME AND CONTEXT

Effective and efficient instructional sequences will depend upon two important variables. Firstly, the context and type of retrieval activities should begin as restrictive tasks and move slowly towards wider application. Secondly, retrieval will be distributed over time in order to ensure long-term retention.

Figure 3.3 shows the relationship between the two variables and how specific retrieval tasks may be more appropriate at the start or the end of an instructional sequence:

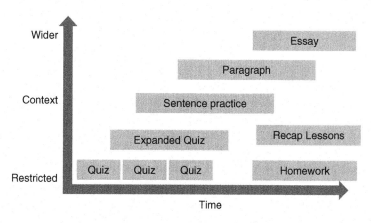

Figure 3.3   The relationship between type of retrieval and time

At the start of an instructional sequence, a 'quiz' of restrictive closed questions may be most appropriate; at the end of a sequence and closer to the final test, wider retrieval tasks like paragraph and essay writing may be more suitable. As time progresses, the retrieval tasks should become wider, eventually mirroring the intended final outcome of the instructional sequence: extended writing.

ADDITIONAL BENEFITS OF RETRIEVAL PRACTICE

The benefits of retrieval practice have been demonstrated across a range of learning materials, including prose passages and tests that involve the kind of tasks that occur in the English classroom like comprehension questions (Fiorella and Mayer, 2015, p. 103). Retrieval practice has also been shown to be an effective strategy for learners of different ages, levels of prior knowledge and ability as well as being a relatively easy and time efficient method of learning (Dunlosky et al., 2013).

In addition to helping students retain information, retrieval practice confers a number of other benefits (Roediger et al., 2011):

1. **Retrieval practice can identify gaps in student knowledge**
   This can help students better identify areas in need of further study. As we have already seen, students are often bad at evaluating what they know and regular retrieval practice can help make them aware of their weaknesses. It also provides valuable feedback to teachers so that they can decide on their steps in learning: this is where the distinction between *performance* and *learning* is so

important. If students cannot successfully recall information after a delay, then even they *performed* well in class when the content was initially taught, we cannot assume that they have *learned*. Repeated, distributed retrieval practice is a useful way of making inferences about *learning* so that we are not tricked into equating good *performance* with good *learning*.

2. **It produces better organisation of knowledge**

   Compared to rereading or restudying, retrieval practice requires students to think more about how the information is organised. If a student is asked to engage in a free recall activity about a poem, then they will need to organise, group and connect different categories of information including things like quotations, thematic ideas, socio-historical context, techniques and vocabulary to use in their response. It may be appropriate to use extended quizzing as a means of supporting this organisation, at least in the earlier stages of learning.

3. **Retrieval practice improves transfer**

   One of the misconceptions about retrieval practice is that it results in inflexible, rote learning where students engage in a reductive 'stimulus-response' chain of behaviour. This, however, is wrong: regular retrieval practice can help increase the flexibility of knowledge so that it can be transferred to new settings.

4. **Retrieval practice can help with retrieval of material that was not tested**

   Our memories work in strange and deeply counter-intuitive ways. We have already seen that retrieving information can make it harder to retrieve other similar or connected information – a phenomena known as 'retrieval induced forgetting'. The opposite phenomena are known as 'retrieval-induced facilitation' where taking a test can actually improve retention of non-tested but related material. Both of these ideas are directly contradictory. As we have already seen, 'retrieval induced forgetting' confers an evolutionary advantage, helping us to efficiently and accurately recall what is relevant without getting confused by similar information. This advantage may well not translate to studying though as presumably we want students to remember as much as possible; luckily, 'retrieval induced forgetting' doesn't seem to occur on tests that are delayed a day or more past the point of initial study (Macleod and Macrae, 2001).

TROUBLE SHOOTING

Table 3.2 demonstrates what to do if students are failing to either remember or understand what you are teaching:

Table 3.2   Trouble shooting table

Student behaviour	Remembering	Understanding	Type of learning	Detriment	What next?
Students performed badly in class and can't remember what they learned	No	No	None	Nothing has been learned at all	Reteach
Students performed well in class but cannot recall the information at a later date	No	At the point of teaching	Crammed	Because students can't recall what they have learned, they cannot use the information	Reteach followed by distributed retrieval practice

Table 3.2 Trouble shooting table *(Continued)*

Student behaviour	Remembering	Understanding	Type of learning	Detriment	What next?
Students can recall information but cannot explain what it means	Yes	No	Rote (inflexible)	Learning is based on a very narrow set of cues. Students will likely be flummoxed by even the slightest change from the original context	Elaboration Examples Explanation Varied practice
Students can recall information which they are able to explain fully	Yes	Yes	Good Learning		Distributed retrieval practice in order to prevent forgetting

SUMMARY

- If we want students to retain and understand what we teach them, retrieval practice can be an effective approach to use.
- For retrieval practice to be most effective, students should receive corrective feedback, tests should be distributed across time and students should be given the least amount of support that results in successful retrieval.
- Student performance in complex tasks like extended writing can be improved through the use of retrieval practice but careful thought needs to be given as to the approach that is used.

REFERENCES

Agarwal, P. K. (2019). Retrieval practice & Bloom's taxonomy: Do students need fact knowledge before higher order learning? *Journal of Educational Psychology, 111*(2), 189–209.

Bjork, R. A., & Bjork, E. L. (1992). A new theory of disuse and old theory of stimulus fluctuation. In A. Healy, S. Kosslyn & R. Shiffrin (Eds.), *From learning processes to cognitive processes: Essays in honor of William K Estes* (Vol. 2, pp. 35–67). Hillsdale, NJ: Erlbaum.

Bjork, R. A. (2011). On the symbiosis of remembering, forgetting, and learning. In A. S. Benjamin (Ed.), *Successful remembering and successful forgetting: A festschrift in honor of Robert A. Bjork* (pp. 1–22). Psychology Press.

Butler, C. (2010). Repeated testing produces superior transfer of learning relative to repeated studying. *Journal of Experimental Psychology: Learning, Memory and Cognition, 36*(5), 1118–1133.

Butterfield, B., & Metcalfe, J. (2006). The correction of errors with high confidence. *Metacognition Learning, 1,* 69–84.

Carpenter, S. K., & DeLosh, E. L. (2006). Impoverished cue support enhances subsequent retention: Support for the elaborative retrieval explanation of the testing effect. *Memory & Cognition, 34*(2), 268–276.

Christodoulou, I. (Spring 2014). Minding the knowledge gap the importance of content in student learning. *American Educator, 27–33.*

Dunlosky, J. (Fall 2013). Strengthening the student tool Box. *American Educator, 37.*

Dunlosky, J., Rawson, K. A., Marsh, E. J., Nathan, M. J., & Willigham, D. T. (2013). Improving students' learning with effective learning techniques: Promising directions from cognitive and educational psychology. *Psychological Science in the Public Interest, 14*(1), 4–58.

Fiorella, L., & Mayer, R. (2015). *Learning as a generative activity: Eight learning strategies that promote understanding.* Cambridge: Cambridge University Press.

Karpicke, J. D. (2017). *Retrieval-based learning: A decade of progress learning and memory: A comprehensive reference* (2nd ed., Vol. 2). Cambridge, MA: Elsevier.

Karpicke, J. D., & Bauernschmidt, A. (2011). Spaced retrieval: Absolute spacing enhances learning regardless of relative spacing. *Journal of Experimental Psychology: Learning, Memory, and Cognition, 37*(5), 1250–1257.

Karpicke, J. D., Butlet, A. C., & Roediger, H. L. (2009). Metacognitive strategies in student learning: Do students practise retrieval when they study on their own? *Memory May, 17*(4), 471–479. https://doi.org/10.1080/09658210802647009

Lemov (2017). https://teachlikeachampion.org/blog/blooms-taxonomy-pyramid-problem/ #:~:text=Familiarly%20known%20as%20Bloom's%20Taxonomy,Analysis%2C%20Synthesis%2C%20and%20Evaluation

Macleod, M. D., & Macrae, C. (2001). Gone but not forgotten: The transient nature of retrieval-induced forgetting. *Psychological Science, 12*, 148–152.

Roediger, H. L., & Karpicke, J. D. (2006a). Test-enhanced learning taking memory tests improves long term improvements from quizzing. *Journal of Experimental Psychology Applied, 17*(4), 382–395.

Roediger, H. L., & Karpicke, J. D. (2006b). The power of testing memory basic research and implications for retention. *Psychological Science, 17*(3), 181–210.

Roediger, H. L., Putnam, A. L., & Smith, M. A. (2011). Ten benefits of testing and their applications to educational practice. *Psychology of Learning and Motivation, 55*, 1–36.

Rowland, C. A. (2014). The effect of testing versus restudy on retention: A meta-analytic review of the testing effect. *Psychological Bulletin, 140*(6), 1432–1463.

Shipstead, Z., Hicks, K. L., & Engle, R. W. (2012). Cogmed working memory training: Does the evidence support the claims? *Journal of Applied Research in Memory and Cognition, 1*(3), 185–193.

Wiliam, D. (2018). *Memories are made of this.* https://www.tes.com/news/memories-are-made-3

4

NOVICES AND EXPERTS

In this chapter, we will explore

- Cognitive Load Theory
- What is the difference between novices and experts?
- What are schema and what role do they have in learning?
- The Worked Example effect
- The Alternation Strategy
- Completion problems
- Backwards fading: moving from I to We to You
- The Expertise Reversal Effect
- The Instructional Hierarchy

INTRODUCTION

According to Cognitive Load Theory (CLT), novices and experts learn differently and teachers should take this into account when making instructional choices. This chapter will explore some of the important findings from CLT and other related ideas.

WHAT IS COGNITIVE LOAD THEORY?

In Chapter 1, I explained how Willingham's simple memory model can be useful for teachers and how learning can be described as 'a change in long-term memory'. Chapters 2 and 3 built on this model and definition, further explaining the important distinction between working memory and long-term memory as well as exploring strategies to help students to remember and understand the content that we teach. We can think of our working memory as being roughly equivalent to what we are conscious of at any one time (Sweller et al., 1998) and as we have seen, working memory is limited.

CLT is also based upon this model of cognition. According to CLT (Sweller et al., 1998), if instructional procedures are to be effective, they need to respect the limits of working memory so as to not confuse or overwhelm students – after all, we can only pay attention to so much information at once. Additionally, CLT suggests that the optimal instructional choice will be largely determined by the level of expertise of the students that we are teaching: novices should study worked examples and models; more expert learners should be given problem solving, application and freer practice.

WHAT IS THE DIFFERENCE BETWEEN EXPERTS AND NOVICES?

What is it that makes experts proficient? A study was conducted by Chase and Simon (1973) to investigate what made grandmaster chess players superior to other players. While an intuitive answer may have attributed their dominance to more proficient problem solving abilities, the application of a generic 'means-ends' analytical approach or the fact that they weighed up and considered a wider range of alternative strategies, the reality was a difference in their memories. Players, both expert and novice, were shown a chess board with pieces arranged in plausible and typical game situations for five seconds. When asked to recall the positions of the chess pieces, expert players were significantly and consistently better than novices. However, if the pieces were arranged randomly, then this gap in performance disappeared: experts and novices performed the same. With the random configurations, experts could not rely upon recalling thousands of game configurations as the pieces did not conform to or fit game patterns that they had stored in long-term memory.

This effect is not specific to the game of chess. If you were asked to repeat the previous sentence from memory, you would more than likely find this to be an easy task, despite the fact that the sentence contains 39 separate letters. However, if those 39 letters were arranged in random configurations, you would likely find the task impossible (Sweller et al., 2011). Like the expert chess players, your ability to recreate the sentence with fidelity is down to the information stored in your long-term memory – as an expert reader, you will have read many sentences that contain similar or even identical syntax and you will know how to spell each individual word.

Similar results to the chess study have also been found in other domains, including recall of text (Chiesi et al., 1979) and algebra (Sweller and Cooper, 1985). The conclusion of these studies is that when solving problems or engaged in cognitive work, experts rely upon their larger and more developed long-term memory deposits, patterns of information that are also called schemas.

WHAT ARE SCHEMA?

Schema can be seen as structured webs of knowledge within our long-term memories, serving to select and organise incoming information (Mayer, 2008, p. 79). If our schema are detailed, systematised and readily accessible, they will allow us to engage in the three stages of cognitive processing:

Stage 1: *Selecting* relevant information to attend to
We are far more likely to select the correct information if we know something about it: what we already know determines what we see (Kirschner and Hendrick, 2020, p. 6).

Stage 2: *Organising* the material into a coherent cognitive structure in working memory

If we have automatized aspects of relevant knowledge – something that is a core part of schema construction – then we will no longer need to pay any conscious attention to them, potentially freeing up capacity within our working memories. Additionally, if we have the relevant prior knowledge, this will help us to interpret and organise it into a coherent structure (Alba and Hasher, 1983).

Stage 3: *Integrating* it with relevant prior knowledge activated from long-term memory

The more detailed and organised a schema is within long-term memory, the more likely that you will be able integrate new information within it and the more you know, the quicker you will be likely to learn new information, provided that there is some connection to what is already within your long-term memory. For example, if you already know some English social history of the early 19th century, you might be quicker to grasp the meaning behind Shelley's *The Masque of Anarchy.*

In a landmark study focusing on Schema theory, Bartlett (1932) asked a participant to read a short Native American folklore narrative. The participant was then asked to recreate as much of the story as they could from memory for a second participant, who was asked to do the same for a third participant. This chain of narrative reconstruction continued until a total of ten participants had read and recorded their memory of the previous person's retelling of the passage. Bartlett found that by the end of the chain, many details had been left out, others had been emphasised and the entire story had been transformed from a story about spirits and ghosts into something more akin to a traditional war story. What had happened was that the participants – who knew next to nothing about Native American culture – had reconstructed the story through the prism of their own schemas. Obvious things – at least to these participants – were accentuated further; things that were unknown or incomprehensible were omitted and finer details were glossed over in favour of the gist or structure of the story. The sense making process of the participants was led by their long-term memories or schema. Had the participants known more about the culture that they were reading about, the omissions and refinements would not have happened in the same manner.

According to schema theory, skilled performance in any domain is developed through building ever greater numbers of increasingly complex schemas (Centre for Education Statistics and Evaluation, 2017). Novices, however, have less relevant knowledge stored in their long-term memory and therefore need to use 'thinking skills' (Sweller et al., 2011). Because *'thinking* skills' rely upon working memory, an aspect of cognition that has a small and fixed capacity for holding and manipulating items, novices soon become overwhelmed and find tasks difficult or impossible as a result. The implications of these findings are striking for teachers. In a general sense, we should be spending much if not most of our time as teachers trying to increase our students' background knowledge so that we can help them overcome the seemingly unalterable capacity in their short-term memory and instead recall, apply and use relevant knowledge from their long-term memories. Sweller et al. (2011) posit that 'we should provide learners with as much relevant information as we are able' and that 'assisting learners to obtain needed information during problem solving should be beneficial'. They also posit that 'Providing them with that information directly and explicitly should be even more beneficial'. Explicit teaching, at least for novices, is almost certainly preferable to asking students to discover things for themselves. If we are not explicit, there is a greater chance that students will not retain and understand what we are teaching, resulting in a missed opportunity for them to increase their knowledge.

However, experts not only know *more* than novices, they also think differently (Kirschner and Hendrick, 2020, p. 9), their schema being deeper, more conceptual and containing a great deal of information regarding the explicit conditions as to when they will or will not be applicable to a specific problem. In a seminal study that explored the difference between how novices and experts represent, interpret and categorise different physics problems, researchers found that experts were faster to categorise problems and link them to possible solutions (Chi et al., 1979). Experts see problems in terms of their deep structures: these are the underlying principles that transcend specific examples. Novices see problems in terms of their surface structure, or the particular aspects of a specific example (Willingham, 2002).

In English, this effect can be seen when novice students are confused by examination questions that contain vocabulary or turns of phrase that they don't understand or were not expecting. Perhaps you have spent time teaching students about Macbeth's ambition but when students are asked to 'Explore the theme of desire in *Macbeth*', they don't realise that this question is very similar to what you have taught them and that writing about ambition here would be a successful approach. By focusing on the word 'desire', they are blinded to the deep thematic similarity to what they have learned in class.

Similarly, students are often confused by different variations of text response questions when they are asked to analyse unseen extracts. As novices, they are slow to realise that the deep structure of different questions are often highly similar and the optimal solutions will require highly similar approaches, components and skills. Experts will not only have more developed schema that they can apply to these novel situations, but they will also be quicker to realise that their schema are applicable. This difference can also be thought of as experience – an expert will have accrued substantially more practice and will have applied their knowledge to a far wider range of situations and tasks than a novice. Because of this, their knowledge can be said to be more flexible and it is this flexibility that gives them an advantage. Novices, in comparison, are limited by the inflexible and more limited nature of their schema. Perhaps the most effective method of developing expertise is through deliberate practice and we will explore this in detail in Chapter 9.

Novices often fail to see similarities between questions, instead seeing a task as being unconnected to others; therefore, it can be really useful to group questions for students so that they begin to see the deep structure of what is being asked such as shown in Figure 4.1.

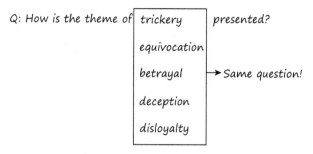

Figure 4.1   Showing how questions are similar

Similarly, demonstrating the similarity between tasks makes it far more likely that students will succeed. Telling students what skills they will need to use and prompting them to do so can be an effective initial approach (Butler, 2010).

Here are two examples:

1. **Comparing texts**
   The deep structure of text comparison tasks are often the same, irrespective of the text type that is to be compared (see Table 4.1).
2. **Persuasive writing**
   Although the text type and purpose (Argue? Persuade? Speech? Article?) may be ostensibly different, the deep structure is often highly similar. If I were to write an answer to either of the questions in Table 4.2, I would use many of the same components and skills. Even if the question asked me to write a letter, then this would still be the case. Unless the mark scheme specifies that students need to present a balanced argument, then both questions can be written in a polemical and impassioned tone, an approach that not only invites the use of rhetorical devices, figurative language and captivating imagery, but also permits students to add their own creative stamp to what can sometimes be seen as a dull task (see Table 4.2).

The link between deep structure and schema is important here. If a student is aware of the deep structure of text comparison, then this is because their schema acts as a kind of template that permits them to effortlessly complete the task. The more practice they get with applying this schema, the easier and more effortless their performance will seem. Anyone who has acquired this schema – and therefore can be said to see the deep structure – will treat tasks as the same, despite any surface level differences like wording, syntax or text type (Sweller et al., 2011).

There is also an important link between the ideas of deep structure, schema and curricula: well sequenced and efficient schemes of learning will teach students 'high-utility' knowledge, concepts and skills that are maximally applicable. In Chapter 8, we will explore Direct Instruction and how some things have higher utility than others. Similarly, in Chapter 5, we will look at how to choose which words to teach and practice. Yes, an expert's ability to see the deep structure may well be synonymous with experience – something that develops incrementally over

Table 4.1 Comparing texts

Text type	Comparing two poems	Comparing two non-fiction texts
Typical question (Surface structure)	*Compare the ways poets present ideas about power in 'Ozymandias' and 'London'*	*Compare how the two writers convey their different attitudes to parenting*
Similarities (Deep structure)	• Whole text structure: introduction, blocked sections on each text and then conclusion • Comparative introductions using 'Both' and 'While' • Analytical compoments, covering WHAT, HOW and WHY (see Chapter 11)	
Differences (Deep structure)	• Different techniques to be analysed according to text type. • Different background knowledge required for each text	

Table 4.2 Similarity across writing tasks

Text type	Writing a speech	Writing an article
Typical question (Surface structure)	*Write a speech arguing for or against banning cars from urban areas.*	*Write an article explaining your position on the use of cars in urban areas.*
Similarities (Deep structure)	• Whole text structure: personal-general-personal (see Chapter 9) • Rhetorical components • Formal tone • Both can be polemical	

time, but this doesn't mean that we cannot take steps towards accelerating this ability within novice students too.

We should teach high-utility, generalisable content combined with a meticulous focus on explicitly demonstrating similarities across different tasks, providing students with the tacit knowledge that experts have and helping to illuminate the deep structure of tasks. One effective method of doing this is by asking students to study worked examples instead of attempting to do the task themselves. A worked example acts as a schema substitute, essentially providing a novice learner with a representation of the schema held in the minds of experts (Clark et al., 2006).

THE WORKED EXAMPLE EFFECT

The worked example effect refers to the idea that if you want novices to succeed in a domain, they would be better studying the solutions to problems rather than attempting to solve them. Asking novice students to repeatedly write extended answers to questions 'unnecessarily adds problem-solving search to the interacting elements, thus imposing an extraneous cognitive load' (Sweller et al., 2011, p. 99). In the absence of well-developed background knowledge, students flounder because they have little stored in their long-term memories to help them. Comments in class such as 'I don't know how to start' and 'what do I write' are sometimes indicative of this scenario.

Responding analytically to texts is a complex activity containing multiple components, many of which are abstruse for novice learners. If you try to describe these elements, you are forced to use abstract phrases like *sophisticated analysis* or *judicious use of quotations* and, in the absence of examples, these terms merely serve to mystify the process further. This is the language of mark schemes, terminology that may make sense to experts but leaves novices confused. Asking students to study worked examples – in English this may mean sentences, paragraphs or essays – exemplifies these opaque terms, converting the abstract into the concrete.

Sweller et al. (2011, p. 99) posit 'worked examples can efficiently provide us with the problem solving schemas that need to be stored in long-term memory'. Studying worked examples is beneficial because it helps to build and develop students' background knowledge within their long-term memories, information that can then be recalled and applied when attempting problems. The grandmasters in the chess study were successful because of the breadth and depth of their background knowledge. Similarly, English teachers find writing (one of the problems in our domain) easy because we have long-term memories that contain myriad 'problem solving schemas' and mental representations of different forms of writing within our long-term memories.

RESEARCH INTO THE WORKED EXAMPLE EFFECT IN ENGLISH

In *Cognitive Load Theory* (2011, p. 102), Sweller et al. refer to English, the Humanities and the Arts as 'ill structured learning domains' to distinguish them from mathematics and science. They make the point that in maths and science problems, we can 'clearly specify the various problem states and the problem solving operators', essentially rules that dictate process and approach; whereas 'ill structured domains' do not have such rigid constraints. Although there are subjective elements within English and often innumerable ways of approaching a task, different approaches may be considered of equal worth and demonstrate a comparable level of proficiency. The variables within analytical writing can, like the colours within a painter's palette, be arranged in numerous and diverse patterns; however, these different configurations can be judged to contain equivalent skill and quality. Despite this, the researchers make the important point that 'the cognitive architecture…does not distinguish between well-structured and ill-structured problems' meaning that the findings of CLT apply to all domains (Sweller et al., 2011, p. 102).

The researchers also posit 'the solution variations for ill-structured problems are larger than for well-structured problems but they are not infinite and experts have learned more of the possible variations than novices'. Over the years, teachers have read, thought about and produced innumerable pieces of writing and, as a result, have developed rich schemata of this kind of knowledge which we can recall, choose from and apply when dealing with problems. Sweller et al. (2011, p. 100) point out that 'even though some exposure to worked examples is used in most traditional instructional procedures, worked examples, to be most effective, need to be used much more systematically and consistently to reduce the influence of extraneous problem-solving demands' A curriculum that systematically and consistently uses worked examples should help students build a rich schemata of 'possible variations', moving them quicker and more efficiently along the continuum from novice to expert than if they had just completed lots of writing tasks.

The constant studying of concrete worked examples is far superior to describing proficiency using abstracted and often vague success criteria before then asking students to attempt to produce them. When describing complex performance in the absence of concrete examples, which is the purpose of an examination mark scheme, the sheer breadth and possible variation of what is being described necessitates a wide lens of representation. While this is advantageous to the expert, allowing complexity to be summarised and condensed, it is obfuscatory and perhaps even meaningless for students. Experts have detailed schema that exemplify abstract terms like *critical analysis, judicious references, contextual factors*, novices do not.

In *Cognitive Load Theory* (2011, p. 103), two studies directly relevant to English are referenced. In the first, students were given extracts from Shakespearean plays, half receiving texts with accompanying explanatory notes, the other half receiving no additional notes (Oksa et al., 2010). Perhaps unsurprisingly, the group who were given the notes performed better on a comprehension task. In another study (Kyun et al., 2013), students were given an essay question to answer. One group received model answers to study, the other did not. The study found that the worked example group performed significantly better than the conventional problem-solving group.

Although CLT contains a number of other different effects, the worked example effect is described by the researchers as being 'the most important'.

WHAT DOES THIS LOOK LIKE IN ENGLISH?

If we want students to perform well in complex tasks like writing, we should be giving them the necessary information. CLT points to the superiority of explicit, direct instruction, approaches that are more efficient and effective for novice learners.

VOCABULARY AND SENTENCES

In the English classroom, we should be explicitly teaching sentence structures and vocabulary and we should provide this information to students when they are completing extended writing: one way of doing this is through vocabulary tables that contain definitions and examples. Not just examples of how the vocabulary words are used, but also examples of the sentence styles that students should include. Each of these example sentences is a worked example in itself and, with effective teacher questioning and annotation, can be a powerful way of turning abstract and amorphous success criteria (use sophisticated sentences/use a range of complex sentences, and so on) into concrete examples that the learner can 'study and emulate'. Table 4.3 is a section of a vocabulary table to be used when studying William Blake's poem, *London*.

Students should have these tables when they are annotating the poem, allowing them to make the link between text and interpretation. In Chapter 5, we will explore how these tables can be used to support students when studying texts.

Table 4.3 Example of part of a vocabulary table

Denounce (v) **Denunciation (n)**	Publicly declare to be evil or wrong *A romantic poet who denounced exploitation and oppression, Blake wrote London to highlight the omnipresence of suffering in the city.*
Exploit (v) **Exploitation (n)** **Exploitative (adj)**	To take advantage of; to use someone *Blake was appalled at the exploitation of the marginalised*
Marginalise (v) **Marginalisation (n)** **Marginalised (adj)**	People on the edges of society: the poor, minorities and those thought of as insignificant *The 'charterd' streets exclude the marginalised and the destitute, benefiting only the wealthy and privileged.*

PARAGRAPHS

Students should regularly read, discuss and annotate model paragraphs, labelling transferable components that they can then use in paragraphs of their own. This will help develop their mental representation of what successful writing can look like. Here's an example:

> Macbeth exclaims 'O full of scorpions is my mind' as if he seems traumatised and paranoid, despite the fact that he is now king. The word 'scorpions' reminds us of venom as if his hubristic and sacrilegious actions have harmed him. It is as if his evil actions have poisoned not only his conscience, but also his mental stability. Perhaps Shakespeare is hinting at the dire ramifications of regecide.

THE ALTERNATION STRATEGY

The Alternation Strategy, also known as 'worked example problem pairs', is the idea that 'for an example to be most effective, it had to be accompanied by a problem to solve' (Sweller et al., 2011, p. 104). The most effective use of worked examples is to present a worked example and then immediately follow this example by asking the learner to solve a similar problem. Interestingly, the researchers found that if you give students a number of massed worked examples and follow that later with a similar massed set of problems, then this led to poorer outcomes. For The Alternation strategy to work effectively, both example and problem need to be presented simultaneously.

One of the specific benefits of using worked example problem pairs is that they accelerate learning, reducing the time required for instruction. In *Efficiency in Learning Evidence Based Guidelines to Manage Cognitive Load* by Clark et al. (2006, p. 192), the authors explore a study by Sweller and Cooper which used algebra problems. Students were assigned to two groups: one in which students completed eight problems and the other in which they studied four sets of example problem pairs. The findings are shown in Table 4.4.

The 'all practice' group took nearly six times as long to complete the instructional sequence. Students in the example problem pair group were not only faster at completing the lessons, but they were also faster at completing the test which followed. Additionally, the number of test errors was less for those students who

Table 4.4 Worked example problem pairs compared with only practice (Clark et al., 2006, p. 192)

Outcome	Worked example-practice	All practice
Training time (Sec)	32.0	185.5
Training errors	0	2.73
Test time	43.6	78.1
Test errors	0.18	0.36

had studied using the Alternation Strategy. Another study (Zhu and Simon, 1987) was conducted in Chinese middle schools in which a traditional three-year course consisting of two years of algebra and one year of geometry were successfully completed in two years by replacing some practice with worked examples. This confirms the findings of the previous study and suggests that the technique can be adapted to real-life classrooms and learning.

So what is it that makes the alternation strategy so effective? If a student can study a worked example prior to attempting a similar problem, then the worked example can be used by the student as an analogy to help them solve the problem (Clark et al., 2006, p. 193). As we have already seen, worked examples can be seen as schema substitutes and by studying them, a student can build a schema of how to perform the task. Not only does the worked example present an indication of the 'best solution approach', providing students with a clear idea as to what is expected when they attempt the problem, but it also exemplifies the level of quality that they are to aim for.

COMPLETION PROBLEMS

An intermediate approach, completion problems are an attempt to alleviate the concerns and possible shortcomings with fully worked examples and problem solving. While problem solving may create excessive cognitive load, completion problems could help to mitigate this. While fully worked examples may be ignored or glossed over by students, completion problems require more mental effort, hopefully resulting in students thinking harder about them and therefore building schemas that can be then applied to subsequent problems. Completion Problems are tasks that include 'a partial worked example where the learner has to complete some key solution steps' (Sweller et al., 2011, p. 105).

Table 4.5 displays the results from a study where students were taught statistical concepts like mean, median and mode. Students were placed in one of three instructional set ups: all problems; worked example and practice pairs (The Alternation strategy); and completion problems and practice pairs.

Table 4.5 Worked examples compared with completion problems and all practice (Clark et al., 2006, p. 196)

Outcome	Worked examples	Completion examples	All practice
Test score (0–24)	18.8	16.1	12.4
Time in training	32.3 mins	39.8 mins	42.5 mins
Effort during test (0–9)	3.8	3.1	4.9

EXAMPLES OF COMPLETION PROBLEMS

The following is an example of using completion problems when teaching multiple interpretations:

> Owen describes the gas as a 'green sea', making it seem huge and powerful as it envelops the soldiers. Not only does he want us to..., but he also creates a feeling of...

Here are some examples of completion problems when teaching students to write absolute phrases:

1. He froze in terror, his hands..., his face...
2. The rain lashing down, the wind howling, they couldn't wait to...

So, if both worked examples and completion problems are *'equally effective'*, then how are we to know which one to use? This is an important question, and there is a possible solution in an approach known as 'backwards fading'.

BACKWARDS FADING

A lesson, or series of lessons, that involves 'backwards fading' will begin with worked examples, providing concrete models of what is being taught. The next worked example could be a 'completion problem' where students are expected to finish a particular task that has been started for them; eventually, learners will be asked to attempt entire problems for themselves.

Figure 4.2 shows a conceptual model of this process (Clark et al., 2006):

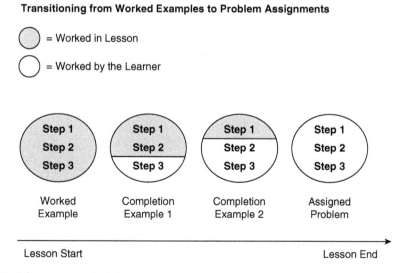

Figure 4.2 Backwards fading

While this conceptual model describes a single lesson, backwards fading will often span multiple lessons as concepts are taught and practised through extended instructional sequences where support is gradually faded out. Chapter 10 will demonstrate what these multi-lesson sequences can look like.

Backwards fading seems like a sensible approach when teaching almost anything as, if it is done correctly by spending sufficient time on each stage, it seems to hit a sweet spot where cognitive load is managed and student effort is maintained. The 'backwards fading' continuum is a sequence of tasks that slowly increases learner application and effort whilst simultaneously reducing the need for worked steps. As students grow in proficiency, they are required to solve more of the problem themselves, a shift that represents the transition from novice to expert.

THE EXPERTISE REVERSAL EFFECT

CLT – and specifically the 'worked example effect' – is dependent upon treating students as being somewhere upon a continuum between 'novice' and 'expert'. The difference between expert and novice is more than a mere labelling exercise and has real implications for instructional and curriculum design.

Clark et al. (2006, p. 249) explain that 'prior knowledge is the one individual difference that has been consistently shown to interact with different instructional methods'. Novices learn best by studying worked examples, model answers that build up their schemas and background knowledge and effectively act as analogous solutions to subsequent problems. While worked examples are optimum for novices, they can actually hinder the learning of more competent learners. Once students have acquired a basic schema for whatever it is that they are learning, they will learn best by applying that schema, thereby making it stronger and more effective. For students who have acquired the necessary schema, studying a worked example will be a redundant activity: instead, they should be applying their knowledge and skills to problems or tasks.

Table 4.6   Novices and experts require different instructional approaches

Broad level of expertise	Instructional choice
Novices	**Worked examples** • Reduces cognitive load for novice learners who lack sufficient background knowledge • Used for building schemas • Exemplifies success criteria or goal
Developing in expertise	**Completion problems** • A hybrid of worked examples and problem solving • Ensures students process worked parts sufficiently
Experts	**Problems** • Allows students with sufficiently developed schemas to apply their knowledge

THE INSTRUCTIONAL HIERARCHY

When teaching something new, what should be the goal of instruction? What kind of measures can be used to indicate proficiency or expertise? While a student's prior knowledge is important when choosing an instructional approach (worked examples for novices and problems for experts), is there anything else that teachers can use to help them make judgements about student proficiency, choose the optimal instructional approach or decide upon the next steps in learning? Is background knowledge the only measure of expertise? The Novice-Expert continuum is often described as if it is a dichotomy – is there any way of adding further nuance to what can often seem like a simplistic polarisation?

One possible approach is the 'Instructional Hierarchy' (Haring et al., 1978). This framework splits learning into five distinct stages (although some adaptations reduce this to 4), each with distinct goals, broad descriptors of competence and suggested instructional approaches.

The five stages:

1. Acquisition
2. Fluency
3. Retention
4. Generalisation
5. Adaptation

Describing the incremental development of expertise, the stages also focus on a number of the important aspects of learning that we have explored in the previous two chapters, including transfer, the change from inflexible to flexible knowledge and memory.

As well as potentially fleshing out the bit in between novice and expert, the stages of learning can help teachers make more precise decisions regarding instructional choices. Teaching is clearly not as simple as choosing between worked examples and problems, and learners are often somewhere in between the absolute descriptors of novice and expert.

Each of the stages may span many lessons and students will be at different stages with different skills. While the end goal of most instruction will always be creative, generalised performance where students deftly choose, adapt and refine what they have learnt in a way that fits whatever context they are presented with, the most efficient way of achieving this will involve multi-lesson instructional sequences that move students through the preceding stages. It is probably impossible to be a fluent performer in a particular discipline if you are inaccurate. Similarly, if you haven't even acquired whatever it is you are learning – perhaps because you failed to select the correct information, then accuracy cannot be developed either. While experts have better organised and more developed knowledge at their disposal, it is how they are able to apply that knowledge that also sets them apart from novices.

STAGE 1: ACQUISITION

This stage of learning refers to students who are learning a skill for the first time. The objective at this stage is for students to learn how to complete the skill accurately and repeatedly.

Acquisition should always begin with modelling where students are shown exactly what they are expected to do before attempting the skill themselves. Students can then use these models as exemplars to consult when attempting to produce their own versions. Teachers should make their thought process explicit when writing live models, discussing their choices and the reasons why they are doing what they are doing. Initial practice activities must allow the teacher to give instant corrective feedback so that errors do not become ingrained and restrictive activities are an efficient way of doing this.

The goal of this stage of learning is for students to be able to accurately perform the skill without any form of support. While tasks will begin with lots of scaffolding, support and prompts, these should be faded out as quickly as possible.

STAGE 2: FLUENCY

Fluency is an important part of expertise in any domain. Expert performance is rapid, smooth and accurate, and seems almost effortless and automatic to an observer. Once students have demonstrated the ability to perform accurately, the next focus for instruction will probably be fluency. Fluency, defined here as accuracy+speed, can be built by engaging in regular, short, practice activities that include a specific focus on speed by setting time limits or counting the number of successful completed trials within a specific time limit. Feedback should be focused on speed and accuracy and students should be praised for increased fluency. Like in the preceding stage, corrective feedback should be instant in order to make sure that students don't ingrain errors.

Asking students to write five specific sentence constructions within a limited time can be a useful fluency starter.

At this stage, students can also be asked to combine skills together in practice activities.

Example 1: Ask students to combine embedded evidence with appositive phrases like this: *The writer describes where the giraffes live as 'nine small puddles', a metaphor that hints at their vulnerability and the fact that their habitats are slowly being destroyed.*

Example 2: Ask students to combine present participles, multiple interpretations and tentative language like this: *Upon hearing the witches' prophecies, Macbeth says 'cannot be ill, cannot be good' as if he is not only intrigued and fascinated by their predictions, but is also slightly horrified by the possible ramifications of usurping King Duncan.*

With these combinatory practice activities, it is important for students to have demonstrated accurate performance in each of the separate components before they are asked to combine them.

STAGE 3: RETENTION

To ensure that students retain the skill, practice should be distributed over weeks, months and even years. Like with fluency practice, periodic review does not need to make up an entire lesson and distributed practice activities can make ideal starters to lessons.

STAGE 4: GENERALISATION

An important aim for instruction is for students to gain a generalised understanding of what is being taught. The ability to generalise is quite similar to the idea of transfer and transfer is the goal of this stage. Distributed and varied practice across the widest possible range of relevant contexts can go some way towards helping students achieve near transfer. Initially, prompts or success criteria can help remind students to apply what they have learned to new contexts.

STAGE 5: ADAPTATION

The adaptation stage builds upon the generalisation stage: at this point students can typically apply the skill in novel situations without prompting from the teacher. Being the final stage in the hierarchy, this stage doesn't end and will typically see students making small modifications and adaptations to the skill, widening its applicability even further and seeking out new creative ways of using it. This stage represents independence and true proficiency-students will be accurate, fluent and able to use the skill with flair and originality.

SUMMARY

- If instruction is to be maximally effective, it should respect the important difference between novices and experts: novices should study worked examples, ideally using the alternation strategy, while experts should be asked to apply what they know. As most students are novices, worked examples should be commonplace within lessons.
- Experts have well organised and extensive schema that they can draw upon when completing tasks; novices do not. For novices, worked examples can act as schema substitutes, helping to build and develop students' background knowledge that they can eventually apply to later tasks.
- Completion problems, partially completed examples, can be a useful stepping stone on the way towards independent application.
- Instructional sequences should go through a process of backwards fading where support is gradually removed as students develop in expertise.
- Expertise can be conceived as being more than just background knowledge: fluency and the ability to generalise are also important attributes of expert performance.

REFERENCES

Alba, J. W., & Hasher, L. (1983). Is memory schematic. *Psychological Bulletin, 93*(2), 203–231.

Barlett, F. C. (1932). *Remembering: A study in experimental and social psychology.* Cambridge: Cambridge University Press.

Butler, C. (2010). Repeated testing produces superior transfer of learning relative to repeated studying. *Journal of Experimental Psychology: Learning, Memory and Cognition, 36*(5), 1118–1133.

Centre for Education Statistics and Evaluation. (2017). *Cognitive load theory: Research that teachers really need to understand.*

Chase, W. G., & Simon, H. A. (1973). Perception in chess. *Cognitive Psychology, 4*, 55–81 in Sweller.

Chi, M. T. H., Feltovich, P. J., & Glaser, R. (1979). Categorisation and representation of physics problems by experts and novices. *Cognitive Science, 5*, 121–152.

Chiesi, H. L., Spilich, G. J., & Voss, J. F. (1979). Acquisition of domain-related information in relation to high and low domain knowledge. *Journal of Verbal Learning and Verbal Behavior, 18*, 257–273.

Clark, R. C., Nguyen, F., & Sweller, J. (2006). *Efficiency in learning evidence based guidelines to manage cognitive load*. San Francisco, CA: Pfieffer.

Kirschner, P., & Hendrick, C. (2020). *How learning happens: Seminal works in educational pyschology and what they mean in practice*. Oxford: Routledge.

Kyun, S., Kalyuga, S., & Sweller, J. (2013). The effect of worked examples when learning to write essays in English literature. *The Journal of Experimental Education, 81*(3), 385–408.

Mayer, R. (2008). *Learning and instruction* (2nd ed.). Upper Saddle River, NJ: Pearson Merrill Prentice Hall.

Oksa, A., Kalyuga, S., & Chandler, P. (2010). Expertise reversal effect in using explanatory notes for readers of Shakespearean text. *Instructional Science, 38*, 217–236.

Sweller, J., Ayres, P., & Kalyuga, S. (2011). *Cognitive load theory explorations in the learning sciences, instructional systems and performance technologies*. New York, NY: Springer.

Sweller, J., & Cooper, G. A. (1985). The use of worked examples as a substitute for problem solving in learning algebra. *Cognition and Instruction, 1*, 59–89.

Sweller, J., Van Merrienboer, J. J. G., & Paas, F. G. C. (1998). Cognitive architecture and instructional design. *Educational Psychology Review, 10*(3).

Willingham, D. (Winter 2002). Ask the cognitive scientist: Inflexible knowledge: The first step to expertise *American Educator, 26*(4), 31–33.

Zhu, X., & Simon, H. (1987). Learning mathematics from examples and by doing. *Cognition and Instruction, 4*, 137–166.

5

TEACHING VOCABULARY

In this chapter, we will explore

- The benefits of vocabulary instruction
- The importance of both incidental and explicit instruction
- Which words should we focus on?
- The importance of morphology
- Approaches to explicit vocabulary instruction

INTRODUCTION

Students who have a wide and accessible vocabulary have an advantage when studying English. Although there are many other important things that we can teach, helping students to broaden their vocabularies is an important focus.

BENEFITS OF VOCABULARY INSTRUCTION

VOCABULARY AND READING

Being a successful reader is heavily dependent upon vocabulary. When we read, we need to understand most of the words we encounter if we are to understand the text as a whole (Perfetti et al., 2005), and this is why students with larger vocabularies are more likely to understand things that they read (Wright and Cervetti, 2017). As a result, teaching vocabulary can help improve students' reading comprehension (Shanahan, 2005). Having a broad vocabulary also gives students a second important advantage: compared to students who have smaller vocabularies, such students are far more likely to learn new vocabulary from their reading (Hirsch, 2003), and this is because there is a reciprocal relationship between vocabulary and reading comprehension: the development of vocabulary knowledge massively helps reading comprehension and reading is a major mechanism in the development of vocabulary knowledge (Oakhill et al., 2015, p. 54). Because of this, English lessons should involve systematic and explicit vocabulary instruction as well as a high volume of reading (Cunningham and Stanovich, 1998).

VOCABULARY AND WRITING

While writing expertise is made up of many things, including transcriptional fluency (Santangelo and Graham, 2016), knowledge of genre (McCutchen, 2011), and the ability to consider multiple mental representations at once (Kellogg, 2008), vocabulary also plays an important role and teaching it can improve students' writing (Graham et al., 2016). If students are to think critically about a topic, they will need sufficient domain specific knowledge about the topic they are writing about (Willingham, 2016) and vocabulary makes up a large part of this knowledge base. Expert writers are able to rapidly and effortlessly retrieve this knowledge (Kellogg and Whiteford, 2009); novice writers, however, often struggle with their writing because they lack such relevant and accessible knowledge (McCutchen, 2011).

HOW SHOULD WE TEACH VOCABULARY?

Everything we read, discuss and write about is reliant upon vocabulary and as a result, we are nearly always teaching it, no matter what we are doing. So how can we ensure that the way that we teach vocabulary is as efficient and effective as possible? Vocabulary is best taught through a combination of incidental and explicit instruction, using a variety of complementary methods designed to explore the relationship among words, their structure, origin and meaning (Moats, 2020).

INCIDENTAL INSTRUCTION

Students will learn lots of words without any form of explicit instruction through rich language interactions like conversation, discussion and reading. Reading, however, has a special importance because many words and language patterns rarely occur in spoken language. Weaker readers may only have access to more advanced or recondite vocabulary if they read texts above their reading level, for example in shared class reading (Oxford Language Report, 2018). This is where a teacher, through careful annotation, explanation and elaboration, can unlock challenging texts for students.

This could be done in advance by explaining vocabulary like this:

> Peyton Farquhar was a well-to-do planter, of an old and highly respected Alabama family. Being a slave owner and like other slave owners a politician he was naturally an original **secessionist** and **ardently** devoted to the Southern cause. Circumstances of an imperious nature, which it is unnecessary to relate here, had prevented him from taking service with the **gallant** army that had fought the disastrous campaigns ending with **the fall of Corinth**, and he chafed under the **inglorious** restraint, longing for the release of his energies, the larger life of the soldier, the opportunity for distinction. That opportunity, he felt, would come, as it comes to all in war time. Meanwhile he did what he could. No service was too humble for him to perform in aid of the South, no adventure too perilous for him to undertake if consistent with the character of a civilian who was at heart a soldier, and who in good faith and without too much qualification assented to at least a part of the frankly villainous **dictum** that all is fair in love and war. (Extract from *An Occurrence at Owl Creek Bridge* by Ambrose Bierce 1890)

Table 5.1 An example of a vocabulary box

Condemned	Sentence (someone) to a particular punishment, especially death	*Apprehension*	Anxiety or fear that something bad or unpleasant will happen
Evade	Escape or avoid something	*Secessionist*	Member of the Confederates, generally in favour of slavery
Ardent	Very enthusiastic or passionate	*Fall of Corinth*	Battle in US Civil war. Unionists defeated Confederates
Inglorious	Causing shame or a loss of honour	*Dictum*	A short statement that expresses a general truth or principle

In the example above, different words have been chosen for different reasons. Some have been chosen because they are crucial for understanding this particular text (Fall of Corinth/Secessionist); others because they seem like useful, formal words that students may encounter and be able to use in the future (condemned/ inglorious).

If you explain vocabulary in advance like in the example above, it is important to use clear, simple definitions that avoid new or complex words. When reading, it can be helpful to stop at a relevant point – perhaps at the end of the sentence where the defined word is found – before asking students to silently read the definition to themselves. You can then ask them to explain what it means using synonyms or by paraphrasing the definition, making it more likely that they engage in meaningful cognitive processing – if you think back to Chapter 2 where we explored The Levels of Processing Model, this approach is more likely to result in understanding and retention than merely reading the existing definition.

EXPLICIT INSTRUCTION

As well as a rich diet of reading, students should also receive explicit vocabulary instruction, which can enhance reading fluency and comprehension, especially for struggling readers (Elleman et al., 2009) and second language learners (Seok and DaCosta, 2014).

WHICH WORDS SHOULD WE CHOOSE TO TEACH THROUGH EXPLICIT INSTRUCTION?

If students are to engage in meaningful, nuanced and sophisticated responses to texts, they need to be taught a more comprehensive field of reference which will include vocabulary and terminology. Similarly, if pupils' aesthetic appreciation is to mature, they need to be taught relevant vocabulary and concepts so that they can apply reason to their feelings and articulate their responses coherently and with precision. We should teach vocabulary and terminology that pupils can use to furnish and refine their own interactions with texts: widening pupil's frames of reference and linguistic schema will develop their aesthetic and emotional responses, allowing pupils to enter into a more sophisticated dialogue with both texts and each other (Warwick and Speakman, 2018).

One way of classifying vocabulary is by placing words into tiers (Beck et al., 2013, p. 23).

TIER 1

These are everyday, functional words that would be familiar to most and used regularly in spoken language. These include words like 'eat, work, house, sad, late etc.'

TIER 2

These are formal or academic words that students are likely to need and use across a range of contexts and subjects. They are high frequency yet ambitious words like 'analyse, statement, repression, vulnerability, concealed'. Such words would be commonplace in journalism, non-fiction and prose and often have a sense of nuance or sophistication that Tier 1 words may lack. Tier 2 words are not typically used in functional, everyday speech, although this will depend upon the context and purpose of what is being said.

TIER 3

These are subject specific words that are unlikely to be used outside of a particular domain. This includes words like 'metonymy, synechdoche, anagnorisis, plosive, bathos'.

Although it will be important to focus on words across all three tiers, the words that we choose to teach through explicit instruction should be those that have the highest utility and the widest possible application: if we are to spend time teaching specific words, we need to maximize the return that students get. Some words are more useful than others and more often than not, words chosen for explicit instruction will fall within Tier 2.

When choosing words to teach, it can be useful to ask a number of questions:

1. Will the word be useful when responding to this text?
2. Will it be useful when responding to other texts?
3. Will it be useful for students to use in different types of writing?

If you can answer yes to two or three of the above questions, the word is almost certainly worth teaching through explicit instruction.

Here's an example:

The word 'domineering' has high utility and could be taught, revisited and applied across multiple texts and years (Table 5.2):

Think back to Chapter 1 which outlined the ideas of flexible knowledge and transfer – if students can transfer and apply a word to multiple texts, then their knowledge can be said to be flexible. Similarly, cast your mind back to Chapter 3 which explored the benefits of distributed retrieval practice: if a word is applied

Table 5.2 High utility vocabulary

Year	Text	Example sentence
7	Animal Farm	**Domineering** and tyrannical, Napolean asserts his authority, expecting total obedience from the other animals.
7	Antigone	Creon, a **domineering** and despotic leader, is enraged when Antigone undermines his authority.
8	Julius Caesar	Proclaiming 'Danger knows full well That Caesar is more dangerous than he', Caesar demonstrates his hubristic and **domineering** nature.
8	Lord of the Flies	Jack **domineers** and controls the choir, a group who obey and even fear him.
9	Romeo and Juliet	A **domineering** father and husband, Lord Capulet commands both his wife and his daughter.
10	My Last Duchess	The Duke is a **domineering** figure who seems to treat his wives as possessions to boast about.

across texts, units and years, this will necessarily involve such practice, ensuring that vocabulary is retained for longer.

Let us now discuss some useful vocabulary categories to select words from.

CHARACTER ATTRIBUTES

Analytical writing often requires students to comment on characters within texts and explicitly teaching vocabulary connected to character attributes, behaviour and emotions can help students to increase the precision and sophistication of their writing. Here are some examples:

Supercilious	Sinister	Defiant	Obsequious
Duplicitous	Vindictive	Authoritarian	Insouciant

WORDS FOR EXPRESSING THE TONE OF A TEXT, AUTHORIAL INTENT OR THE WRITER'S OPINION

Sardonic	Indignant	Nostalgic	Irreverent
Provocative	Mournful	Assertive	Exposes
Undermines	Accentuates	Subverts	Juxtaposes
Admonishes	Satirises	Warns	Hyperbolises

THE IMPORTANCE OF MORPHOLOGY

Morphology is the study of word structure and words are made up of smaller parts called morphographs, which are the smallest possible units of meaning. These units include roots, base words, suffixes and prefixes. Some words only contain one morphograph such as *cat, house, giraffe, piano*; others contain more than one like *photography, transportation, psychosomatic*.

Teaching students about morphology and the structure of words can be a really useful approach as morphographs often have fixed spellings and meanings across different words. As a result, morphological instruction is an efficient and generative approach to building students' vocabularies which can then help students comprehend successfully (Oakhill et al., 2015, p. 66).

As over two-thirds of English words are comprised of Latin or Greek affixes or roots, teaching these morphographs can help them to generalise their understanding to new words. For example, if a student is taught that the prefix 'mal' means 'bad, badly or evil' and how prefixes combine with root words, it is much more likely that she will be able to understand untaught words like 'malcontent, maladjusted and malnutrition'. Morphological knowledge can also help pupils decode novel words that contain taught roots and affixes because the spelling and pronunciation of morphographs are often constant (Flanigan et al., 2012).

APPROACHES TO EXPLICIT VOCABULARY INSTRUCTION

While pre-explaining or defining vocabulary like in the example above from *An Occurrence at Owl Creek Bridge* can be really useful, teachers will often need to explain and define words off the cuff, meaning that they will have to think on their feet. When doing this, it is important to consider the utility of the word as well as what you want students to get out of a particular reading in order to judge how to approach the instruction. When we read texts, we may be trying to understand the gist of what has been written or we may be taking a more fine-grained approach where we are interested in the effects of specific words or patterns of language: each of these reading goals will involve a different approach to the reading of the text. Similarly, the purpose of vocabulary instruction will vary and as a result, so will the approach that teachers adopt.

Let's have a look at some examples.

1. **Aim = Reading a text for an overview or to learn more about the narrative**

   When reading a text for the first time, it is often important to read with minimal interruptions so that students are able to follow without being distracted. Vocabulary instruction may still be important though and should be focused upon words that students have to know in order to understand and follow what they are reading.

   THE "Red Death" had long devastated the country. No pestilence had ever been so fatal, or so hideous. Blood was its Avatar and its seal—the redness and the horror of blood. There were sharp pains, and sudden dizziness, and then profuse bleeding at the pores, with dissolution. The scarlet stains upon the body and especially upon the face of the victim, were the pest ban which shut him out from the aid and from the sympathy of his fellow-men. And the whole seizure, progress, and termination of the disease, were the incidents of half an hour.

The extract above contains the opening paragraph from Poe's *The Masque of the Red Death*. It is probably important that students know the word 'pestilence' in order to understand the rest of the opening paragraph, but also to begin to engage with Poe's symbolism and how the story can be read allegorically.

This is how you could teach the word with minimal interruption:

TEACHER (italics = reading; **bold = talking**):*The 'Red Death' had long devastated the country. No pestilence,* **which means plague or disease** *had ever been so fatal, or so hideous.*

To do this a lot would be highly distracting and annoying and so this approach should be reserved for vocabulary that is crucial for students to understand.

2. **Aim = analysing in more detail**

When adopting a close reading approach, it is important to read line by line, stopping to explain and discuss regularly so that students can understand and analyse meaning. Perhaps you decide that in the opening to Poe's tale, the word 'profuse' is important for your students to know. Not only is it important for their understanding of the severity of the red death, but it is also a useful word that can be applied beyond this text. Think back to when we discussed transfer – one way of increasing the likelihood that students develop flexible knowledge that can be transferred is to explicitly show them how a word can be applied to different contexts. With vocabulary, this often means giving a range of example sentences, demonstrating how the word can be used.

This is how you could approach it:

Teacher: 'Ok so let's return to the opening paragraph, the Red Death causes 'profuse bleeding at the pores'. The word 'profuse' means a lot or large amounts. If I swear profusely, then I use a lot of bad language. When you hurt someone, you should apologise profusely. What can we learn about the Red Death from Poe's use of the word 'profuse'?'

VOCABULARY TABLES

For explicit vocabulary instruction to be effective, continual review is important and words should be learned in context so that students are able to see how the words can be applied (Butler et al., 2010). Distributed retrieval practice is important if pupils are to retain new vocabulary (Roediger and Karpicke, 2011, pp. 23–48). It can also develop their understanding and improve their ability to transfer their knowledge to new contexts (Roediger et al., 2011). In addition, it is vital that students practice using the words (Oxford Language Report, 2018).

Vocabulary tables are a useful way to present new vocabulary, whilst also acting as a resource for practice.

At secondary school, perhaps the most common form of writing in English lessons is text response where students write analytically about what they have read. As a result of this, it is a good idea to focus vocabulary instruction on words that will help students improve this type of writing.

Let's have a look at an example:

Macbeth Act 2 Scene 2 Vocabulary

Table 5.3 A vocabulary table for teaching Macbeth

Conscience (n)	A person's moral sense of right and wrong, viewed as acting as a guide to one's behaviour. *After murdering Duncan, Macbeth's conscience torments him, causing him to exclaim 'I could not say Amen'.*
Torment (v) **Torment (n)**	Severe physical or mental suffering/cause severe physical or mental suffering *Macbeth is tormented by what he has done, exclaiming that he can 'sleep no more'.*
Dismiss (v) **Dismissive (adj)** **Dismissively (adv)**	Feeling or showing that something is unworthy of consideration *While Macbeth is horrified by what he has done, his wife dismisses his concerns.*
Insouciant (adj) **Insouciance (n)**	Showing a casual lack of concern. *Insouciant and nonchalant, Lady Macbeth tells Macbeth that 'a little water clears us of this deed' as if what he has done is trivial.*
Indifferent (adj) **Indifference (n)**	Lack of interest, concern, or sympathy. *Lady Macbeth seems indifferent to Macbeth's horror; she seems to be only interested in avoiding detection or culpability.*
Sacrilege (n) **Sacrilegious (adj)**	Violation or misuse of what is regarded as sacred. *Macbeth exclaims that he 'could not say Amen', a statement that demonstrates the sacrilegious nature of his crime: killing the King is a direct offence against God himself.*

FEATURES OF VOCABULARY TABLES

Presenting words in this way makes continual review and retrieval much easier and the approaches to retrieval that we explored in Chapter 2 are perfect for ensuring that students retain new vocabulary. New words should be repeated and recycling vocabulary is really important if students are to understand and apply the words that they learn (Butler et al., 2010). As an example, in the table above, words are repeated within the table as well as repeating words that were taught in previous units. As explained earlier, words are chosen based on utility – all of the words listed in the table above could be considered Tier 2 and can be applied not only to this scene and the rest of the play but also when students respond to other texts.

Each word is given a simple, concise definition as well as an example sentence. The example sentences contain constructions that students are expected to use in their writing, each acting as a mini worked example:

- Macbeth is tormented by what he has done, *exclaiming that he can 'sleep no more'.* – Present participle
- *Insouciant and nonchalant,* Lady Macbeth tells Macbeth that 'a little water clears us of this deed' as if what he has done is trivial. – 2 adjective start
- Lady Macbeth seems indifferent to Macbeth's horror; she seems to be only interested in avoiding detection or culpability. – Semi-colon
- Macbeth exclaims that he 'could not say Amen', *a statement that demonstrates the sacrilegious nature of his crime: killing the King is a direct offence against God himself.* – Noun Appositive

Chapter 10 explains how some of these constructions can be taught and practised through multi-lesson instructional sequences.

The content of the example sentences are often interpretations of the text and
can act as supports or prompts for analysis and discussion. As we saw in Chapter
4, novices learn best through studying worked examples and teachers of such
students should focus upon building background knowledge. The example sentences in vocabulary tables fulfil both of these conditions and providing students
with some initial interpretations can be a useful starting point for developing
their analysis. This does not, however, mean that teachers should only offer one
authoritative or definitive reading of a text, an approach that would clearly
impoverish students' experiences and disrespect the discipline of literary analysis
(Elliot, 2021). Rather than acting like a straightjacket, coercing students into
thinking the same as the teacher, explicitly taught interpretations allow students
to critique, discuss and deconstruct ideas, unlocking challenging texts and
making them accessible.

The table also presents and labels all relevant forms of the word, allowing
students and teachers to focus on morphology.

HOW TO USE VOCABULARY TABLES

After reading a section of a text with a class, we often want to focus on an interesting part in order to practice close reading and developing interpretations. Based
upon a specific section of a text, the vocabulary table provides words and ideas for
students to use in their analysis, whether it be spoken or written. Students can be
asked to read rows of the table out loud. The teacher can annotate their table under
the visualiser, providing further explanations, synonyms, antonyms or other useful
background knowledge.

Choral drills can be really useful to practice pronouncing trickier words, using
the 'Model-Lead-Test' approach (Engelmann and Carnine, 2016, p. 483). Let's have
a look at an example:

Teacher: 'Ok, the word is *sack-rell-ijj-uss*, let's say it together'.

At first, segmenting the syllables can be helpful so students hear all the
sounds

Teacher and Class: 'Sack-rell-ijj-uss'

Teacher: 'Again'.

Class: 'sack-rell-ijj-uss'

Teacher: 'sacrilegious'

Class: 'sacrilegious'

This process should be repeated until the class are firm. The teacher can then
ask more confident students to say it on their own, providing further models for the
class to hear.

Choral pronunciation drills may help with phonemic processing but, as we saw in Chapter 2, if we want students to understand what we are teaching them, we need to ensure that they engage in deep, semantic processing where they focus on meaning. Here are some ways to do this:

1. **Questioning and discussing the example sentences**

   a. Using 'Think Pair Share' (see Chapter 7), teachers could ask students questions about the example sentences, ensuring that they use the vocabulary word in their answers.
   b. Using 'ABC questioning' (see Chapter 7), students could be asked to agree, add to or challenge the example sentences.
   c. Teachers could ask students to connect the words to other texts: *What is it that torments Jekyll? How is Ozymandias dismissive?*

2. **Focusing on morphology**

   The teacher can draw attention to specific affixes, before asking students for other examples so that they begin to generalise. *The prefix 'in' can mean not or no as in insignificant and incomplete...can you think of some others?*

3. **Because, But, So** (Hochman and Wexler, 2017)

   This is a simple yet effective way of practising vocabulary so that students focus on meaning and application. Let's have a look at some examples:

   a. Spoken practice

   Teacher: 'Ok, we've read and discussed the definition and example sentence; now I want you to finish my sentence, ensuring that you add as much information as you can. Here's an example of what I'm looking for:

   Macbeth is tormented by his conscience *because* he has committed regicide. Not only does this offend God, but he has murdered a King who was universally loved and who praised him highly.

   Notice how I have included additional information from the table and previous lessons in order to develop my point further'.

   Teacher: 'Ok, Ruby, your turn...'

   Students could either be called on to finish the sentence in front of the class or they could practice in pairs before doing so.

   b. Written practice

   Students could be asked to complete specific sentences like this:

   Macbeth's conscience torments him, *but....* .

- What about Lady Macbeth?
- Include sacrilegious
- Include *'not only. . . . .but'*

The bullet points ask students to include additional things in their answer, helping them to make connections between separate bits of knowledge and reminding them to use specific sentence structures in their answer, which, as a result of these success criteria, will probably be a mini paragraph response.

4. **Vocabulary table as a scaffold for writing**
The words in the vocabulary table, along with the example sentences, can be deliberately used in model paragraphs that students annotate, discuss and deconstruct, allowing them to see how these tiny analytical building blocks fit into paragraphs and essays. When students write their own paragraphs or essays, they can use these tables as a resource to improve the precision and sophistication of their writing. Weaker students are able to use the example sentences as starting points for their own analysis, borrowing the entire example sentence and then expanding upon it; more confident students can transform or adapt the sentences into their own words.

SUMMARY

- Vocabulary instruction can benefit students' reading and writing ability.
- In order to develop students' vocabularies, English lessons should involve a high volume of reading as well as systematic, explicit vocabulary instruction.
- The optimal approach to vocabulary instruction will depend upon the purpose served by focusing on a word: high utility words that are applicable across texts and writing tasks will be a useful focus for explicit instruction and practice.
- Morphological instruction is a useful and efficient way to build students' vocabularies as well as helping with reading comprehension.
- Vocabulary tables are a useful way to present, organise, discuss and practice words chosen for explicit instruction.

REFERENCES

Beck, I. L., McKeown, M. G., & Kucan, L. (2013). *Bringing words to life: Robust vocabulary instruction*. New York, NY: Guilford Press.

Butler, S., Urrutia, K., Buenger, A., Gonzalez, N., Hunt, M., & Eisenhart, C. (2010). *A review of the current research on vocabulary instruction*. National Reading Technical Assistance Center.

Cunningham, A., & Stanovich, K. (1998). *What reading does for the mind*. American Educator.

Elleman, A. M., Lindo, E. J., Morphy, P., & Compton, D. L. (2009). Intervention, evaluation, and policy studies: The impact of vocabulary instruction on passage-level comprehension of school-age children: A meta-analysis. *Journal of Research on Educational Effectiveness, 2*(1), 1–44.

Elliot, V. (2021). *Knowledge in English: Canon, curriculum and cultural literacy.* Oxford: Routledge.

Engelmann, S., & Carnine, D. (2016). *Theory of instruction: Principles and applications.* Adi Press; revised, Subsequent edition.

Flanigan, K., Templeton, S., & Hayes, L. (2012). What's in a word? Using content vocabulary to generate growth in general academic vocabulary knowledge. *Journal of Adolescent and Adult Literacy, 56*(2), 132–140.

Graham, S., Harris, K. R., & Chambers, A. B. (2016). Evidence-based practice and writing instruction: A review of reviews. In C. A. MacArthur, S. Graham & J. Fitzgerald (Eds.), *Handbook of writing research* (pp. 211–226). The Guilford Press.

Hirsch, E. D. (2003). Reading comprehension requires knowledge — of words and the world. *American Educator,* 10–45.

Hochman, J., & Wexler, N. (2017). *The writing revolution: A guide to advancing thinking through writing in all subjects and grades.* San Francisco, CA: Jossey-Bass.

Kellogg, R. T. (2008). Training writing skills: A cognitive development perspective. *Journal of Writing Research, 1*(1), 1–26.

Kellogg, R. T., & Whiteford, A. P. (2009). Training advanced writing skills: The case for deliberate practice. *Educational Psychologist, 44*(4), 250–266.

McCutchen, D. (2011). From novice to expert: Implications of language skills and writing-relevant knowledge for memory during the development of writing skill. *Journal of Writing Research, 3*(1), 51–68.

Moats, L. C. (2020). *Teaching reading is rocket science: What expert teachers of reading should know and be able to do.* American Educator.

Oakhill, J., Cain, K., & Elbro, C. (2015). *Understanding and teaching reading comprehension a handbook.* Oxford: Routledge.

Oxford University Press (2018). *Why closing the word gap matters: Oxford language report overview.* OUP. http://fdslive.oup.com/www.oup.com/oxed/Oxford-Language-Report-Overview.PDF?region=uk

Perfetti, C. A., Landi, N., & Oakhill, J. (2005). The acquisition of reading comprehension skill. In M. Snowling & C. Hulme (Eds.), *The science of reading: A handbook* (pp. 227–247). Blackwell.

Roediger, H., & Karpicke, J. (2011). Intricacies of spaced retrieval: A resolution. In *Successful remembering and successful forgetting: A Festschrift in honor of Robert A. Bjork.* Psychology Press.

Roediger, H. L., Putnam, A. L., & Smith, M. A. (2011). Ten benefits of testing and their applications to educational practice. *Psychology of Learning and Motivation, 55.*

Santangelo, T., & Graham, S. (2016). A comprehensive meta-analysis of handwriting instruction. *Educational Psychology review, 28*(2), 225–265.

Seok, S., & DaCosta, B. (2014). Oral reading fluency as a predictor of silent reading fluency at secondary and postsecondary levels. *Journal of Adolescent and Adult Literacy, 58*(2), 157–166.

Shanahan, T. (2005). *The national reading panel report. Practical Advice for teachers.* http://eric.ed.gov/ERICWebPortal/recordDetail?accno=ED489535

Warwick, I., & Speakman, R. (2018). *Redefining English for the more able a practical guide.* London: Routledge.

Willingham, D. (2016). *Knowledge and practice: The real keys to critical thinking.* https://knowledgematterscampaign.org/wp-content/uploads/2016/05/Willingham-brief.pdf

Wright, T. S., & Cervetti, G. N. (2017). A systematic review of the research on vocabulary instruction that impacts text comprehension. *Reading Research Quarterly, 52*(2), 203–226.

6

EXPLICIT INSTRUCTION

In this chapter, we will explore

- A definition of explicit instruction
- Some of the evidence in support of explicit instruction
- Some of the ideas within explicit instruction and what these look like in the classroom

INTRODUCTION

The preceding chapters have explored how teachers can use ideas from cognitive science in order to improve their teaching. Explicit Instruction is a pedagogical approach that complements these ideas, highlighting classroom strategies that are likely to improve learning.

EXPLICIT INSTRUCTION IS SUPERIOR FOR NOVICES

Education is fraught with disagreement concerning teaching methods. Some teachers prefer a 'student-centred' approach where students are encouraged to learn through discovery and enquiry; others subscribe to a 'teacher-centred' approach where information is presented in an explicit fashion. Although few teachers exclusively subscribe to one of these schools of thought, instead using methods from both according to the needs of their students, the debate between them has raged for over a hundred years (Chall, 2002, p. 15), with proponents on both sides tending to claim the superiority of their approach.

Teachers are often passionate and unrelenting advocates of the methods that they use in the classroom and rightly so: enthusiasm and commitment are important qualities for any teacher to have. But how are we to judge what is our best bet in the classroom? There must be more for enquiring teachers to base their decisions on than fervent endorsements and earnest beliefs. I hope that in the preceding chapters, I have gone some way towards persuading you that we can use research from cognitive science to increase the probability that our teaching is effective. In this chapter, I hope to do the same by making the case that 'explicit instruction is superior for novice learners'. As we have already seen, novices are students lacking in expertise who have little prior knowledge that they can rely on.

WHAT IS EXPLICIT INSTRUCTION?

This chapter will explain the principles that make up what is commonly known as 'explicit' or 'direct' instruction. It will begin by outlining some of its core methods in order to arrive at a workable definition, before exploring the robust and wide-ranging evidence that supports its effectiveness. Finally, it will explore some of the approaches that are subsumed within this broad methodology, demonstrating how they can be applied to the English classroom.

Explicit instruction refers to classroom practice that is led by the teacher (Rosenshine, 2008) and typically involves whole class teaching.

Students are presented with all the information that they need and, through processes of explanation, questioning, demonstration and guidance, are asked to practice applying it in increasingly wider and freer contexts, eventually resulting in the ability to complete tasks entirely independently of the teacher. Concepts and skills are fully explained and before students attempt problems, tasks or applications, they will have been explicitly taught everything that they need as well as the processes that they are expected to complete (Clark et al., 2012) While independence is the goal, the most efficient means of achieving it is through explicit instruction: a process of highly structured, interactive teaching.

THE EVIDENCE BASE
PROJECT FOLLOW THROUGH

In the 1970s, the United States conducted Project Follow Through, the largest comparative study of teaching approaches that has ever been undertaken. Twenty-two different methods of instruction were examined and the study involved hundreds of thousands of students in nearly 200 different disadvantaged communities. Engelmann's Direct Instruction (also known as DI) was the most effective in reading, spelling, language and maths. Students who learned under DI performed the best in basic academic skills as well as problem solving and higher order tasks. Despite the misjudged criticism that Engelmann's approach was dehumanising, robotic and demotivating, students who learned with DI also reported the highest positive change in self-esteem. Perhaps unsurprisingly, success caused students to feel good about themselves.

More recent studies have confirmed these findings: a 2018 meta-analysis of 328 studies spanning 50 years also demonstrated DI's effectiveness (Stockard et al., 2018).

Engelmann's DI is distinct from direct or explicit instruction in that it exists within extensively tested and rigorously planned off the shelf programs. All aspects of instruction are tightly controlled and it includes elements like scripted lessons and choral responding that do not typically exist within the broader methodology of explicit instruction. However, there is a good deal of overlap with explicit instruction as both involve guided practice, active student participation, scaffolding, modelling and the gradual fading of support (Rosenshine, 2008). Because of this huge overlap, the evidence in favour of DI can be seen as supporting the superiority of explicit instruction in general.

In Chapter 8, I will explore how some of the theoretical principles behind DI can be applied to the everyday classroom.

PROCESS-PRODUCT RESEARCH

From the 1950s until the end of the 1970s, U.S. researchers set out to ascertain what it was that made teachers effective. They visited classrooms in an attempt to draw correlations between the teacher's actions and the resulting academic outcomes. The findings were collated by Brophy and Good (1984). While this is correlative research – and even the most novice student of statistics will point out that 'correlation does not imply causation' – it has been pointed out that 'there has been no observational or correlational research on instruction since that time that has invalidated these findings' (Rosenshine, 2009, p. 201). Additionally, many of the correlative studies were followed by experimental studies where teachers were asked to use the strategies found in the correlative studies. The majority of these studies found that the teachers who used these approaches were more effective than the control group (Coe et al., 2014; Rosenshine, 2009, p. 202). 'The Principles of Instruction' is perhaps the most famous summary of this research and is seen by many as a definitive list of common, explicit teaching strategies – in Chapter 7, I will explore how these explicit instruction principles can be applied in the English classroom.

When summing up their findings towards the end of the paper, Brophy and Good (1984) explain:

> At least two common themes cut across the findings, despite the need for limitations and qualifications. One is that academic learning is influenced by the amount of time that students spend engaged in appropriate academic tasks.

Perhaps unsurprisingly, we should consistently deliver efficient lessons where students spend maximal time thinking deeply about the content: if you think back to the previous chapter, if we want students to remember and understand what we teach them, then this is essential (Craik and Lockhart, 1972). Open-ended group work or convoluted multi-faceted learning activities can make this difficult to achieve as the potential for-off task behaviour and confusion is greater than with explicit whole class teaching.

Brophy and Good (1984) continue:

> The second is that students learn more efficiently when their teachers first structure new information for them and then help them relate it to what they already know, then monitor performance and provide corrective feedback during recitation, drill, practice or application activities.

Whole class teaching – where students typically complete the same tasks – allows the teacher to have more interactions with individual pupils than if students were working in groups or on their own: this means that monitoring and feedback is much easier. Students are also more likely to stay on task as it is far easier to monitor a whole class than multiple groups that are working on different tasks and at different rates (Muijs and Reynolds, 2017, p. 39).

Brophy and Good's statement seems to implicitly describe how to ensure students engage in Fiorella and Mayer's three stages of cognitive processing which, in the opening chapter, I proposed were a good way of thinking about the process of learning:

a. Select information to attend to
b. Organise the material into a coherent cognitive structure in working memory
c. Integrating it with relevant prior knowledge activated from long-term memory

This match between theory and practice is significant. If teachers who achieve favourable outcomes teach in a way that allows students to successfully engage with these three stages-and as argued in Chapter 2, the assumption is that each of these three stages are crucial for fostering learning – then this can be seen as adding further weight to the proposition that 'explicit instruction is superior for novices'.

Explicit instruction is the fastest way to accumulate new knowledge. The more knowledge that we have in our long-term memories, the easier it is to assimilate further knowledge (Muijs and Reynolds, 2017, p. 40).

According to the researchers, the most effective teachers

> instruct actively by demonstrating skills, explaining concepts and assignments, conducting participatory activities, and reviewing when necessary. They teach their students rather than expect them to learn mostly on their own by reading texts and working on assignments. However, they do not stress merely facts or skills; they also emphasize understanding and applications. As students' self-regulation skills increase, they are encouraged to assume more responsibility for managing their own learning. (Brophy and Good, 2008)

The most effective teachers obtained consistently high success rates from their students – 75% of questions were answered correctly and when students engaged in independent practice, this percentage rose to between 90% and 100%.

A common yet misjudged criticism of explicit instruction is that it involves 'rote' learning where students mindlessly repeat things that they have been told; after all, parroting what the teacher has said seems easy and would likely result in similarly high success rates. However, the high percentages achieved by effective teachers are not evidence in support of this mischaracterisation, they are evidence of successful instruction.

By carefully explaining things fully, teaching students everything they need and then creating an instructional sequence where students have to make sense of the material (Fiorella and Mayer, 2015), retrieve it from memory (Roediger et al., 2011) and engage in varied practice (Butler, 2010), teachers create the conditions for flexible, transferable learning, a desirable outcome that is the very antithesis of rote learning.

In the most successful classrooms, an observer will see processes and approaches that are underpinned by our best understanding of cognitive science and how we learn effectively.

THE ACADEMIC ACHIEVEMENT CHALLENGE

Jeanne S. Chall (2000), Professor of Education at Harvard University, wrote *The Academic Achievement Challenge: What Really Works in the Classroom?* In this wide-ranging work that evaluates research and reforms from the past century, Chall compares the effectiveness of teacher-centred, explicit instruction against student-centred methods involving enquiry learning. The overall conclusion that she reaches is that explicit instruction is preferable, particularly for students of lower economic status and those who have special educational needs. Although a thorough discussion of her findings is outside of the scope of this volume, what follows are a few of the research findings that she examines.

Chall (2000, p. 81) cites research from Gage (1978), a quantitative study that demonstrated that overall, students in traditional, teacher-centred schools achieved better than those in student-centred equivalents. Similarly, Chall cites Walberg (1990), a meta-analysis of over 800 studies which demonstrated that the methods with the greatest positive effect were those that contained corrective feedback, frequent testing or quizzes, cues, reinforcement and explicit and direct teaching.

Chall quotes Stevens and Rosenshine (1981) who explain that 'In reading and math, students make more progress when the teacher, not the student, selects and directs the activities, and acts as a strong leader ... approaches the subject matter in a direct, business-like way, organizes learning around questions posed by the teacher, and occupies the center of attention'. Explicit, teacher-led instruction results in good progress.

PISA RESULTS

Every three years, the Organisation for Economic Co-operation and Development run an international study that examines 15-year-olds in science, reading and maths. In 2017, a report was produced analysing the performance of students in 39 of these countries including the EU and surrounding states (Mourshed et al., 2017). The conclusion was that students perform the best in classrooms which have more explicit instruction than enquiry-based learning, classrooms where students receive explicit instruction in many to all lessons and enquiry methods in some to many lessons. To be clear though, enquiry methods does not mean unguided, discovery learning where the teacher takes a back seat: enquiry, if it is to be effective, should be about applying and practicing recently learned content and skills (Clark et al., 2012).

ADDITIONAL EVIDENCE

Explicit instruction has been found to be particularly effective for teaching pupils from disadvantaged backgrounds (Muijs et al., 2014, p. 39). In perhaps the widest ranging synthesis of research that has ever been collected, explicit instruction and teacher-led approaches were found to be more effective than student-centred, enquiry-based methods (Hattie, 2009).

Creemers and Kyriakides (2006) developed 'The Dynamic Model' of educational effectiveness, a model that has been subjected to extensive verification and testing (Coe et al., 2014). A major aspect of this model groups teacher effectiveness into eight factors and, while it has pointed out that the eight factors do not exclusively refer to one particular approach to teaching (Joyce et al., 2000) as their breadth can encompass a range of styles, each factor is of crucial importance to effective explicit instruction.

Table 6.1 Orientation

| 1. Orientation | a. Providing the objectives for which a specific task/lesson/series of lessons take(s) place |
| | b. Challenging students to identify the reason why an activity is taking place |

Effective teachers emphasise academic goals, make these goals explicit and expect students to master them (Ko et al., 2013). Making the purpose of a lesson or task clear to students can help focus their attention as well as helping them to see how individual parts fit together in a sequence of learning (Brophy and Good, 1984). Additionally, the process of clarifying an objective for a task or lesson is of vital importance for the teacher too. If a task is to be effective, the teacher should be able to explain exactly why they are doing a specific thing at that specific time in a sequence of learning.

Let's have a look at some examples:

a. Starting a lesson with retrieval practice. Questions ask about content from the previous week.

As we saw in chapters 2 and 3, retrieval practice is a really powerful learning strategy. Because of this, the purpose of this task should definitely be explained to students including the important nuance that there has been a sufficient time gap between initial learning and this particular quiz, thereby increasing the effort required and giving a bigger boost to retention. Not only do we want them to benefit from this task but ultimately, we want them to begin using this approach themselves when studying independently. After we have explained the theory behind it, we can then 'challenge students to identify the reason' they are doing it in subsequent retrieval tasks, reinforcing the relevance and importance of this vital study strategy.

b. Practising using semi-colons in sentence practice drills.

In Chapter 9, we will explore some of the research behind deliberate practice and how this approach can be highly effective at developing expertise. Initial practice drills should be restrictive so that teachers can give precise feedback, the purpose being to develop accuracy and fluency before students are expected to apply the skill within freer writing. Explaining this to students is really important so that they don't see the practice tasks as mindless drudgery. If the focus of near perfect accuracy is reinforced and, assuming that the teaching and tasks have been set up so that near perfect success rates are achievable, then practice drills can become enjoyable for students – being successful is a powerful motivator.

Table 6.2   Structuring

| 1. Structuring | a. Beginning with overviews and/or review of objectives |
| | b. Outlining the content to be covered and signalling transitions between lesson parts |

Fully guided instruction involves teachers explaining the content as thoroughly and comprehensively as possible so that students are provided with everything that they need. When reading texts, teachers can provide elaborations, further examples and annotations so that students can understand novel, abstract or complex ideas.

Seamless transitions and clear instructions are the hallmarks of pacey, efficient teaching. When reading texts, it can be really helpful to give a quick overview or summary of the content so that students are more likely to understand as they read. 'Written by a WW1 veteran, this article explains some of the horrors of life in the trenches. We are reading it in order to better understand Dulce et Decorum Est'.

Table 6.3   Questioning

1. Questioning	a. Raising different types of questions (i.e. process and product) at appropriate difficulty level
	b. Giving time for students to respond
	c. Dealing with student responses

Questioning is an integral part of effective, explicit instruction, but what kind of questions should a teacher ask? We should expect teachers to ask more lower level questions than higher level questions, even when dealing with higher level content (Brophy and Good, 1984). This may involve questions about the components of a more complex task; questions that typically involve students demonstrating their understanding and questions that can seem focused on factual or conceptual elements. By focusing on lower level questioning, drill and practice, we can help build the necessary foundations for complex academic tasks like extended writing.

Let's have a look at an example:

Imagine you are teaching *London* by William Blake and are focusing on the first stanza:

I wander thro' each charter'd street,

Near where the charter'd Thames does flow.

And mark in every face I meet

Marks of weakness, marks of woe.

Typical higher order questions that could be asked here include:

What is the poem saying? How does Blake use language? How is London presented?

These questions are the kind of thing that students are expected to answer in an examination or assessment, their wide, open-ended nature being the perfect stimulus for extended, analytical writing. However, if these were the only questions that a teacher asked when teaching the poem, it is likely that students would become confused or produce responses that lack substance.

A better approach might involve teaching students some ideas and asking numerous lower level questions about these ideas, thereby incrementally building their knowledge of the stanza and widening their options as to what they can say in response to it. This approach is in perfect alignment with the three stages of cognitive processing that we explored in Chapter 1. Annotating the poem and adding ideas helps students to engage in the process of *selecting* what to attend to as, in this example, the teacher is pointing students towards what might be of interest. By working through the stanza line by line, the content is broken into manageable chunks, an approach that will help students to *organise* the material in their working memories and prevent confusion. Finally, asking lots of lower level questions about the words and annotations will help students to *integrate* the information with their prior knowledge. With novice students, this approach is far more likely to result in 'meaningful learning' (Fiorella and Mayer, 2015).

Table 6.4   Teaching modelling

1. Teaching modeling	a. Encouraging students to use problem-solving strategies presented by the teacher or other classmates
	b. Inviting students to develop strategies
	c. Promoting the idea of modelling

Most of the time, it is more efficient to show students how to do something before then asking them to apply what you have shown them to a similar task.

Table 6.5   Application

1. Application	a. Using seatwork or small-group tasks in order to provide needed practice and application opportunities
	b. Using application tasks as starting points for the next step of teaching and learning

If students are to master something, they will need to engage in well-designed practiced activities – after all, practice makes permanent (Lemov et al., 2012, p. xii). Student success rates for independent practice and application work should be really high and this success should come from 'effort and thought, not mere automatic application of already overlearned algorithms' (Brophy and Good, 1984).

If you think back to the important distinction between performance and learning, it is important that teachers don't rush to interpret high success rates during initial practice activities as evidence of actual learning as what they are probably observing is *performance*. However, if this practice is sufficiently distributed across time, then teachers can be more confident in equating student success with *learning* rather than just *performance*.

Students should be able to instantly grasp what they have to do in a practice or application activity, allowing them to focus all of their concentration on the content that is being learned. If we are to teach challenging and unashamedly academic content, then we should not be adding to the cognitive load by creating complicated methods of delivering that content: tasks should be procedurally simple; if they are not, then students will need to simultaneously work out how to approach the task as well as getting their heads around the content within it. Time spent working out the rules of a convoluted activity is time not spent thinking about what they are meant to be learning.

By looking through student application tasks like extended writing, teachers can make decisions as to which components require more practice or further instruction.

Table 6.6   The classroom as a learning environment

1. The classroom as a learning environment	a. Establishing on-task behaviour through the interactions they promote (i.e. teacher–student and student–student interactions)
	b. Dealing with classroom disorder and student competition through establishing rules, persuading students to respect them and using the rules

Table 6.7   Management of time

1. Management of Time	a. Organising the classroom environment
	b. Maximising engagement rules

For explicit instruction to be effective, the class need to be focused and behaviour needs to be good. If students are not paying attention or the classroom is unruly, it is very difficult to learn properly. Explicit teaching often involves procedures and tasks that have been done many times by the teacher and the students, both being so familiar with the instructions that the teacher is able to devote maximal concentration to behaviour management, misconceptions and questioning, while the student can devote maximal attention to what it is they are learning.

Set precise time limits for tasks – some teachers use timers for this but I usually make it up, telling them 'you've got three minutes left'. The advantage of making it up is that you can speed up or slow down the time they have left based upon what you see the students are doing: if they are struggling, you can stretch the minutes; if they are whipping through it, you can speed up the time.

It is also worth ensuring students know exactly what you expect in terms of output: One page? A paragraph? Six lines? The inclusion of authorial intent?

With regard to behaviour, having relentlessly high expectations of all students at all times will ensure that distractions are kept to the minimum. Explain what you expect, why you expect it and then give consequences to those who deliberately choose to ignore your requests. Assuming what you have asked is reasonable and following your behaviour policy and it is clear that the student has still chosen to misbehave, you shouldn't need to engage in any argument, debate or negotiation.

Table 6.8 Assessment

1. Assessment	a. Using appropriate techniques to collect data on student knowledge and skills b. Analysing data in order to identify student needs and report the results to students and parents c. Teachers evaluating their own practices

In Chapter 8, we will explore some of the theory behind Engelmann's Direct Instruction, an approach to teaching that puts the onus for learning on the teacher. As Englemann says 'if the learner hasn't learnt, the teacher hasn't taught' (Children of the Code, 2009). One of the most useful things that a teacher can do is to regularly look through student work in order to ascertain whether or not instruction has been successful. If the quality of work is poor, then this may be due to faulty instruction. If a sequence of learning is designed effectively, the final freer practice activities will be largely error free, containing all of the necessary components and relevant information. Well-designed instructional sequences will contain frequent opportunities for the teacher to check for understanding, deal with common misconceptions and ensure that student success rates are consistently high.

SUMMARY

- The evidence in support of explicit instruction is robust and wide-ranging.
- Whole class, explicit instruction is an efficient and effective way to teach that is in line with ideas from cognitive science about how we learn.
- Teachers should organise and structure new information for students, helping them to connect it to what they already know.
- Students should be taught everything they need for success and explicit instruction involves consistently high success rates from students.

REFERENCES

Brophy, J. E., & Good, T. L. (1984). *Teacher behavior and student achievement*. Occasional Paper no.73. East Lansing, MI: Institute for Research on Teaching, Michigan State University.

Brophy, J. E., & Good, T. L. (2008). *Looking in classrooms* (10th ed.). Boston, MA: Pearson.

Butler, C. (2010). Repeated testing produces superior transfer of learning relative to repeated studying. *Journal of Experimental Psychology: Learning, Memory and Cognition, 36*(5), 1118–1133.

Chall, J. S. (2000). *The academic achievement challenge.* New York, NY: Guildford Press.

Children of the Code. (2009). *Siegfried Engelmann: Instructional design 101: Learn from the learners!.* https://childrenofthecode.org/interviews/engelmann.htm

Clark, R. E., Kirschner, P. A., & Sweller, J. (2012). Putting students on the path to learning: The case for fully guided instruction. *American Educator, 36*(1), 6–11.

Coe, R., Aloisi, C., Higgins, S., & Major, L. E. (2014). *What makes great teaching? Review of the underpinning research.* London: The Sutton Trust.

Craik, F. M., & Lockhart, R. S. (1972). Levels of processing: A framework for memory research. *Journal of Verbal Learning and Verbal Behaviour, 11,* 671–684.

Creemers, B. P. M., & Kyriakides, L. (2006). Critical analysis of the current approaches to modelling educational effectiveness: The importance of establishing a dynamic model. *School Effectiveness and School Improvement, 17,* 347–366.

Ericsson, A., & Pool, R. (2017). *Peak vintage.*

Fiorella, L., & Mayer, R. (2015). *Learning as a generative activity: Eight learning strategies that promote understanding.* Cambridge: Cambridge University Press.

Hattie, J. (2009). *Visible learning. A synthesis of over 800 meta-analyses relating to achievement.* London/New York, NY: Routledge.

Joyce, B., Weil, M., & Calhoun, E. (2000). *Models of teaching.* Boston MA: Allyn & Bacon.

Ko, J., Sammons, P., & Bakkum, L. (2013). *Effective teaching: A review of research and evidence.* Oxford: CfBt Education Trust.

Lemov, D., Woolway, E., & Yezzi, K. (2012). *Practice perfect.* San Francisco, CA: Jossey Bass.

Mourshed, M., Krawitz, M., & Dorn, E. (2017). *How to improve student educational outcomes, McKinsey & Co.* Retrieved from: www.mckinsey.com/~/media/McKinsey/Industries/Social%20Sector/Our%20Insights/How%20to%20 improve%20student%20educational%20outcomes/How-to-improve-student-educational-outcomes-New-insightsfrom-data-analytics.ashx

Muijs, D., Kyriakides, L., van der Werf, G., Creemers, B., Timperley, H., & Earl, L. (2014). State of the art-teacher effectiveness and professional learning. In *School effectiveness and school improvement: An international journal of research, policy and practice.* London: Routledge.

Muijs, D., & Reynolds, D. (2017). *Effective teaching: Evidence and practice.* London: SAGE.

Roediger, H. L., Putnam, A. L., & Smith, M. A. (2011). Ten benefits of testing and their applications to educational practice. *Psychology of Learning and Motivation, 55,* 1–36.

Rosenshine, B. (2008). *Five meanings of direct instruction.* Lincoln, IL: Center on Innovation & Improvement.

Rosenshine, B. (2009). The empirical support for direct instruction. In S. Tobias & T. M. Duffy (Eds.), *Constructivist instruction: Success or failure?* New York, NY: Routledge.

Stockard, J., Wood, T. W., Coughlin, C., & Rasplica Khoury, C. (2018). The effectiveness of direct instruction curricula: A meta-analysis of a half-century of research. *Review of Educational Research, 88,* 479–507.

7

WHAT CAN ROSENSHINE TEACH US?

In this chapter, we will explore

- The importance of regular review
- The importance of presenting new material in small steps
- The role of questioning and checking for understanding
- The importance of modelling
- The features of guided and independent practice

INTRODUCTION

Rosenshine's 'Principles of Instruction' is often seen as a definitive list of explicit teaching strategies. While the principles themselves are not subject specific, this chapter will demonstrate how they can be applied when teaching English.

TEN PRINCIPLES

Barak Rosenshine's Principles of Instruction outlines a number of approaches and techniques that are seen as the hallmarks of explicit instruction, including regular reviews of prior learning, breaking down learning into manageable steps and utilizing models. The Principles of Instruction comes from three areas of research: research into cognitive science, research on the classroom practices of expert teachers and research on cognitive supports like scaffolding and using models to help students learn complex tasks. Despite the breadth of this evidence base, Rosenshine points out that 'the fact that the instructional ideas from three different sources supplement and complement each other gives us faith in the validity of these findings' (Rosenshine, 2012). This convergence between classroom-based research and cognitive science demonstrates that these strategies are of crucial importance to teachers. Not only are they effective, but they are easy to apply to everyday teaching.

Table 7.1 Three instructions models all point to similar ideas

Broad starting point according to perceived level of learner expertise	Direct instruction/ explicit instruction	Cognitive load theory	Rosenshine's principles of instruction
1 **Novice learners**	**I** • Teacher demonstrates via an explicit instruction approach	**Worked example** • Reduces cognitive load for novices who lack sufficiently developed background knowledge • For building schemas • Exemplifies success criteria or goal	**Provide models** • Clarify and exemplify specific steps • Turn the abstract into the concrete
2 **Developing in expertise**	**We** • Teacher demonstrates and asks student to assist with completion	**Completion problem** • A 'hybrid' of worked examples and problem solving • To ensure students process worked parts sufficiently	**New material in small steps/provide models** • Mastering individual steps one a time prevents cognitive overload
3 **Expert learners**	**You** • Students attempt problem independently	**Problem** • Allows students with sufficiently developed schemas to apply their knowledge	**Independent practice** • Develops automaticity and fluency

This chapter will explore seven principles of instruction.

1. Daily review
2. Weekly and monthly review
3. Present new material in small steps with student practice after each step
4. Ask lots of questions and check the responses of all students
5. Provide Models
6. Guide student practice
7. Require and monitor student practice

REVIEW: DAILY, WEEKLY AND MONTHLY

As we saw in Chapter 2, retrieving information from our long-term memory is a really effective method of slowing down the rate of forgetting as well as providing additional practice for students. For knowledge to become consolidated and therefore more easily accessed and automatized, students need to practice retrieving and applying what they know in different ways (Howard et al., 2018). If pupils rehearse and review what they have learned, their knowledge will likely become more interconnected, making it easier to apply in wider writing or discussion as well as increasing the ease with which new information is learned (Rosenshine, 2012).

Daily review can involve retrieval practice, drills and restrictive practice activities, helping pupils to become accurate and fluent in components like vocabulary, specific sentence structures or analytical skills. Weekly and monthly review is ideal for wider application, helping pupils to broaden their understanding and increase the flexibility of their knowledge. It's a bit like building-each brick of knowledge and each specific skill needs to be accurate and fluent before being connected to others in increasingly larger constructions: sentences, paragraphs and then whole essays.

While Chapter 2 explained a number of retrieval practice techniques, this chapter will explore additional approaches and benefits.

School children's brains are still developing and as a result, their ability to make connections with prior knowledge can be limited (Brod et al., 2013). As novice learners, their knowledge is inert and while it may have already been learned and retained, it may well be inaccessible to them (Shing and Brod, 2016). While an expert – someone who has better organized, more developed and more accessible schema – would likely recognize that specific knowledge is required when presented with a new task, students will often need to be prompted to reactivate their prior knowledge. Perhaps the simplest way of doing this is through written retrieval practice as explained in Chapter 2. All students should be expected to respond, and instant corrective feedback should be given so that all students are provided with the knowledge required and errors are efficiently corrected. Merely asking 'Who can remember what we did last week' is not going to cut it; the keen child will answer and everyone else will switch off.

The process of activating prior knowledge is dependent upon what knowledge is being activated. In some classrooms, teachers may ask open-ended questions designed to elicit the prior knowledge of their students. Imagine the class are currently reading *The Giver* by Lois Lowry and today's lesson is focused on Jonas. The teacher could ask students to list words that they know that could be used to describe Jonas. Although this is an example of activating prior knowledge, the knowledge that is being activated will be unique to each student as they will all have different vocabulary within their memories. While the variance is not a problem in itself (there will always be differences in pupils' prior knowledge), this approach can lead to further problems. Firstly, it will be difficult to continue to retrieve and apply 30 different sets of vocabulary over the next few weeks, meaning that subsequent lessons may not be as effective at helping all pupils to broaden and deepen their understanding. Secondly, this type of brainstorming often favours the children who have the widest vocabularies, giving them further praise for their word knowledge and reminding the pupils who have narrower vocabularies that they are not as successful. Thirdly, if the lesson focuses on words that some pupils already know, can it really be said to be stretching the more erudite pupils?

A more efficient approach would be to activate prior knowledge that all students have been explicitly taught in previous lessons. Reducing the variance here makes it much easier for the teacher to help pupils retain and broaden their knowledge.

Daily review is particularly important for content that is in constant use by students (Rosenshine, 2012), and the goal for daily review activities is retention, accuracy and fluency. In English, this might be high-utility vocabulary, important plot details, quotations or concepts within a text and for such content, retrieval practice, as explained in Chapter 2, will likely be the simplest way of conducting daily review.

For students to master new sentence structures, punctuation or analytical skills, they will also need daily review. However, if students are not already reasonably accurate at producing specific sentence structures, then it may be counter-productive to ask them to review and practice them or they will become confused, demotivated and will practice making errors. Chapter 10 will explore how to create multi-lesson instructional sequences in order to efficiently teach new sentence structures and skills, ensuring that through a process of backwards fading, students are able to maintain consistently high success rates while gradually increasing in independence.

Here are some useful strategies for daily review and practice.

SENTENCE COMBINING

Asking student to combine simple sentences into more complex constructions is an effective method of practice in order to develop writing fluency (Andrews et al., 2006). This approach can be used in either a free-form manner where students are asked to manipulate and play with different possibilities in order to tease out different effects or it can be more restrictive, asking students to create specific constructions through prompts or drill type activities. Let's have a look at some examples:

FREE FORM

Students can be presented with a number of simple sentences and can then combine them into a more complex construction:

- Macbeth hallucinates
- He sees a dagger
- Macbeth talks to the dagger
- It is covered in blood
- Macbeth is psychologically unstable

Some possibilities:

Hallucinating and psychologically unstable, Macbeth sees and talks to a bloody dagger.

Macbeth seems psychologically unstable as he hallucinates, seeing a bloody dagger which he talks to.

Talking to a hallucination, Macbeth seems psychologically unstable as he sees a bloody dagger.

Macbeth talks to his hallucination, a blood covered dagger that symbolizes his psychological instability.

Let's now look at some further examples of simple sentences and some possibilities:

- He stared into the distance.
- Tears welled in his eyes.
- She was gone.
- The future looked bleak.

Some possibilities:

He stared into the distance as tears welled in his eyes; the future looked bleak now that she was gone.

Tears welling in his eyes, he stared into the distance as he realized that she was gone and the future looked bleak.

Because she was gone, tears welled in his eyes as he stared into the distance: the future looked bleak.

This approach allows students to create different effects so that they can see the relationship between different ideas and, through discussion and comparison, can evaluate which constructions are most effective (Dean and Anderson, 2014). When teaching literature texts, this approach can be doubly effective, reviewing content as well as practicing sentence constructions. The process of evaluating which construction is most apt can result in nuanced analysis of the content that is being reviewed: if you think that the dagger soliloquy should primarily be seen in terms of Macbeth's burgeoning mental turmoil, then beginning a sentence with 'Hallucinating and psychologically unstable', may be the most fitting construction.

DRILLS AND PROMPTS

1. Underline what to keep
   This approach asks student to practice being concise, focusing upon the main ideas and cutting out anything that is redundant.
   The monster dropped dead.

- It was twitching.
- It was gasping.
- It was bleeding.

Twitching, gasping, bleeding, the monster dropped dead.

2. Prompts
   This approach asks students to use a specific construction when combining.

- Eggs are versatile.
- You can fry them.
- You can boil them.

- You can poach them.
- *Use 'because'.*

Because eggs are versatile, you can fry, boil or poach them.

SENTENCE AND VOCABULARY DRILLS

Once pupils are able to accurately write specific sentence structures, they can be asked to complete further practice to increase their fluency. They can also be asked to practice specific vocabulary that they have been taught (Figure 7.1).

Misogyny (n)	Dislike, contempt and distrust of women
misogynist (n)	
misogynistic (adj)	*Authoritarian and misogynistic, Creon calls his son a 'woman's slave'*

TASK: Write sentences about Creon that contain the following components:

1) Present Participle
2) Noun Appositive
3) Absolute phrase
4) 2 adjective start

Each sentence must use 'misogyny' or a different form of that word.

Example sentences:

1) <u>Describing his son as a 'woman's slave'</u>, Creon demonstrates his flagrant misogyny.
2) <u>A misogynistic despot who treats women as 'inferior'</u>, Creon disparages, criticizes and denigrates women.
3) Creon defiantly exclaims that he would 'never let some woman triumph over' him, <u>his words filled with misogynistic invective.</u>
4) <u>Tyrannical and despotic,</u> Creon misogynistically refers to women as 'inferior'.

Figure 7.1 Example of combining sentence and vocabulary practice

DESCRIBE THE PICTURE

Pupils can be asked to write specific sentence constructions and include words that they have learned in previous lessons. This approach is particularly well suited to narrative, creative or descriptive writing. Let's have a look at an example:

Task 1: Write a sentence describing the picture, following the sentence styles:

Styles:

1. Appositive at the end
2. Present participle at the start
3. Semi-colon
4. Appositive at the start
5. Two present participles at the end

Examples:

1. The monster clung to the stone, a huge monolith that protruded from the deep.
2. Howling loudly, Dagon emerged from the murky sea.
3. It had laid dormant for a thousand years; the earthquake awoke it from its slumber.
4. A fearsome, immortal demi-god, Dagon flexed his slimy muscles.
5. The sea raged, crashing against the rocks, spraying high into the air.

The example sentences provide further support for pupils; those who are struggling can adapt the examples by changing words or parts of sentences. Later on in an instructional sequence, these examples would be faded out so that pupils are expected to generate their own sentences from the list of styles.

ANALYSIS COMBINATION DRILLS

In Chapter 11, we will explore how analysis can be broken down into a number of sub-skills, each of which can be taught and practiced in isolation before being combined with others. Asking students to combine components and specific content such as quotations and vocabulary is an ideal form of daily review. These daily review items can go beyond mere sentence completion, instead acting as targeted and purposive responses to whatever text you are studying. For example, students could be asked to make links between the target vocabulary and other relevant bits of knowledge. These drills can also make clear your expectations as to technical sophistication or the full development of arguments and ideas. Also, they can be used to make links between different pieces of vocabulary that you have taught them.

Let's have a look at some examples:

1. Mr Birling thinks he is infallible because...

   - Include *pompous*
   - Include a quote
   - Add a semi-colon and a further independent clause

      Possible answer: 'Mr Birling thinks he is infallible because he emphatically states that the "Titanic" is "unsinkable"; alongside his other bold and pompous pronouncements, this makes us doubt his intelligence and question the validity of his position as a man of influence at the top of society'.

2. Eric lives a privileged life so...

   - Include a quote
   - Include a participle phrase

      Possible answer: 'Eric lives a privileged life so he has few responsibilities and immense wealth, enabling him to drink "too much"'.

3. At the beginning of the play, Lady Macbeth seems dominant but...

- Add an appositive
- Add 'Out Damned spot!'
- Add a second sentence discussing Shakespeare's intention
- Include *nefarious, insurrection, plight* and *admonishment*

> Possible answer: 'At the beginning of the play, Lady Macbeth seems domi-nant but her nefarious plan eventually causes her to become mentally unstable as she chants "Out Damned spot!", evidence of her psychological instability. Perhaps Shakespeare wanted her plight to serve as an admon-ishment to those considering insurrection or regicide, potentially flattering King James who had just survived an assassination attempt'.

An additional benefit to these restrictive practice exercises is that they allow the teacher to circulate and give precise feedback to students as they write: 'You need quotation marks around your evidence. Has your appositive got a noun in it? Check your spelling of "assassination". Does you sentence make sense here?' Instead of taking in books, marking and then handing them back – a laborious and lengthy process – corrections can be made instantly and quickly. Because the practice is so defined and restricted, your feedback can be completely purposive and precise. Instead of vague, abstracted comments like 'you need to develop that further or you should extend that point or you need to use better vocabulary', you can refer to the success criteria for each practice item. I tend to do these under a visualiser: modelling several by writing them 'live' is crucial, especially for the ones that contain specific success criteria. Sometimes I take a student's book and we explore their work under the visualiser; sometimes I ask students to read out one that they are proud of (making sure they *say* the punctuation marks so that I can check if they are accurate).

If these review activities are to be maximally effective, pupils need to have the relevant prior knowledge. It will be no good asking them to review and practice writing a present participle sentence or include a specific quotation if they don't know how to do so. These review activities should be about building fluency and broadening understanding by asking pupils to apply what they have learned to increasingly wider contexts.

ERROR CORRECTION

Once pupils have been taught how to construct specific sentences or use punctu-ation and can produce them fairly accurately, they can be asked to correct sentences with errors in them. Useful error sentences will often feature omissions and com-mon misconceptions and can therefore be preplanned fairly easily. Errors can also be compiled from student work, thereby focusing on specific things that students are getting wrong.

WEEKLY AND MONTHLY REVIEW

CUMULATIVE MIXED RETRIEVAL PRACTICE

As well as daily retrieval practice, a weekly or fortnightly version can further support retention and help pupils deepen their understanding. If a class is given weekly retrieval practice, they are more likely to perform well in final examinations (Rosenshine, 2012). If weekly or monthly review is cumulative, this can also help create further connections between different concepts, thereby deepening students' understanding. This process of connection and integration will result in better organized and more comprehensive schemas in students' long-term memories, one of the hallmarks of expertise (Centre for Education Statistics and Evaluation, 2017). The more detailed and connected the knowledge is, the more flexible it will be and therefore the greater likelihood that students will be able to apply it.

CONCEPT MAPPING

Asking pupils to create mind maps or concept maps can be a really useful review activity. Mapping is an effective learning approach because students engage in all three cognitive processes. Firstly, they need to select which concepts to focus on; secondly, they need to organise the information into a spatial arrangement, paying attention to positioning and the links between ideas; thirdly, students integrate the information with their prior knowledge by transforming it from one mode of representation into another as well as connecting it with logical principles from their long-term memory like compare and contrast (Fiorella and Mayer, 2015, p. 38).

PARAGRAPHS/MINI-ESSAYS

Extended writing is an ideal approach for weekly or monthly review. Asking pupils to write at length in response to a question ensures that they combine and apply components that they would have initially been taught in isolation.

ENTIRE RECAP LESSONS

Planning recap lessons into units is a good way to ensure that content from previous units is retrieved, applied and practiced. Such lessons may involve a selection of different retrieval quizzes, restrictive practice activities or more extended writing tasks.

LAGGED HOMEWORK

Homework can also be the perfect opportunity for review. A useful approach is to set homework on previous units to ensure that pupils are engaging in distributed retrieval and practice, thereby increasing the likelihood that there will be 'a change in long-term memory'.

Table 7.2   Lagged homework example

Current unit	Homework
War Poetry	
Romeo and Juliet	War Poetry
The Crucible	Romeo and Juliet
Frankenstein	The Crucible

WHAT IS THE LINK BETWEEN DAILY REVIEW AND MONTHLY REVIEW?

In English literature, most lessons build slowly towards the complex skill of extended analytical writing, daily review providing practice on components and weekly or monthly review providing practice with wider application.

Let's have a look at an example that demonstrates the connection between daily and monthly review over the course of a number of lessons. As explained above, for this to be maximally effective, it needs to involve cumulative review where concepts, skills and knowledge are gradually combined and integrated as students move closer towards a final performance.

EXAMPLE: MACBETH: PLANNING OVERVIEW

Table 7.3   Macbeth planning overview demonstrating link between daily and weekly review

Teaching focus	Daily review	What is reviewed?	Weekly review Possible extended writing questions that involve cumulative review and ask for pupils to make connections
Week 1: Act1:1 Act1:2 Act1:3	Plot details Vocabulary Important lines Interpretations Techniques Context Sentences Punctuation Analytical Skills	Week 1	• What is the difference between how Macbeth is presented in Act 1:2 and how he responds to the witches in Act 1:3 • How are the witches presented in Act 1:1 and Act 1:3?
Week 2: Act 1:4 Act:1:5		Week 1+2	• Explore Macbeth's duplicity, focusing on Act 1:2, Act 1:3 and Act1:4 • Explore Macbeth's ambition, focusing on Act 1:3, Act 1:4 and Act 1:5 • 'Lady Macbeth is similar to the witches' How far do you agree with this? Focus on Act 1:1, Act 1:3 and Act 1:5
Week 3: Act 1:6 Act 1:7		Week 1+2+3	• How is Duncan presented? Refer to Act 1:2, Act 1:4 and Act 1:6 • How is Macbeth perceived by others? Refer to Lady Macbeth and Duncan, using ideas from all preceding scenes • How has Macbeth's state of mind changed in Act 1? Focus on his soliloquies and asides.

PRESENT NEW MATERIAL IN SMALL STEPS WITH STUDENT PRACTICE AFTER EACH STEP

For a novice student, the model paragraph above may contain multiple pieces of novel and complicated information and as a result, it may well be challenging or impossible for them to understand or produce. Think back to Chapter 1 where we explore the process of learning: if students are to make sense of what we teach them, they need to be able to engage in three stages of cognitive processing (Fiorella and Mayer, 2015):

- **Stage 1:** *Selecting* **relevant information to attend to**
- **Stage 2:** *Organising* **the material into a coherent cognitive structure in working memory**
- **Stage 3:** *Integrating* **it with relevant prior knowledge activated from long-term memory**

If students are overwhelmed with too much novel and complicated content, then it is highly likely that they will be unable to engage with stage 2 of the learning process. Our working memories are limited and if students are to successfully cope with new information, we need to ensure that it is presented, taught and practised in small steps. Effective teachers will ensure that pupils master a smaller step before moving onto a subsequent one.

Breaking a complex performance into its components and practising these individually can often be more effective as by doing so, students are less likely to become overwhelmed and confused. If these steps are distributed across multiple lessons, then there will be an additional benefit: students are more likely to retain the content.

Here's how the complex performance of extended writing can be split up into smaller steps.

DAILY REVIEW OF VOCABULARY, QUOTATIONS TO BE MEMORISED (KEY STAGE 4) AND CONTEXT INFORMATION

a. Some questions will be closed, rote style factual recall, perhaps with clues:
   What adjective means flawless or perfect: imp_cc_ble ANSWER: impeccable.
b. Some will be more open, the assumption being less clues are needed for successful recall:
   What noun means good behaviour? ANSWER: propriety.
c. Some will involve students making links, hopefully developing schemas and connections in their minds:
   Name three terms that refer to standards of behaviour ANSWER: decorum, social conformity, propriety.
d. Some will involve even wider links:
   Complete the quotation: 'embarassed in. . . . .'
      Write down another two quotations that describe Utterson's secrecy.
      What context information is relevant here?
      Write down three adjectives to describe Utterson's behaviour.
      ANSWER: Quotations: 'embarrassed in discourse' 'cold' 'never found his way into his talk' Context: Fear of Blackmail and scandal, Repressive Victorian Social Mores. Adjectives: secretive, paranoid, obsessed.

This final answer is essentially the bare bones of an analytical paragraph and asking these freer retrieval questions help students to build mental plans of what to write. You could then ask them to use it to write a paragraph at speed.

DAILY REVIEW OF VOCABULARY OR SENTENCE PRACTICE

Using 'because, but so' (see Chapter 5) or practising specific structures that you want students to use in their wider writing.

LINE ANNOTATION

Applying vocabulary that has been taught, discussing interpretations and using rapid sequences of questions in order to maximise student participation and recall.

WORKED EXAMPLE ANNOTATION

The model answer contains all of the constituent elements mentioned above, exemplifying their usage within wider writing.

FOCUSED PARAGRAPH WRITING

Allowing students to apply the constituent concepts.

This final task may come at the end of a lesson that involves many of the preceding practice activities, allowing the teacher to check that students can accurately and fluently apply and combine the components that have been taught.

However, teachers should treat what students write here as evidence of 'performance' not 'learning'. If you think back to Chapter 2, the distinction between the two is really important. Performance is 'the temporary fluctuations in behaviour or knowledge that can be observed and measured during or immediately after the acquisition process' (Soderstrom and Bjork, 2015). Because the whole lesson has been an 'acquisition process', it will be unsurprising that students will perform well: the knowledge is fresh in their minds and has 'high retrieval strength.'

This is why weekly and monthly review is so important. If students cannot successfully recall information after a delay, then even if they *performed* well in class when the content was initially taught, we cannot assume that they have *learned*. Weekly and monthly review is a useful way of making better inferences about *learning* so that we are not tricked into equating good *performance* with good *learning*.

ASK LOTS OF QUESTIONS AND CHECK THE RESPONSES OF ALL STUDENTS

Asking questions is an important part of teaching but if questions are to be useful, we need to think about why we are asking them. Questions can be asked to check understanding, to push students to develop their answer, to consider alternative viewpoints or to help them make links between ideas. Questions also provide pupils with vital practice on what is being taught.

Most of the time it is far more efficient to teach stuff, then ask students questions about what you have taught. Beginning with eliciting questions like 'Who knows what The Great Chain of Being is?' or 'What do you think "hubris" means?' before teaching them anything is probably not that useful. The worst example of this is 'guess what's in my head' where a teacher asks a question with a specific answer in mind, hoping to elicit that specific answer from the class. This guessing game can go on for ages and is almost certainly a waste of time.

WHAT SHOULD BE THE FOCUS OF QUESTIONING?

Successful teachers ask more useful questions to as many students as possible. Their questions will focus on declarative knowledge (the content that is being taught) as well as procedural knowledge (the processes that students need to follow if they are to complete tasks properly) (Rosenshine, 2012).

Let's have a look at some examples:

Declarative questions:

1. What is the subject of the first sentence?
2. What is the adjectival form of 'benevolence'?
3. If the audience knows something that the character does not, what is this technique called?
4. Why does Macbeth want to kill Duncan?
5. Who is responsible for Macbeth's demise?

Procedural questions:

1. How did you find the answer to that question?
2. What are the five steps you should follow when answering the examination question?
3. What you should include in your first paragraph and why it is important?
4. How do you know that?

Asking procedural questions is really important. Not only does it provide additional practice as students are asked to explain how they have done something, but it allows other students to understand how they did it.

PURPOSE: CHECK FOR UNDERSTANDING

Using mini-white boards. Mini-white boards are ideal for checking an entire class' answers at once. They are especially useful for lower order, closed and factual questions, their size prohibiting answers that are anything more than a few sentences.

Cold call. This technique helps to ensure that all students are engaged and thinking about what you have asked (Lemov, 2010, p. 111). Assuming you have taught them what they need in order to answer the question, this can be an equitable and appropriate means of ensuring everyone thinks of an answer, an outcome that is more difficult to achieve with traditional 'hands up' style questioning.

Let's have a look at an example.

Teacher: 'How do you know that Ozymandias was arrogant'?
The teacher should then pause, allowing everyone the opportunity to think of answer
Teacher: 'Korede. . . . . .what do you think'?

Choral response. Asking an entire class to respond at the same time means that everyone answers the question. This allows for far more practice as well as providing the teacher with more comprehensive information about whether their students have understood. Choral response questions are ideally suited to lower order, closed and factual questions. For this approach to be successful, students need to respond at the same time. If some students are faster than others, the slower students can just copy the answer they hear instead of thinking for themselves. If you are thinking that this approach sounds weird or won't work with teenagers, you may be pleasantly surprised: typically, they enjoy choral response, especially if the teacher is enthusiastic.

Let's have a look at an example:

Teacher: 'Which rhetorical technique involves three ideas in succession'?
The teacher then needs to give a cue: clicking fingers, saying 'Go', or dropping a raised arm all work well.
Whole class: 'Tricolon'.

THE FIRST PURPOSE OF QUESTIONING: DEVELOPING THINKING

THINK PAIR SHARE

This approach is ideal for developing student thinking about more complex ideas and is ideally suited to higher order questions involving explanation, comparison, analysis, synthesis or evaluation.

Imagine you are teaching *Musee des Beaux Arts by W. H. Auden* and have already spent some time teaching and discussing the poem.

Teacher: 'I want you all to think in silence for 20 secs. *What does the poem have to say about suffering*'?
It is important to wait, giving them sufficient thinking time.
Teacher: 'Remember to include specific reference to the poem and some of the vocabulary that we have learned. When you are done, I will call for a random

student to share their thoughts so make sure your discussions are fruitful. *Ok, discuss your ideas with your partner for 1 minute. Go!'*

The inclusion of specific success criteria is vital so that students know what is expected of them. Deliberately frontloading the instructions with the details and ending with the actual question or the instruction can help ensure that pupils listen properly. If I began with the italicised parts, lots of students might begin and therefore ignore the other parts.

A/B/C QUESTIONING

Discussion is a crucial means of developing ideas. Alex Quigley (2013) popularized a useful way to structure student responses by giving them three options:

- A = Agree: If a student agrees with a point has been made, they will need to verbally summarise and paraphrase what has been said. The process of transforming a previous assertion into their own words ensures that they engage in appropriate cognitive processing.
- B = Build upon: Alternatively, a student could be asked to build upon a previous point, adding additional ideas.
- C = Challenge: Finally, they could be asked to challenge what has been said, instead offering an alternative interpretation or explanation.

SOCRATIC QUESTIONING

Socrates loved questions, famously claiming that *'the unexamined life is not worth living'*. In Socratic Questioning, there are six different types of questions that teachers can use in order to develop student thinking. After each one are some example questions.

1. Clarification

   - 'What do you mean'?
   - 'Could you explain that further'?
   - 'How does this relate to our discussion'?

2. Challenging Assumptions

   - 'Is this always the case'?
   - 'Why do you think that'?

3. Asking for Evidence

   - 'How do you know this is the case'?
   - 'What evidence do you have for this'?
   - 'Can you give me an example'?

4. Alternative viewpoints and perspectives

- 'What is the counter argument here'?
- 'Another possibility for this is ...., what do you think'?
- 'What is the difference between these two interpretations'?

5. Implications and consequences

- 'If this is the case, then what about...................'
- 'How does............................. link to.........................?
- 'What is the effect of..?

6. Questioning the question

- 'Why is that an important question'?
- 'Why did I ask that question'?

PURPOSE: HIGH EXPECTATIONS

NO OPT OUT

When asked a question by a teacher, students often choose to opt out by answering 'I don't know' or by shrugging their shoulders. Sometimes this will be because the genuinely don't know how to answer; other times, however, this response is given in the hope that the teacher will then move on to someone else. Thinking requires effort and all of us, teachers and students alike, are prone to avoiding doing so if given the chance. As soon as students realise that 'I don't know' is a shield that can protect them from taking part or exerting effort, then it can be difficult for the teacher to expect them to do so. Teachers who use No Opt Out are doing so in order to minimise the likelihood that pupils will try to avoid participation as well as providing students who don't know an answer additional repetition and practice.

The aim of this questioning technique is to ensure that 'A sequence that begins with a student unable to answer a question should end with the student answering that question as often as possible' (Lemov, 2010, p. 28).

Let's have a look at some examples:

1. **You provide the answer; the student repeats it**
   Teacher: 'What is the name of a speech given by a character when they are on their own so that the audience can know what they are thinking'?
   Olamide: 'I don't know'.
   Teacher: 'Olamide, the answer is soliloquy. Now you tell me, what is the name of the speech'?
   Olamide: 'It is called a soliloquy'.
   Teacher: 'What is a soliloquy'?

Olamide: 'It's a speech given by a character on their own so that. . ...errr. . ..so we can know what they are thinking'

2. Another student provides the answer, the student repeats it

3. You provide a cue that the student can use

Teacher: 'What reasons does Macbeth consider as to why he shouldn't kill Duncan'?

Olamide: 'I don't know'.

Teacher: 'Some of the reasons are about Duncan's character'

Olamide: 'He is a good and kind King and. . ..err. . .this would make the crime even more shocking'.

Teacher: 'Yes, but even if he was a bad king, it would still be shocking though, why is this. . ..'?

Olamide: 'Because of The Divine Right of Kings. . ..people thought that the King was chosen by God'.

4. Another student provides a cue that the student can use

Teacher: 'What reasons does Macbeth consider as to why he shouldn't kill Duncan'?

Olamide: 'I don't know'.

Teacher: 'Who can give Olamide a clue'?

Xin: 'Some of the reasons are to do with Macbeth's conscience and what might happen if he did it'.

Olamide: 'He's concerned that everyone will find out'.

If possible, cues should be chosen over asking students to repeat answers and this is because providing cues requires students to think more than merely repeating an answer. As a general rule, the teacher should always try to offer the least amount of support that still results in the correct answer.

FORMAT MATTERS

When students give answers to questions, teachers should expect them to answer with precision, clarity and use standard English (Lemov, 2010, p. 47). Although there is much contention surrounding the exact meaning of 'standard English', it is the kind of formalized language that would widely be accepted as correct.

Spoken language is different to written language: there are many language structures that are rarely found in speech at all and written texts typically contain more formal and complex syntax (Montag, 2019). When we speak, we often use incomplete sentences, more repetition and simpler constructions. Classroom talk is different though. Spoken answers given in class can be used by teachers as a useful opportunity for students to practice quickly generating complete sentences (Lemov, 2010), to practice using specific sentence constructions or to practice applying specific vocabulary. If these opportunities are to be utilised, it can often be necessary to insist upon a style of talk in the classroom that is at odds with common conventions of spoken language. Classrooms where students are expected to use full sentences, formal constructions and academic vocabulary will see students engaging in considerably more practice than those that don't. This additional practice will likely result in greater retention, more flexible knowledge and more fluent application of what has been taught.

PROVIDE MODELS: PROVIDING STUDENTS WITH MODELS AND WORKED EXAMPLES IS FASTER FOR LEARNING

In Chapter 3, we explored some of the research behind studying worked examples. This approach is effective because it helps to build and develop students' background knowledge within their long-term memories, which can then be recalled and applied when they write independently. Whatever it is that we are teaching, whether it be a piece of vocabulary, a specific sentence construction, a genre of writing or even a means of approaching a specific examination question, beginning instruction by studying models and examples is likely to be far more effective than asking students to begin by attempting the task without this guidance.

MODEL AND DESCRIBE

Effective teachers combine modelling with description (Lemov et al., 2012, p. 86). While the model exemplifies the skill that the student is expected to replicate, the accompanying description helps them to understand the reasons behind the choices and steps that the teacher has demonstrated.

Let's have a look at an example:

Imagine you are modelling how to approach an extract-based essay question on *Lord of the Flies*. The students are presented with an extract from the novel and have to write an analytical essay in response to this question:

Explore the theme of savagery in *Lord of the Flies*

If students are to succeed at this question, they will likely need to follow a process. While there may be many different ways of approaching the task, some will be more efficient and effective than others. The most useful one to teach will be the simplest and most transferable approach and if students are to master it, the teacher will need to model and describe it to them.

What follows is a six-step approach to answering this style of question. For each of the steps described below, the teacher needs to show students how to do it as well as explaining why it is important. Using a document camera or visualiser makes modelling really clear as the teacher can easily show students how to do each step.

STEP 1: READ THE QUESTION AND UNDERLINE THE KEY WORD

In this case, the key word is 'savagery'.

Why:

- To ensure that you are focused on the question
- You then know what to look for in the extract in the next step

STEP 2: READ THE EXTRACT AND FIND EVIDENCE THAT FITS THE QUESTION

How:

The teacher should demonstrate reading and annotating, deliberately describing their thought process so that students can see how to approach this step.

Teacher: 'Ok so the question is about savagery. I'm going to read the extract and find bits that exemplify savagery. I know that there may be some words or phrases that I don't fully understand: this is ok though. I should concentrate on the bits I do understand, choosing evidence that I am able to say developed, interesting things about. If I choose well here, then writing will be much easier. I also need to ensure that my evidence is as short as possible-each piece will probably be only a few words but none will be longer than a sentence. Remember I only want to analyse and interpret interesting words and phrases.'

Why:

- This evidence will be used in the section of your essay that focuses on the extract

STEP 3: MAKE A PLAN

How:

Students should then list ideas about savagery from the rest of the novel. The teacher should demonstrate how to plan by listing useful ideas, describing their thought process so that students understand what to do.

Teacher: 'Now that I've annotated the extract, I need to think about how savagery is presented in the rest of the novel. I need to list big ideas that I will be able to write about. Remember, a big idea is often something abstract like "atavistic regression", it is not a specific thing from the text like the fact that the boys look dirty and disheveled. These specific things show the big idea of "atavistic regression". Each paragraph should be about a big idea. Each paragraph should have lots of specific examples that illustrate these big ideas'.

Possible Paragraph Plan:

1. Innate Capacity for Evil
2. Atavistic Regression
3. Civilisation vs Anarchy
4. Deindividuation and group psychology

Why:

- A sophisticated, analytical essay is often pitched at a conceptual level, dealing with abstract notions and nominalized ideas. Instead of commenting on a violent character, it will delve into the savagery of an archetype; instead of merely exploring the cruel treatment of Piggy, it will comment on dominance and competitive urges. Characters become constructs; language becomes symbolic and the tenor of the essay will be pitched far in excess of a mere analytical commentary where students move from quotation to quotation.
- The paragraph plan essentially lists big ideas connected to the question. Students will use these in their analytical introduction.

STEP 4: WRITE THE ANALYTICAL INTRODUCTION

Why:

- Analytical Introductions will sketch out the big ideas that students have identified with regard to the question. They will often touch upon authorial intent and will contain a few succinct, well-chosen quotations to demonstrate that even at this level of abstraction, the interpretations are still based upon a close reading of the text. Appositive sentences lend themselves well to these introductions, allowing students to hit the examiner with thematic commentary from the very beginning.

Here is an example:

A novel that explores humanity's innate capacity for evil, Lord of the Flies conveys how a group of school children quickly descend into 'darkness' and become increasingly atavistic and 'bloodthirsty'. As anarchy replaces civilisation, Golding warns us of the importance of benign authority.

STEP 5: WRITE ABOUT THE EXTRACT

Using the evidence that they found in step 2, students should write about how savagery is portrayed in the extract.

STEP 6: WRITE ABOUT THE REST OF THE NOVEL

Using the big ideas that they came up with in step 3 and then included in their analytical introduction, students should then write at least a paragraph about each one.

CALL YOUR SHOTS (LEMOV ET AL., 2012, P. 87)

If we want students to get maximum benefit from models and worked examples, we need to tell them what to focus on and pay attention to. Just showing an example of something and asking students why it is good will not cut it: a novice may not know enough about what is being shown to understand which bits make it effective.

MODELLING 'LIVE' IN CLASS VS PREMADE, MODELS

Writing examples 'live' in class under a visualizer or document camera can be a really useful approach as it allows you to talk through your decisions and process. You may make mistakes when doing so but this should not be seen as a bad thing: students benefit from seeing how writing is a messy process. It is also important for them to realize that proficient writers are constantly editing what they write, changing words or rephrasing sentences in order to maintain a specific focus, tone or perspective (Kellogg, 2008).

To make live modelling easier, you can prewrite an example which you can then copy and write during the lesson. This allows you to ensure that your model contains whatever it is you want to demonstrate while still allowing you to give the impression that you are writing it 'live'. With this approach, you can preplan questions and explanations too. I tend to have my prewritten model next to the visualiser as I write it again live on a new piece of paper.

WHAT TO MODEL?

For modelling to be truly effective, the model needs to exemplify transferable things that the students can then apply in later tasks. The more transferable something is, the more useful it is to students and the more important it is to teach. These may be analytical components, specific sentence constructions or whatever else makes up a quality response. These can be highlighted in the model and then used as success criteria for student writing so that they are clear as to what is expected. Using clear success criteria – things like you must zoom in on a word or you must include an analytical appositive sentence is far clearer than vague comments like you must develop your ideas.

Here's an example of a model introduction to an essay that compares texts. The Both/While sentences are the transferable constructions that I want students to use in their answers:

Q: Compare how Source A and Source B convey their perspectives on racial identity.

Both texts explore how people stereotype others and label them as things that they are not. Both writers describe how they have been told by white people that they are a certain culture or that they should act a certain way. While the writer in source A describes how they grew up not really thinking about race because it wasn't important, the writer in source B writes about how race has defined her.

The purpose of this model is to demonstrate to students how they can combine and apply the two constructions in extended writing.

Table 7.4 provides some useful strategies for modelling writing.

Table 7.4 Useful strategies for modelling writing

Do you teach and ask students to practice the components of extended responses before students attempt to create the whole?	• Are you teaching and practising vocabulary at word and sentence level, then paragraph level? • Are you teaching and practising sentence forms initially in isolation? • Are you distributing practice of components over enough time (see Chapter 10 which explains how to create multi-lesson instructional sequences)? • When teaching components, do you name the component so you have a shared language? The choice of name probably doesn't matter as long as you are consistent.
Do you demonstrate your thought process when deconstructing or creating a model?	• Do you 'call your shots', telling students what to look for before they see the model? • Do you live model in class, writing an example and making the implicit process explicit by narrating your choices and explaining what you are doing? • Have you tried using a visualiser: this might make your life much easier! • Do you label models to highlight components, draw attention to links, sequences, choices or application of concepts or constructions?
Do you use 2 or 3 models to demonstrate different levels of quality or competence?	• Have you tried writing a crap one and a good one? The comparison can be really useful. • Have you tried asking students to improve a crap one by improving or adding content? • Have you tried asking students to correct errors in a crap one? • Grading/marking here is probably not as useful as talking about and practising the thing itself
Do you use student made models?	• Feedback can be given via a model: instead of telling Students they need a more developed argument, SHOW them this. • Have you tried deconstructing a model under a camera, labelling why it is good, then asking Students to look for these things in their own work? What they have left out will be what they need to do to improve. • Are you building up a collection of student models as a teaching resource? • Do you use examination board marked scripts as exemplars?
Do you use the *alternation strategy* (present a model followed by a minimally different analogous question for students to attempt)?	• In the first instance, copying a model may be suitable. Students can then label it. Students could also paraphrase it. • Are you giving questions/problems that are minimally different to the model so that students can use the model as an analogy? • I-We-You...success rate throughout should be really high. If you move to 'we' and they muck it up, perhaps you need more 'I'? • When asking for independent practice (The You stage), are you asking students to apply the model to a sufficiently wide range of contexts/tasks?
Do you use backwards fading as an instructional sequence continues?	• I-We-You is a model of backwards fading. Initially the teacher works all the steps, then the students work some of the steps, then they do most of the steps before students complete all the steps in the task. • Do you use success criteria as an intermediate form of scaffolding (only AFTER you have shown them concrete examples though)? • Do writing expectations become longer and more complex over time?

(Continued)

Table 7.4 Useful strategies for modelling writing *(Continued)*

Do you model and teach planning, processes and metacognition?	• Do you model essay planning? • Do you model knowledge organisation? Do you use concept maps or visual methods of organising ideas? • Do you model exam techniques, explaining the step by step process to approach a task? • Do you model redrafting/editing? • Do you address the deep structure of a question by grouping similar questions together (e.g. fear/horror/evil in Jekyll and Hyde are very similar)
Do you directly address common misconceptions?	• These may be unique to the class. For example, if you have read their work and it is clear that many struggle with something, then addressing this common misconception will be useful. • These may fit the content. For example 'infer vs imply'.

GUIDE STUDENT PRACTICE

Table 7.5 provides an overview of guided practice.

Table 7.5 Overview of guided practice

WHAT?	• Students practice with support from the teacher
HOW?	• Ask students to help you complete a task; they are applying what you have just modelled • Focus questioning/teaching on things that will be confusing/hard to understand • Ask students to do 1 or 2 sentences or write for a short time and then stop. Teacher can then give feedback, showing their answers (explaining why they are good) and get students to compare/fix errors/plug gaps)
WHY?	• To instantly correct errors/prevent misunderstanding • To check that students have acquired information from modelling (I stage) • Students are more likely to be successful/engaged in independent practice if they spend time on purposive, guided practice • Guided practice is about developing connections, building and refining schema and promoting understanding

WHY IS GUIDED PRACTICE IMPORTANT?

Think back to Chapter 1, which outlined two useful definitions of learning:

1. Learning is 'a change in long-term memory' (Kirschner et al., 2006).
2. Learning is when students 'actively make sense of the material so they can build meaningful learning activities to transfer what they have learned to solving new problems' (Fiorella and Mayer, 2015).

If students are to master and retain new content and skills, they will need sufficient practice. As we will see in Chapter 9, for practice to be truly effective, it needs to be purposive or deliberate. We want students to retain and understand what we are teaching them; we also want them to be able to retrieve and fluently apply what they have learned. Practice is essential if we are to meet these goals

(Great Teaching Toolkit Evidence Review, 2020). Even though we eventually want students to be able to work independently without support, before they are able to do so, they will need to engage in guided practice.

If we were to skip this stage and move straight to independent practice, it is highly likely that students will flounder and much of this failure will be due to the limits of working memory. For example, imagine you were teaching pupils a method for approaching an unseen poem. If you demonstrated the whole method before asking students to independently practise it themselves, you may find that when they do, they have forgotten or confused some of the steps because you have presented too much new information at once. Skipping guided practice can also result in disengagement as students will find the independent practice work too difficult and, as a result, will quickly give up (Rosenshine and Stevens, 1986).

Instead, successful teachers spend more time on guided practice, providing further explanations, correcting errors, asking questions in order to develop students' thinking, giving prompts or cues and checking for understanding (Rosenshine 2012).

Similar to questioning, guided practice will differ according to the material that is being taught (Rosenshine and Stevens, 1986) and guided practice of a procedure such as attempting an examination question will look different to practising using a specific sentence construction. Think back to the six-step approach to answering an extract-based essay question that I outlined earlier. After demonstrating a step or the whole process, the teacher could then ask students to recreate a step or sequence of steps, asking lots of procedural questions to check whether they know what they should be doing, how they could complete each step and why each step is important.

WHAT ARE THE FEATURES OF GUIDED PRACTICE?

Initial practice of new knowledge or skills should involve teacher guidance, but what does this look like?

HIGH FREQUENCY OF QUESTIONS AND OVERT STUDENT PRACTICE

- Teachers should ask questions that are directly relevant to the new content or skills, ensuring that they choose the correct category of questions: procedural questions for processes and skills; declarative questions for content and knowledge.
- Practice activities should be 'overt' in that it should be simple for the teacher to ascertain whether the student is performing correctly or not. Written work is ideal here as the teacher can move around the class to check all student responses.
- Teachers should regularly check for understanding. This could be through oral questions or through checking written work as students are completing it.
- If it is clear that a student or students do not understand something, the teacher should offer a repeated or additional explanation or relevant feedback as necessary.
- If it is clear that lots of students do not understand, it may be necessary to stop the guided practice and then reteach the whole class.

PROMPTS

Prompts are hints or reminders that encourage students to do the work when they have temporarily forgotten how to do something. They can be phrased as statements or questions and are designed to guide student thinking. Sometimes telling students the answer before asking them to apply it is much faster and this approach will be useful if you want pupils to practice using specific content like vocabulary – this is the approach taken in the restrictive practice activities that I described in the daily review section of this chapter. However, it will sometimes be more useful to guide their thinking rather than just telling them the answer. Over time, this approach may see students incorporating these new metacognitive thought processes into their own habits so that they can use them in different contexts. Here are some different types of prompts (Fisher and Fray, 2014, p. 44):

Table 7.6   Different types of prompts

Types of prompt	Definition	Examples
Background Knowledge	Reference to content that the student already knows but has either temporarily forgotten or is not using correctly	*When a student is writing about a poem but has forgotten to write about methods or techniques:* **'How has the poet expressed her ideas? Which techniques have been used?**
		When a student forgets an important piece of contextual information in their paragraph about Romeo and Juliet: **What about courtly love?**
Process or Procedure	A reminder of the process that has either been forgotten or is not being followed properly	*When a student is responding to another in a discussion but forgets to acknowledge the previous point:* **We are using ABC questioning here, what did you miss out at the start of your point?**
		When a student is tackling an unseen poem and forgets to use an effective procedure: **Step 1 is really important. Don't forget step 1.**
Reflective	A reminder to students to think metacognitively	*When a student has just read something incorrectly:* **you read 'She lives in a horse' Does that make sense?**
		When a student has forgotten to include all of the success criteria: **Remember to check your work against the criteria**

CORRECT ERRORS

Guided practice should continue until students are able to perform accurately and error correction is a crucial part in this process. If errors are not corrected at this point, students may practice doing the wrong thing. The old adage that 'practice makes perfect' isn't really true-instead, practice makes permanent. If early errors are not corrected, they can end up being stored and retrieved as errors (Guzzetti and Others, 1993).

Guided practice is essential in order to prevent students from learning misconceptions (Rosenshine and Stevens, 1986). As we saw in Chapters 1 and 2, learning often involves connecting new information to our prior knowledge and building our schemas. If a student's prior knowledge is not sufficiently developed and they are not supported or sufficiently guided when they begin to practice, they may *select* the wrong information, fail to *organise* it properly and *integrate* it with their prior knowledge in a disorganised or piecemeal fashion: any one or combination of these problems will likely result in the student learning misconceptions.

Here are some ways that teachers can correct errors during guided practice:

- If your class are doing sentence-level practice, it can be useful to ask them to write the first couple of sentences first then stop. You can then check these answers before asking them to continue.
- You could walk around the class giving live oral feedback as students are working.
- Use restrictive practice activities. These make it easy to give precise corrective feedback.
- Use model answers in order to give feedback: students can compare their work with the model and correct their errors accordingly.

REQUIRE AND MONITOR INDEPENDENT PRACTICE

Table 7.7 provides an overview of independent practice.

Table 7.7 Overview of independent practice

WHAT?	• Students practice without support.
HOW?	• Students complete tasks to a time limit. • Teacher is available to answer questions, **although if the teacher needs to stop and provide additional explanations at this point, it suggests that guided practice was not sufficient or effective!** • Feedback can be given in the lesson: the teacher can show a model answer (explaining what makes it good) and get students to compare/fix errors/plug gaps.
WHY?	• Overlearning is really important for developing fluency/automaticity in a skill. • Independent practice promotes 'thinking hard', helping with retention and understanding. • Independent practice is about applying schema.

Rosenshine and Stevens (1986) point out that guided practice should usually be continued until a success rate of around 80% is achieved. After guided practice, students should then begin independent practice which should result in a much higher success rate of perhaps 95%.

WHY IS INDEPENDENT PRACTICE IMPORTANT?

FLUENCY

Students need a lot of practice, a process called 'overlearning', with new content and skills if they are to become fluent and automatic. When material is 'over-learned', it will make less demands on working memory, meaning that students can devote their attention to higher order processes like comprehension and application (Rosenshine, 2012). As an example, if you want pupils to make good choices when they write, it will be useful if they are able to select from a wide range of sentence structures and vocabulary. For students to recall and apply these components accurately and with minimal effort, they will need sufficient independent practice. By reducing the attentional demands on the components, independent practice can free up pupils' attention so that they can concentrate on the whole performance, allowing them to respond flexibly and effectively to the task at hand.

INTEGRATION

Guided practice may have involved a list of reminders or success criteria, asking students to include specific things in their writing. During independent practice, however, students should be expected to combine and apply components such as sentence structures, analytical skills and vocabulary without prompting. For example, if you have taught a number of lessons on the use of embedding quotations, a useful independent practice activity would involve a writing task that would require students to use this skill. Students could be asked to write a paragraph or more extended response to a text. As a final reminder, you could ask them to specifically check that they have embedded their quotations when they have finished writing.

Knowing how to embed a quotation in a drill activity is a 'splinter skill' and is a means to an end; being able to embed quotations in extended writing is a useful and transferable skill. Integration tasks are really important and if they are left out, restrictive or guided practice activities can be rendered ineffectual as students learn 'splinter' skills without learning to combine and apply them (Archer and Hughes, 2011, p. 20).

TRANSFER AND FLEXIBLE KNOWLEDGE

We want students to develop flexible knowledge that they can transfer to the widest range of relevant contexts and tasks. Independent practice should ask students to practice applying their knowledge and skills to a sufficiently wide range of situations if this is to happen (Butler, 2010).

WHAT ARE THE FEATURES OF INDEPENDENT PRACTICE?

LINK WITH GUIDED PRACTICE

Independent practice will often involve similar activities to guided practice except students are given no support, prompts, scaffolding or models (Rosenshine, 2012).

Initially, independent practice tasks may be highly similar, helping students to apply the schema that they have constructed during guided practice. As independent practice continues, tasks can become increasingly wider. Initial independent practice tasks should also be easy before gradually moving towards more complex tasks (Archer and Hughes, 2011) This is 'backwards fading', as explained in Chapter 4 where support is faded and complexity is slowly increased.

TEACHER CIRCULATES

While students are working independently, the teacher can circulate to give brief support and feedback, although if this help is anything more than brief, it strongly suggests that guided practice was ended too early. At this stage of practice, students should be able to work without assistance.

DISTRIBUTED/SPACED PRACTICE

As explained in Chapter 2, distributing practice can help students retain content better. It can also help teachers make better judgements about whether content has been learned properly

SUMMARY

- The principles and strategies outlined in this chapter are based upon a convergence of classroom-based research and cognitive science.
- All of the principles explained in this chapter conform to the definition and process of learning explained in the first two chapters of this book.
- Teachers who carefully and purposively apply these principles may increase the efficiency with which their students learn.

REFERENCES

Andrews, R., Torgerson, C., Beverton, S., Freeman, A., Locke, T., Low, G., Robinson, A., & Zhu, D. (2006). The effect of grammar teaching on writing development. *British Educational Research Journal*, 32(1), 39–55.

Archer, A. L., & Hughes, C. H. (2011). *Explicit instruction: Effective and efficient teaching.* New York, NY: Guildford Press.

Brod, G., Werkle-Bergner, M., & Shing, Y. (2013). The influence of prior knowledge on memory: A developmental cognitive neuroscience perspective. *Frontiers in Behavioral Neuroscience*, 7, 139.

Butler, C. (2010). Repeated testing produces superior transfer of learning relative to repeated studying. *Journal of Experimental Psychology: Learning, Memory and Cognition, 36*(5), 1118–1133.

Centre for Education Statistics and Evaluation. (2017). *Cognitive load theory: Research that teachers really need to understand.*

Coe, R., Rauch, C. J., Kime, S., & Singleton, D. (2020). *The great teaching toolkit evidence review.*

Dean, D., & Anderson, J. (2014). *Revision decisions: Talking through sentences and beyond.* Stenhouse Publishers.

Fiorella, L., & Mayer, R. (2015). *Learning as a generative activity: Eight learning strategies that promote understanding.* Cambridge: Cambridge University Press.

Fisher, D., & Fray, N. (2014). *Better learning through structured teaching a framework for the gradual release of responsibility* (2nd ed.).

Guzzetti, B. J., Snyder, T. E., Glass, G. V., & Gamas, W. S. (1993). Promoting conceptual change in science: A comparative meta-analysis of instructional interventions from reading education and science education. *Reading Research Quarterly, 28,* 117–159.

Howard, P., Ioannou, K., Bailey, R., Prior, J., & Jay, T. (2018). Applying the science of learning in the classroom. *Impact, 2,* 9–12.

Kellogg, R. T. (2008). Training writing skills: A cognitive developmental perspective. *Journal of Writing Research, 1*(1), 1–26.

Kirschner, P. A., Sweller, J., & Clark, R. E. (2006). Why minimal guidance during instruction does not work: An analysis of the failure of constructivist, discovery, problem-based, experiential, and inquiry-based teaching. *Educational Psychologist, 41*(2), 75–86.

Lemov, D. (2010). *Teach like a champion.* San Francisco, CA: Jossey Bass.

Lemov, D., Woolway, E., & Yezzi, K. (2012). *Practice perfect 42 rules for getting better at getting better.* San Francisco, CA: Jossey Bass.

Montag, J. L. (2019). Differences in sentence complexity in the text of children's picture books and child-directed speech. *First Language, 39*(5), 527–546.

Quigley, A. (2013). https://www.theconfidentteacher.com/2013/12/disciplined-discussion-easy-abc/

Rosenshine, R. (Spring 2012). The principles of instruction research-based strategies that all teachers should know. *American Educator, 36*(1), 12–39.

Rosenshine, B., & Stevens, R. J. (1986). *Teaching functions handbook of research on teaching.*

Shing, Y., & Brod, G. (2016). Effects of prior knowledge on memory: Implications for education. *Mind, Brain, and Education, 10*(3), 153–161.

Soderstrom, N. C., & Bjork, R. A. (2015). Learning versus performance: An integrative review. *Perspectives on Psychological Science, 10*(2), 176–179.

8

INSIGHTS FROM DIRECT INSTRUCTION

In this chapter, we will explore

- Some of the philosophical principles that underpin Direct Instruction
- The elements of a well-designed curriculum that teaches to mastery
- The importance of faultless communication
- How generalisation works
- The six shifts of task design

INTRODUCTION

Direct Instruction contains a number of powerful approaches that can be applied when teaching English. The ideas in this chapter can help teachers to present and explain new content efficiently, reduce the possibility of confusion and sequence teaching so that students gradually become more independent.

In Chapters 6 and 7, we explored the evidence base behind direct or explicit instruction as well as some of the key principles and components that make up this instructional approach. This chapter will explore principles from Engelmann's Direct Instruction. So what's the difference apart from the capitalization? Are they all saying the same thing? Rosenshine explains that they share lots of commonalities:

> There is a good deal of overlap in the three instructional meanings: Guided practice, active student participation, and fading of teacher-directed activities appear in all three meanings. Scaffolds, modeling by the teacher, and coaching of students also appear in all three. (Rosenshine, 2008)

Despite these huge overlaps, there are a number of additional insights that we can learn from Engelmann's Direct Instruction, many of which are not found within the broader frameworks of explicit or direct instruction. Put bluntly, Engelmann's DI is far more rigorous, precise and detailed than its lowercase cousins. While DI programmes can be bought and delivered in schools (and I would highly recommend investigating *Expressive Writing* 2 as a powerful writing intervention for weak writers who enter secondary school), teachers can apply some of the principles to everyday lessons in order to improve their teaching.

Before we explore some of the key ideas that DI employs, we need to outline the core philosophical principle that underpins it.

PHILOSOPHICAL PRINCIPLE: ALL CHILDREN CAN BE TAUGHT

DI puts the onus for learning and success on the instructional designer and teacher (Engelmann, 2017, p. 2). As Engelmann says 'if the learner hasn't learnt, the teacher hasn't taught'. This is a refreshing and interesting position, putting full responsibility for success upon instructional design, clarity of communication and teaching quality. Although we may not like to admit it, I'm sure we have all asked ourselves *why don't they get it!* when presented with students who struggle to understand, our incredulity and frustration causing us to settle for the easiest explanation which, as a result of our exasperation, may end up being the students themselves. Blaming students, the alternative to taking full responsibility for the success of instruction, can often lead to the soft bigotry of low expectations where disadvantage, need, class set or other such labels and categories are blamed for underperformance. This can lead to other related issues such as the dumbing down of content or the *Golem Effect* where a student's performance drops as a result of their teacher's lowered expectations.

But can you teach anyone anything? Surely this can't be true? If it is true, what does a teacher need to know about a student and their teaching if they are to succeed?

a. ***The Importance of prior knowledge***
    David Ausubel (1968, p. vi) would point out that 'The most important single factor influencing learning is what the learner already knows. Ascertain this and teach him [or her] accordingly'.

    As we saw in Chapter 1, learning can be defined as a three-stage process:

    *   **Stage 1: *Selecting* relevant information to attend to**
    *   **Stage 2: *Organising* the material into a coherent cognitive structure in working memory**
    *   **Stage 3: *Integrating* it with relevant prior knowledge activated from long-term memory**

    If students are to successfully engage with stage three, they will need sufficient prior knowledge in their long-term memories. For example, teaching students how to use semi-colons will be difficult if they don't know what a subject, verb or sentence is. Similarly, teaching students how to structure complete essays may be a futile pursuit if they don't have a firm understanding of paragraphing. If instruction is to be successful, lessons must be pitched at the student's current level of understanding.

b. *The importance of analysing student mistakes*

Teachers constantly monitor and assess student work, giving them feedback so they know what and how to improve, assigning grades and noting down what needs to be retaught or given extra practice. But how often are student errors and misconceptions used to refine teaching and curriculum planning? Engelmann (2017) points out that 'You need to look at their mistakes for qualitative information about what you need to change in your instruction to teach it right'.

Engelmann's point about looking at mistakes and output in order to make inferences and judgements about the quality of the teaching is crucial. DI programmes like *Expressive Writing* are extensively field tested before they are published in order to check that they are effective. Although we cannot create an actual DI programme, we can and should analyse student responses carefully, both successes and mistakes, in order to inform our instructional decisions and adaptations. During a sequence of teaching, this could be through the use of whole class feedback where common errors are compiled and addressed through extra teaching or practice in subsequent lessons. At a curriculum level, this could be through the analysis of summative assessments in order to draw inferences as to which elements of a course have been misunderstood.

Both whole class feedback and the analysis of summative tests are reactive approaches, responding to student outcomes; however, the latter approach, if done thoroughly, is preventative: the adaptation of instructional sequences 'based strictly on feedback' should progressively refine the curriculum so that the errors picked up through whole class feedback become less frequent and less complex. In an ideal world, reactive feedback – especially complex, multifaceted corrective work – would be largely unnecessary as student success rates would be consistently high. In DI programmes, students should be at least 70% correct on anything that is completely new and 90% correct on items that have been introduced earlier in the programme. These statistics should make us pause for thought. If what we ask students to do consistently results in lesser percentages, can this be adequately remedied through reactive feedback? If students initially fail to reach a similar success rate, will our feedback reliably ensure that they will close the gap? The problem with trying to perfect reactive feedback approaches is that it may prevent us from fixing the imperfections within our teaching.

Feedback to the teacher about the effectiveness of a programme of study is vitally important. As Engelmann bluntly puts it: 'If they make mistakes, they're telling you, fundamentally, that you goofed up and they're also implying exactly what they need to know'.

ALL CHILDREN CAN IMPROVE ACADEMICALLY AND DEVELOP A STRONGER SELF-IMAGE

Low attaining students often have low self-esteem and poor levels of motivation, but which direction does causation run? Does their lack of motivation cause low attainment or does their low attainment cause poor motivation?

There are lots of reasons why students can become demotivated, many of which are outside of the control and influence of the teacher. One huge factor, and one that the teacher can and should influence, is whether or not students succeed or fail in their lessons. Rob Coe puts it like this:

> In fact the poor motivation of low attainers is a logical response to repeated failure. Start getting them to succeed and their motivation and confidence should increase. (Coe et al., 2014)

Think back to when you were at school: I bet there is a strong positive correlation between the subjects that you enjoyed and those that you were successful at.

ELEMENTS OF WELL-DESIGNED CURRICULA THAT TEACH TO MASTERY

Think back to Chapter 4 where we explored *The Instructional Hierarchy*, a framework that explains the development of expertise. The final stages, 'Generalisation and Adaptation', where students are able to creatively apply the knowledge or skill to novel situations without prompting, can be seen as the point where they have mastered what it is you are teaching. But how can we help students to reach this stage of expertise?

LESSONS SHOULD TEACH EVERYTHING STUDENTS WILL NEED FOR SUCCESS

Writing sophisticated analytical responses to texts is complex: paragraphs and essays are made up of multiple strands of knowledge, all playing a vital role and each conspicuous in their absence. As an adult, it is easy to forget that essays are made up of so many individual yet interconnected components. Our expertise not only blinds us to the fact that these parts exist, but also to the fact that we most likely achieved our expertise through extended, deliberate and purposive practice.

So what exactly do we need to teach students to help them succeed at writing analytical essays?

Imagine you are teaching a unit on Jekyll and Hyde and want students to be able to successfully answer this question 'How is Utterson presented at the start of the novella'?

Here is a list of some of the constituent components that may require explicit teaching and practice before a student can successfully attempt this task. Each component should have been taught, retrieved and practised in restrictive practice activities until students are accurate and fluent.

1. **Vocabulary words**: reputation, decorum, obsessed, exemplifies, secrecy, frivolity, impeccable, propriety, social conformity, disdaining, conveys, paranoia, repressing, repression, social inhibitions.
   All of these words could be initially presented via vocabulary tables and practised using because, but, so or other focused drills as explained in Chapter 5. Although some of these words will have been taught in previous units, having been chosen due to their high-utility nature, others will have been taught for the

first time in this unit. Not only do we want students to use these words in the lesson that sees them writing an answer to the question above, but we also want them to remember and apply these words across units and years: for this to happen, regular retrieval practice is important.

2. **Contextual information**: Fear of Blackmail and scandal, Repressive Victorian Social Mores, Upper Class

3. **Quotations**: 'was never lighted by a smile', 'austere', 'cold', 'embarrassed in discourse' , 'drank gin. . .to mortify a taste for vintages', 'when the wine was to his taste, something eminently human beaconed from his eye', 'never found its way into his talk'.

Closed book exams like GCSEs require students to learn some apt quotations that they can use in their essays. Instead of just memorising them, a process that may only result in structural or phonemic processing and may well not engage in all three stages of learning (flick back to Chapter 2 if you have forgotten these ideas!), students should also explore, manipulate and apply the quotations so that they engage in 'meaningful learning' (Fiorella and Mayer, 2015). If your students have to sit closed book exams, it can be really useful to compile a core exam list of quotations. Memorising, manipulating applying and mastering 20 or 30 short quotations from the novella is infinitely preferable to being exposed to hundreds, the latter approach being condemned by Engelmann (2017, p. 16) as he says 'the expectations for student performance are low because the teachers understand that students will not actually master the material. They will simply be exposed'.

While the first three categories of knowledge that I covered are about the content of the analysis-some of which is text-specific – the next three are about the form and structure of analytical writing. This knowledge has even higher utility as students can use, adapt and apply these concepts across units, texts, years and key stages.

4. **Grammatical constructions**: noun appositive phrases, past participle phrases, present participle phrases.

Once students have mastered the concept of a sentence (subject + verb), they can be taught these more advanced constructions, building on Key Stage 2 and what they are taught at primary school and following Engelmann's assertion that 'For mastery teaching to be possible, programs must be thoroughly coordinated from level to level' Engelmann (2017, p. 32).

See Chapter 10 for instructional sequences that teach participle phrases and noun appositives.

5. **Embedded evidence**

If students cannot embed quotations properly, they are effectively locked out of sophisticated analytical writing and because of this, embedding should be explicitly taught and practised from the beginning of Year 7. One of the unintended limitations of PEE and other formulaic analytical frameworks is that students do not have to learn how to manipulate or embed quotations, instead following the predictable and clunky framework: My evidence for this is '. . . . .'

See Chapter 11 for a fully explained instructional sequence that teaches embedding.

6. **Analytical components**: multiple interpretations, tentative language, evidence in explanation
   See Chapter 11 for explanations as to how to teach these skills.

Here is a model paragraph that exemplifies how these components fit together:

The archetypal Victorian gentleman, Utterson cares deeply about his reputation and attempts to act with the upmost decorum at all times. His face 'was never lighted by a smile', a description that exemplifies his serious nature and desire to be respected by his peers. Obsessed with secrecy and the opinions of others, Utterson is 'austere' and 'cold.', avoiding all forms of frivolity in order to project an image of impeccable propriety. Like other upper class gentlemen, he was expected to display social conformity at all times because Victorian social mores were incredibly restrictive. He was 'embarrassed in discourse', disdaining gossip, conversation and small talk. Perhaps he does this in order to remain secretive and private; it is as if his reputation is the most important aspect of his life and he doesn't want people to judge him. The Upper Class, concerned as they were with their reputations, greatly feared blackmail and scandal and Utterson's behaviour conveys this fear and lack of trust. He 'drank gin…to mortify a taste for vintages', repressing his desire for pleasure. However, this repression and mask of seriousness occasionally slips as 'when the wine was to his taste, something eminently human beaconed from his eye', meaning that he sometimes loses his social inhibitions. Interestingly though, this lack of inhibitions 'never found its way into his talk', suggesting he is guarded, paranoid and incredibly secretive.

So how are you meant to teach all these different components and get students to combine them into a complex piece of extended writing like the model above?

An English lesson could contain multiple activities that attempt to practise many of the constituent parts listed above.

Here is an example plan:

1. Cumulative retrieval practice of vocabulary, quotations to be memorised (Key Stage 4) and context information.
   a. Some questions will be closed, factual recall, perhaps with clues:
      What adjective means flawless or perfect: imp_cc_ble ANSWER: impeccable.
   b. Some will be more open, the assumption being less clues are needed for successful recall:
      What noun means good behaviour? ANSWER: propriety.
   c. Some will involve students making links, hopefully developing schemas and connections in their minds:
      Name three terms that refer to standards of behaviour ANSWER: decorum, social conformity, propriety.
   d. Some will involve even wider links:
      Complete the quotation: 'embarrassed in………………' Write down another two quotations that describe Utterson's secrecy. What context information is relevant here? Write down three adjectives to describe Utterson's behaviour.

ANSWER: Quotations: 'embarrassed in discourse' 'cold' 'never found his way into his talk' Context: Fear of Blackmail and scandal, Repressive Victorian Social Mores. Adjectives: secretive, paranoid, obsessed.

This final answer is essentially the bare bones of an analytical paragraph and asking these freer retrieval questions help students to build mental plans of what to write. You could then ask them to use it to write a paragraph at speed.

2. Sentence practice, using 'because but so' or practising phrases and other relevant structures that you want students to use in their applications. These sentences will frequently require embedded evidence as success criteria, providing practice of this vital skill.
3. Line annotation, applying vocabulary that has been taught and using rapid sequences of questions in order to maximise student participation and recall.
4. Worked example annotation. The model answer contains all of the constituent elements mentioned above, exemplifying their usage within extended writing.
5. Focused paragraph writing, allowing students to apply the constituent concepts.

LESSONS SHOULD TEACH GENERALIZABLE THINGS (BIG IDEAS/HIGH UTILITY STUFF)

One of the most important decisions when designing curricula is to consider the utility and importance of what is being taught. According to DI theory, we should design curricula by 'identifying central organizing ideas and generalizable strategies that enable student to learn more in less time' (Watkins and Slocum, 2003). Although a wide curriculum that exposes students to myriad ideas, concepts and knowledge may seem optimal, if students merely experience the content at the expense of any real attempt to master or retain it, is it worthwhile? If a concept takes a long time to teach, yet its utility is limited to one specific unit or section of a curriculum, is it worth teaching and could the curriculum time be used for something that is more 'generalizable'? If students are regularly taught concepts that they will never be expected to use in later lessons or applications, is this a good use of lesson time?

While all bits of knowledge are useful, some bits of knowledge are more useful than others.

Here are some high utility things that we can teach in English. These ideas, skills and concepts can be applied across units, years, and key stages, as well as helping students to 'further develop their expertise in a subject.'

SPECIFIC SENTENCE CONSTRUCTIONS

Explicitly teaching specific sentence styles and grammatical constructions to students can help them to broaden their range of expression, moving them from functional and simplistic written communication to sophisticated, nuanced and complex writing. Teaching phrases (participles, appositives and absolutes) is one high utility strategy because they can be used with all of 'The Big Three' genres of writing (analysis, rhetoric and creative/descriptive). If you teach the component parts of a sentence, then they can be combined, manipulated and generalised by students into an immense number of combinations. Table 8.1 shows some of the ways that phrases can be combined:

Table 8.1   Example of combining phrases within sentences

Combinations	
Double absolute	*His words verging on the prophetic, his 'fire blood and anguish' rhetoric lifted straight from the Bible,* the Inspector's final speech is a dire warning about the consequences of an atomised society.
Double noun appositive	*A 'hard headed man of business',* Mr Birling is convinced that sacking Eva Smith, *an action that began the chain of events that led to her death,* was the correct thing to do.
Double present participle	*Speaking in a commanding tone, interjecting 'massively',* the Inspector exudes authority and expertly deals with 'one line of enquiry at a time.'
Present participle at the start. Noun apposite at the end	*Subscribing to a hierarchical model of society,* Mrs Birling clearly enjoys the power that she gets not only from her wealth, but also from being chairwoman of a charity, *a position that she uses to assert her authority rather than as a means of genuinely helping the poor.*

Choosing sentence styles that are high-utility is important and if students are to master them, they will need extended, distributed and varied practice, ideally spread across texts, units and years. Chapter 10 will explain how to create instructional sequences that teach some of these phrases.

VOCABULARY TO BE USED IN ANALYSIS

As we saw in Chapter 5, instead of only teaching the vocabulary that you *encount*er within a text, teach the vocabulary required when *responding* to a text. Although it will be useful to teach some of the words within a text as they will be integral to comprehension and analysis, other words may be so recondite, anachronistic or genre specific that their utility is limited. Focusing on Tier 2 words – formal vocabulary that spans contexts and domains – is one way of promoting generalisations.

A GENERALISED ANALYTICAL FRAMEWORK

Chapter 11 will explore how to teach analytical components. This approach is generalised in that the components can be combined in different ways and used when responding to any text.

IN ORDER TO MAXIMISE LEARNING, ALL DETAILS OF INSTRUCTION MUST BE CONTROLLED TO MINIMISE STUDENT MISINTERPRETATIONS

Engelmann states that 'years of research on how children learn show that even minor changes in teachers' wording can confuse students and slow their learning' (Engelmann, 2017, p. 3): the idea of 'faultless communication' is a central part of DI theory. To explain 'faultless communication' and give you an idea of what it must be like to be a novice learner, here is an example from Clear Teaching by Shepard Barbash (2012):

> Try this experiment. Make up a nonsense word for a familiar concept and try teaching the concept to someone without using its regular name. Engelmann holds up a pencil and says, "This is glerm." Then he holds up a pen and says, "This is glerm." Then he holds up a crayon—also glerm. So what is glerm? A student responds: "Something you write with." Logical, but wrong, Engelmann says. Glerm means up. The student learned a misrule—Engelmann's examples were deliberately ambiguous, exemplifying both the concepts for up and for writing implements, and the student came to the wrong conclusion. This is one of the exercises Engelmann uses to teach instructional design. His point is to make us aware of the minefield teachers must navigate to avoid generating confusion in their students. Next he wanders around the room giving examples of the concept graeb, without success. At last he opens the door, walks out and shouts: "This is not graeb." Graeb means in the room. To show what something is, sometimes you have to show what it's not. He points to a cup on his desk and says, "That's glick." Then he holds up a spoon and says, "Not glick." He points to a book on a student's desk—glick—then raises a pen—not glick. What's glick? No one is sure. Finally he puts the spoon on his desk—that's glick—lifts it—not glick—puts the pen on the student's desk—glick—and lifts it—not glick. Everyone gets it: glick means on. (p. 23)

For a novice learner, normal communication and instruction is riddled with ambiguity. As shown in this example, students are unaware as to which points are important and instructions may contain multiple terms that, despite being clear to the teacher, are vague, ill-defined or meaningless to the student.

One of the main controversies surrounding DI programmes is the fact that lessons are scripted and that all teachers are expected to teach the same thing in the same way. Critics believe that this removes teacher autonomy, replacing it with a mechanical and sclerotic approach, dehumanising students and deskilling practitioners. However, it is precisely because we are not robots that scripts and standardisation can be helpful: teaching is incredibly complex, containing numerous variables and requiring hundreds of split-second decisions and sequences of communication every lesson, each one fraught with the potential for errors regarding interpretation.

Before you spit your tea onto this book in horror and disgust, I am not suggesting that English lessons should be scripted. Later on in this chapter, we will explore the importance of carefully choosing, manipulating and sequencing examples so as to ensure that communication is clear. For now though, here are some additional ways that can help with instructional clarity:

a. **Write down and pre rehearse explanations**
   When you write down and redraft an explanation, you will almost certainly produce something that is far more concise than if you had attempted it in a class for the first time. When we talk, we often produce meandering, protracted

explanations, filled with unnecessary digressions, unhelpful tangents and confusing or even contradictory terminology. While synonyms are useful to an expert, ensuring that an explanation is not repetitive and boring, they will be confusing for a novice learner: for initial explanations to be clear, they should generally avoid synonyms.

Equally confusing for novice students is the use of antecedents and referents. Here is an example from *Reading Reconsidered* (Lemov et al., 2016, p. 78), demonstrating how these can make understanding difficult. Although this example focuses on reading, if this was a spoken explanation, it would be equally confusing as each of the numbered words is ambiguous.

The Greeks besieged the city of Troy for nearly ten years. *They (1)* could not take *it (2)* because the walls were so high and strong-some said that *they (3)* had been built by the hands of gods-but *they (4)* kept the Trojans inside. *This (5)* has not always been so. There had been a time when the Trojans had gone out and fought with *their (6)* enemies on the plain, sometimes *they (7)* had beaten *them (8)* in battle, and once *they (9)* had very nearly burnt *their (10)* ships. But *this (11)* was all changed. *They (12)* had lost some of the bravest of their chiefs, such as Hector, the best of the sons of Priam, and Paris the great archer, and many great princes, who had come from the countries round about to help *them (13)*.

b. **Avoid contradictions**
   If you tell a student that a verb is 'an action word', this will cause a problem when they begin to look at multi-word verb constructions like 'He *had been thinking*' or 'They *will have been chosen*'.

c. **Scripting some parts of a lesson**
   English requires accuracy and there are some aspects of the subject like writing sentence constructions and the use of punctuation where inaccuracy will hinder meaning and make student writing look sloppy. When teaching this type of content, it can be really helpful to script what the teacher says so that students can rapidly acquire, understand and apply what it is they are being taught. Chapter 10 will present some instructional sequences, demonstrating how scripting some short explanations can be really helpful.

EACH LESSON SHOULD INTRODUCE ONLY A SMALL AMOUNT OF NEW MATERIAL: THE BULK OF LESSON TIME SHOULD BE SPENT PRACTISING, APPLYING AND RECAPPING PREVIOUS CONTENT

In DI programmes, new content accounts for only 10%–15% of each lesson; the remaining 85%–90% of each lesson is spent reviewing, recapping and practising content from previous lessons (Engelmann, 2017, p. 12). Your average English teacher, however, is often expected to plough through a content heavy curricula in a limited time: as a result, students often fail to retain what they learn or engage in sufficient practice in order to reach acceptable levels of proficiency.

Additionally, we make it difficult for students to master things because we think of learning in terms of discrete, separate lessons combined with a fixation on variety, novelty and pace at all costs. Quickly moving through content with no thought as to the necessity of recap and extended practice will almost always result in a lack of mastery and proficiency from students.

So what can we do in order to reduce the amount of content that is introduced in each lesson and therefore increase the amount of practice pupils undertake?

Table 8.2 How to increase practice

What can we do	Where can you read more?
Create efficient multi-lesson instructional sequences	Chapter 10
Break down learning into small steps	Chapter 7
Choose high utility content to teach	Chapters 5 and 10
Overlearning and extended practice	Chapters 7 and 9
Cumulative practice activities	Chapters 7 and 9

INITIAL TEACHING OF NEW CONTENT ACROSS TWO OR THREE CONSECUTIVE LESSONS

If you present new information to students once, you can make a fairly safe bet that they will forget it. Think back to Chapter 4 where we explored the Instructional Hierarchy. The first stage is 'Acquisition' where the goal is for students to accurately perform whatever it is you are teaching them. If initial teaching spans at least two or three lessons, the massed practice that students will undertake is far more likely to result in them acquiring the knowledge or skill.

TEACHING THROUGH EXAMPLES AND SEQUENCING THEM EFFECTIVELY

When we introduce new concepts to students, we need to be aware of the problems with using definitions. Beginning with a definition may be confusing for a novice student as the words that are used to describe the concept may be abstruse or complex. Explaining that a relative clause is 'a clause that is attached to an antecedent by a relative pronoun such as who, which, or that' may do little to help a student understand how to recognize or apply such a construction. While an expert will understand things like 'antecedent', 'attached' and 'relative pronoun', these may be confusing for novice. This is why dictionary definitions are often little help to students with limited background knowledge: words are merely symbols for the underlying concept and if examples are not presented, allowing the learner to experience the quality that the words symbolise, the teaching sequence will not provide a solid basis for the student to understand which quality the word represents.

For most things that we teach, we want students to develop a generalized understanding so that they are able to apply what they have learned to the widest possible range of relevant contexts and the ultimate goal of most instruction is flexible knowledge. Think back to Chapter 4 where we explored expertise. Compared to novices, experts not only have more comprehensive and better organized schema that they can use, but they also possess the conditional knowledge required in order to decide which knowledge applies to which context. In the next chapter, we will see how this fluent, generalized understanding can be developed through deliberate practice. Additionally, it can be developed through the careful sequencing of examples and non-examples.

We have already seen how models and worked examples are really useful for teaching novices, acting as schema substitutes and helping them see what abstract processes like 'analysis' or 'the judicious use of evidence' really look like.

However, we can also use examples in order to help students understand the breadth and boundaries of whatever it is we are teaching them:

> In order to teach a general case, it is necessary to show students a set of items that includes examples and non-examples arranged so that similarities and differences are readily apparent. Irrelevant aspects of the teaching must be held constant to minimize confusion, and relevant aspects must be carefully manipulated to demonstrate important differences. (Watkins and Slocum, 2003)

So what does this mean? How can we use examples and non-examples in order to help students understand what it is we are teaching them?

HOW EXACTLY DOES GENERALISATION WORK?

Before we look at some general principles about how to sequence examples and non-examples, it is important to outline three specific processes that underpin this approach:

INTERPOLATION. Interpolation involves treating examples of a concept that lie along a continuum in the same way. Imagine you were teaching 'greyness' to a learner, and you presented examples that were broadly on a continuum of 'greyness' like this (Figure 8.1):

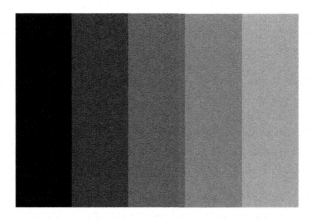

Figure 8.1   Continuum of greyness

If the examples that you presented were found at the edges of the continuum, then if a learner was presented with a shade that came in the middle of the scale, they would logically identify it as grey.

EXTRAPOLATION. Extrapolation involves treating large differences as being at least as important as small differences. If a small change results in an example becoming a non-example, then by extrapolation, any larger change will also result in the item being labelled as a non-example.

STIPULATION. This process involves repeatedly presenting lots of examples that are highly similar and treating them in the same way. If the examples have a limited range, then the learner will come to think that most or all of their qualities are essential. This means that when a later example is presented that falls outside this range, the learner-through the process of stipulation-will treat it as a non-example. Usually, stipulation is something to be avoided as it limits a student's ability to generalise. Stipulation can be avoided by presenting a sufficiently wide range of examples and non-examples, perhaps through multiple sets and distributing them over time.

This all sounds very interesting but what does this have to do with teaching English? Examples and non-examples can be used in order to teach the components of writing including punctuation, sentence forms, analytical skills and much more. Chapters 10 and 11 will demonstrate how to apply these ideas to multi-lesson instructional sequences.

For now though, here are some general principles for sequencing examples:

1. **The Setup Principle**
   According to this principle, 'Examples and non-examples selected for initial teaching of a concept should share the greatest possible number of irrelevant features' (Watkins and Slocum, 2003). This means that examples and non-examples should vary in only one way with all other aspects and features held constant. By doing this, you create a situation where interpretations and inferences are controlled, ensuring that only one interpretation is possible.

   Here is an example of how to apply the setup principle to teaching present participles (Table 8.3):

Table 8.3   Applying the setup principle

Following the setup principle		Not following the setup principle	
Present participle	Avoiding gossip, Enfield is secretive and obsessed with privacy.	**Present participle**	Avoiding gossip, Enfield is secretive and obsessed with privacy.
Not a present participle	Enfield is secretive and obsessed with privacy.	**Not a present participle**	Victorian gentlemen were repressed by strict social mores.

The first column contains only one difference between the example and non-example, meaning that a learner can only make one logical inference about the meaning of 'present participle'. In the second column, there are numerous

differences between the example and non-example. Although there may be many more inferences, a learner could logically infer that 'present participle' means:
a. The inclusion of the word 'Enfield'.
b. A sentence that is in the present tense.
c. A sentence that is in the active voice.

2. **The difference principle**
   Carefully choosing non-examples is a crucial factor in helping students understand the limits or boundaries of a concept. To understand what something is, it is helpful to comprehend what it is not.

   Here is an example of how to apply the difference principle to teaching participle phrases (Table 8.4):

Table 8.4   Applying the difference principle

Following the difference principle		Not following the difference principle	
Present participle	Avoiding gossip, Enfield is secretive and obsessed with privacy.	**Present participle**	Avoiding gossip, Enfield is secretive and obsessed with privacy.
Not a present participle	Avoiding gossip was Enfield's obsession.	**Not a present participle**	Victorian society was strict; gentlemen were expected to conform.

In the left-hand column, the non-example is a gerund phrase (the subject of the verb 'was'). Gerund phrases are often confused with participle phrases and the juxtaposition of these two examples demonstrates why that is: they are incredibly similar. The non-example here is helpful as it gives precise information as to the delineation between 'present participle' and 'not present participle'. In the right-hand column, the non-example is massively different, making it harder for a student to ascertain the boundaries of the concept being taught.

Like with the setup principle, to avoid stipulation (the idea where a student thinks that the examples in a sequence encapsulate the full range of the concept and that other, different examples will therefore fall outside of it), subsequent sequences would follow where the examples are changed, perhaps by using different sentence constructions or subject matter, demonstrating that 'present participle' is a wide ranging concept.

3. **The sameness principle**
   In order to demonstrate the range and scope of a concept, we should juxtapose maximally different examples. If we were trying to teach the concept of 'dog', then we should choose examples that represent the widest possible variety of dogs, perhaps showing pictures of a chihuahua, an Irish wolfhound and a poodle.

   Although we could debate whether there are more strikingly different examples of dogs that we could use, these three have been chosen because, despite all being dogs, they are massively different. If we had merely shown different breeds of terrier, then a student may infer that any future examples that are not terriers would fall outside of the concept of 'dog': this is the process of stipulation.

   Here is an example of how to apply the sameness principle to teaching participle phrases:

Table 8.5   Applying the sameness principle

Following the sameness principle		Not following the sameness principle	
Present participle	Exclaiming 'The more it looks like Queer street, the less I ask', Enfield demonstrates his desire for secrecy.	Present participle	Avoiding gossip, Enfield is secretive and obsessed with privacy.
Present participle	Deliberately avoiding gossip, Enfield is secretive and obsessed with privacy.	Present participle	Disdaining gossip, Enfield doesn't ask questions of anyone.
Present participle	Enfield is obsessed with secrecy, wishing to avoid scandal and maintain his impeccable reputation.	Present participle	Eschewing gossip, Enfield explains how he never judges the actions of others.

The right-hand column only demonstrates a tiny range of possible examples of the concept. If we had merely shown these examples, then a student may infer that any differing future examples fall outside of the concept of 'present participle'. They may logically infer that present participle sentences:

a. Always contain two words.
b. Always begin with a word that ends in 'ing.'
c. Always precede the subject of a sentence.
d. Always begin a sentence.
e. Always contain the word 'gossip'.

The left-hand column demonstrates a far wider range of examples. I have deliberately inserted an example that includes a quotation as this is how students will frequently apply these constructions. The second example begins with an adverb, preventing students from inferring the misrule that all present participle phrases begin with an 'ing' word. The third example has the phrase at the end of a sentence, demonstrating that these constructions are not always used at the beginning.

4. **The testing principle**

Think back to the Instructional Hierarchy from Chapter 4, the first stage of learning is 'acquisition' where students need to be able to accurately and repeatedly perform whatever it is that you are teaching them. One way of checking whether students have acquired what we have taught them is to juxtapose new, untaught examples and non-examples in random order and test students on those (Watkins and Slocum, 2003).

For example, imagine you are teaching students how to write a comparative introduction to an essay that explored and compares two poems. The first stage of this process will probably involve showing students what comparative introductions look like by presenting a good range of worked examples. This is the worked example effect where studying models allows students to build an initial mental representation of what it is you are teaching. If you are being really rigorous, you should also show them non-examples and these non-examples (bad introductions) will often contain the kind of things that students include by mistake. Juxtaposing good examples with bad examples can help students to refine their understanding of what it is that makes a good introduction. However, if we want to test whether they have grasped this distinction, we would need to present further examples and non-examples that have not been previously taught.

By doing so, we are effectively testing whether they have grasped the 'deep structure' as explained in Chapter 4. This also links to the idea of transfer: students who can accurately perform on untaught examples are beginning to demonstrate near transfer as their knowledge becomes more flexible.

Although this may be obvious, in order to ensure that we receive accurate information about a student's understanding of a concept, we need to create tests that do not follow a predictable pattern.

We also need to keep in mind the important distinction between 'performance' and 'learning' and avoid using evidence of the former as a reliable indicator of the latter. To avoid this, it is always useful to delay and distribute tasks that are to be used to make inferences about whether students have actually learned what it is you are teaching them.

All of these five principles are presented here as separate guidelines. Creating sequences of communication through examples and non-examples often requires multiple sets of juxtaposed examples and non-examples, which helps to avoid misrules and faulty inferences, ensuring that students not only learn the precise point when something stops being a concept, but also that they learn that a concept can contain innumerable varieties and differences yet still have the same label (like a Chihuahua and an Irish wolfhound: massively different, but still dogs.)

THE SIX SHIFTS IN TASK DESIGN

Direct Instruction points to six 'shifts' that should occur in any well-designed programme of study (Watkins and Slocum, 2003).

THE SHIFT FROM 'OVERTISED' TO 'COVERTISED' PROBLEM-SOLVING STRATEGIES

In the last chapter, we explored the importance of splitting up complex skills like writing into smaller, more manageable steps. In Theory of Instruction, Engelmann explains the difference between physical and cognitive operations. A physical operation includes things like 'fitting jigsaw puzzles together, throwing a ball, "nesting" cups together, swimming, buttoning a coat' – essentially any process that involves a series of steps that may include motion or the manipulation of matter, and one that receives immediate 'feedback' from the environment. If you are trying to hammer a nail and not doing it properly, the environment will give you 'feedback' and prevent you from completing the physical operation. Perhaps you missed the nail. Perhaps you didn't use a hammer. Maybe you didn't hit the nail hard enough. Perhaps you used the wrong striking technique. The important idea is that it is easy for an instructor to observe the reason behind your failure because the entire process is overt and each step is observable.

For cognitive operations, 'there are no necessary overt behaviors to account for the outcome that is achieved' (Engelmann and Carnine, 2016, p. 40). Essentially, we do not know how an outcome has been reached unless all the individual steps are made overt. A student may have got lucky; they may have relied upon a rule that, while being effective in this instance, may end up causing problems as a sequence becomes more complex. Unlike with physical operations like hitting a nail with a hammer, the physical environment does not provide feedback for cognitive operations. This passage from Theory of Instruction explains this idea further:

> The physical environment does not provide feedback when the learner is engaged in cognitive operations. If the learner misreads a word, the physical environment does nothing. It does not prevent the learner from saying the wrong word. It does not produce an unpleasant consequence. The learner could look at the word 'form' and call it 'Yesterday' without receiving any response from the physical environment. The basic properties of cognitive operations-from long division to inferential reading-suggest both that the naïve learner cannot consistently benefit from unguided practice or from unguided discovery of cognitive operations. Unless the learner is provided with some logical basis for figuring out possible inconsistencies (which is usually not available to the naïve learner), practising the skills without human feedback is likely to promote mistakes. (Engelmann and Carnine, 2016, p. 51)

Making the steps of a cognitive operation overt allows precise feedback to be given as the instructor can easily see the reason behind a particular outcome. During the acquisition phase of learning – the initial stage where, in the absence of teacher support, a student would soon become confused – precise and immediate feedback is of crucial importance, preventing errors from becoming embedded and ensuring accuracy is achieved.

HOW DO THESE IDEAS APPLY TO ENGLISH?

1. When students complete sentence practice activities, ask them to feedback orally by saying the punctuation when they read out their sentence. For example 'Avoiding contact with both friends and family COMMA Romeo begins the play infatuated with Rosaline FULL STOP'.
   This turns the covert into the overt, allowing you to quickly and efficiently ascertain if they have succeeded without having to actually mark or look at their book. If appropriate, other students can listen and give feedback about accuracy too!
2. Live modelling: creating example sentences, paragraphs or even essays under the visualiser whilst narrating your thought process is a really powerful way of letting students observe the process of writing. When this process is made interactive with lots of teacher–student questioning, it can be even more effective.

THE SHIFT FROM SIMPLIFIED CONTEXTS TO COMPLEX CONTEXTS

When teaching something for the first time, it is often far more efficient and effective to do so through restrictive practice tasks. As we have seen in Chapter 4, one of the early goals of instruction and an early stage on the journey towards expertise is accurate performance: this is far easier to achieve if tasks involve initial massed practice combined with instant, efficient corrective feedback.

As we saw in Chapters 2 and 3 when we explored remembering and understanding, most instructional sequences should begin with restrictive practice activities and will slowly move towards wider application. If you want students to write concise and sophisticated introductions to their essays, it will be much more efficient to start by only focusing on this section of the essay instead of expecting students to apply it within a complete piece of writing.

THE SHIFT FROM PROMPTED TO UNPROMPTED FORMATS

In the early stages of instruction, tasks and resources should include prompts to help focus students' attention on important aspects of what it is they are learning in order to increase their success rates. These prompts should be gradually and systematically removed as students increase in competence. By the end of the instructional sequence, students should be able to apply what it is they have learned without any prompts (Watkins and Slocum, 2003).

HOW DOES THIS APPLY TO ENGLISH?

1. In the earlier stages of instruction, worked examples should be labelled clearly, identifying relevant bits and making clear to students which parts are important.

   Here are some examples:
   As we saw in Chapter 7, when modelling it can be really helpful to 'call your shots' when modelling (Lemov et al., 2012, p. 87) so that students know what they should be focused on. You could reduce extended writing into an abstract formula like this:

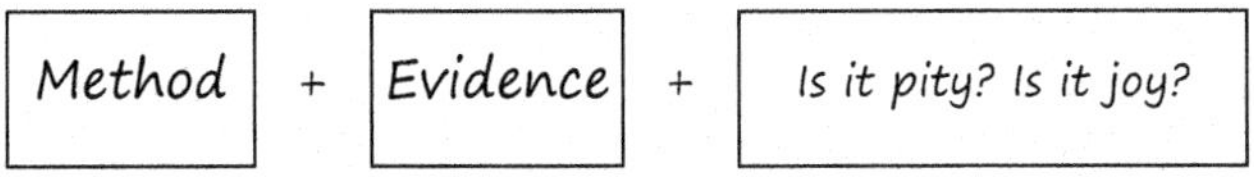

Figure 8.2   Abstract plan for writing

...before demonstrating how this abstraction is realised in actual writing by using prompts and labels:

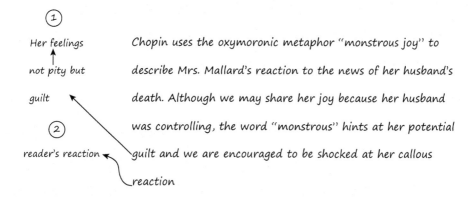

Figure 8.3 Concrete model that demonstrates how the components from the plan fit together

When teaching sentence styles, arrows and labelling can help make the implicit interactions and relationships between different components obvious to students:

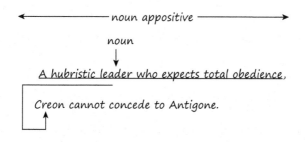

Figure 8.4 Labelling constructions

THE SHIFT FROM MASSED PRACTICE TO DISTRIBUTED PRACTICE

As we will see in the next chapter, practice, and specifically purposive or deliberate practice, is crucial if students are to master what it is we are teaching them. But what form should practice take? Should practice be massed or distributed? Exactly like the choice between model answers and attempting problems, the answer depends upon the expertise of the student. Initially students will learn a skill best when they undertake massed practice and complete many practice opportunities in a short period of time. In later learning, retention is enhanced by practice opportunities conducted over a long period of time (Watkins and Slocum, 2003). During the acquisition stage of learning, it will probably be helpful to have multiple practice opportunities in order for students to become accurate and proficient. As the sequence of learning progresses, this practice should become increasingly more distributed. This table explores the difference between massed and distributed practice:

Table 8.6   The difference between massed and distributed practice

	Massed	Distributed
When	• During initial teaching	• During the rest of the sequence of learning
What	• Repetitive, often sequential practice	• Distributed over time: daily? weekly? monthly? Intervals should be as long as possible whilst still allowing retrieval and performance success
How	• Instant feedback and error correction • Guided practice • Restrictive practice activities	• Delayed feedback • Independent Practice • Cumulative practice • Wider application
Why	• So that students can acquire what you are teaching them and can perform accurately	• So that student retain, become fluent and are able to generalise
1. Memory Implications 2. Performing or Learning	• High Retrieval Strength but low storage strength (Crammed) • Initial inflexible knowledge • Because of all the cues, models and support, student output here should be considered 'performance' not learning	• High Retrieval Strength and High Storage Strength (Learned Well) • Developing flexible knowledge • Consistently good performance in distributed practice tasks is a more reliable proxy for 'learning'

THE SHIFT FROM IMMEDIATE FEEDBACK TO DELAYED FEEDBACK

At the beginning of an instructional sequence, feedback should be immediate and precise in order to prevent errors and misconceptions from becoming learned. Once students are able to perform accurately, feedback should be increasingly delayed so that they are able to apply what you have taught them without interruption and in increasingly wider contexts. Delaying feedback can also lead to increased retention (Soderstrom and Bjork, 2015).

HOW DOES THIS APPLY TO TEACHING ENGLISH?

1. Initial practice activities of all concepts (analytical skills, vocabulary, context knowledge, sentence styles, punctuation, etc.) should be through restrictive and isolated practice, allowing precise and immediate feedback to be given. The teacher can either circulate, giving verbal feedback, or write a model and, by displaying it under the visualiser, provide students with an answer with which to check their own efforts against.

2. Regular recap activities at the start of lessons provide the perfect opportunity for immediate feedback regarding conceptual understanding and spelling. Referring to the 'hypercorrection effect' which we explored in Chapter 2, Dylan Wiliam (2018) explains that 'The benefits of testing come from the retrieval practice that students get when they take the test, and the

hypercorrection effect when they find out answers they thought were correct were in fact incorrect. In other words, the best person to mark a test is the person who just took it.'

THE SHIFT FROM AN EMPHASIS ON THE TEACHER'S ROLE AS A SOURCE OF INFORMATION TO AN EMPHASIS ON THE LEARNER'S ROLE AS A SOURCE OF INFORMATION

This shift matches the idea of 'I-we-you', where responsibility and agency gradually moves from teacher to student. While teachers will begin with lots of modelling and explicit instruction, students will increasingly be asked to complete tasks without support.

HOW DOES THIS APPLY TO TEACHING ENGLISH?

Table 8.7, adapted from *Teach Like a Champion* (2010, p. 72), illustrates this shift, focusing on teaching students how to approach an unseen poetry question.

Table 8.7   I-We-You

Step	I/We/You	Who?	Typical statements
1	I	I do	*The first step is to underline the key word in the question before reading the poem: this will provide a focus for our annotations. Then I need to read the poem and find around five interesting parts that fit the question*
2	We	I do, you help	*Okay, now let's try this method. What was the first thing I should do?*
3	We	You do, I help	*Okay Vikki, you show us how to do it and I'll help if you get stuck*
4	You	You do	*Now you can all try one on your own*
5	You	You do (next lesson)	*Here's an unseen poem, before we tackle it, please write down the steps that you will take when answering the question*

Here's another example, focusing on helping students to write paragraphs:

1. The teacher writes a paragraph under the visualiser, narrating their thought process and decisions (The 'I' stage)

   Using a semantic field of light, Dickens describes Scrooge's room with words like 'bright...', symbolising warmth, comfort and opulence. Perhaps the ghost wants Scrooge to experience a convivial and celebratory scene so that Scrooge will not only realise that being as 'solitary as an oyster' is a bad choice, but that he could spend his money and enjoy himself instead.

2. The teacher begins a second paragraph under the visualiser, asking students to help them complete it. (The 'We' stage)

   Using a hyperbolic metaphor, Dickens describes the food as '.....'

- If you use the same structure as the first paragraph, students will be able to use the first example as an analogy. Think back to Chapter 4, this is the alternation strategy in action.
- Asking for assistance from students is a useful way to catch misconceptions: if students offer poor suggestions, they can be discussed or corrected.
- The teacher can prompt students to use taught vocabulary, analytical skills or specific sentence styles.

3. Students now have two models to use as analogies. They should then write their own paragraph using different evidence but following the same process and structure (The 'You' Stage).

SUMMARY

- For teaching to be successful, it needs to be pitched at a student's current level of understanding.
- Student errors should be analysed in order to draw inferences about and improve the quality of teaching and the curriculum.
- Well-designed curricula should teach high-utility, generalisable content, providing students with everything they will need for success.
- Student success often results in increased motivation.
- New content should be introduced in small steps and sufficient time should be allocated to recap, practice and application.
- Teaching through examples and non-examples can help students to understand and master new content.
- As students gain in competence, the learning tasks that they are asked to complete should gradually change.

REFERENCES

Ausubel, D. P. (1968). *Educational psychology: A cognitive view.* New York, NY: Holt, Rinehart & Winston.

Barbash, S. (2012). *Clear teaching: With direct instruction, Siegfried Engelmann discovered a better way of teaching* (p. 23). Education Consumer Foundation.

Coe, R., Aloisi, C., Higgins, S., & Major, L. E. (2014). *What makes great teaching? Review of the underpinning research.* London: The Sutton Trust.

Engelmann, S. (2017). *Successful and confident students with direct instruction.* Oregon: NIFDI Press.

Engelmann, S., & Carnine, D. (2016). *Theory of instruction: Principles and applications revised edition.* Oregon: NIFDI press.

Lemov, D. (2010). *Teach like a champion.* San Francisco, CA: Jossey-Bass.

Lemov, D., Driggs, C., & Woolway, E. (2016). *Reading reconsidered.* San Francisco, CA: Jossey-Bass.

Lemov, D., Woolway, E., & Yezzi, K. (2012). *Practice perfect.* San Francisco, CA: Jossey-Bass.

Rosenshine, B. (2008). *Five meanings of direct instruction.* Lincoln, IL: Center on Innovation & Improvement.

Soderstrom, N. C., & Bjork, R. A. (2015). Learning versus performance: An integrative review. *Perspectives on Psychological Science, 10*(2), 176–179.

Watkins, C. L., & Slocum, T. A. (Summer 2003). *The components of direct instruction in journal of direct instruction* (p. 78). California State University, Stanislaus and Utah State University.

Wiliam, D. (2018). *Memories are made of this.* https://www.tes.com/news/memories-are-made-3

9

TEACHING WRITING

THE CASE FOR DELIBERATE PRACTICE

In this chapter, we will explore

- The meaning and importance of purposive or deliberate practice
- How practising components can help build expertise

INTRODUCTION

Practice is often seen as a key driver of academic success but what does effective practice actually look like? How can we ensure that practice is efficient and effective and if we want students to get better at extended writing, what exactly should we be practising? This chapter will argue that deliberate practice can be an effective approach to improve student writing.

One of the main goals of teaching English is to help pupils become better at writing. Expert writers seem to be able to write with minimal effort. They write quickly, accurately and effectively, their sentences well-constructed, their ideas expressed with clarity, producing texts that appeal to the reader whilst also being suited perfectly to the task at hand. This is, however, no easy feat. Expert writing involves the control of cognitive, perceptual and motor processes, each of which has become relatively effortless, most likely through extended and deliberate practice.

Deliberate practice can help to reduce the attentional demands of particular processes. Simple perceptual-motor processes can, through deliberate practice, become completely effortless. If you have ever trained in a particular sport, you will recognise this process of automisation. I play football and, as a result of sustained deliberate practice, do not have to think about the position of my feet, the angle of my leg or where my foot will meet the ball when kicking. Someone who has never kicked a ball before will need to concentrate on all of these things. The sheer number of things to consider (and we haven't even talked about positioning or anything to do with other players) will mean that this may be a difficult task to execute proficiently and consistently. Writing, however, is not a simple perceptual-motor process. Because of this complexity, effective writing instruction should seek to reduce rather than entirely eliminate the relative effort required for each of the components and processes involved (Kellogg and Whiteford, 2009).

Deliberate practice can do exactly that. By reducing the attentional demands on the components, it can free up pupils' attention so that they can concentrate on the whole performance, allowing them to respond flexibly and effectively to the task at hand.

If we want students to improve at writing, we should increase the amount of practice that they undertake (Graham et al., 2018). Effective teachers regularly ask students to practise writing for a variety of useful purposes. Although this may seem a little reductive, much of GCSE English writing, spanning both literature and language, can be grouped into three main genres: rhetoric, descriptive/creative and responding to texts. These are broad categories, each containing a range of typical tasks that require slightly different approaches, but there are more similarities than differences within each one. Teachers should ensure that students are given enough opportunities to practice each type and increasing the amount of time students spend practising writing will likely increase the quality of their writing. To be maximally effective, practice needs to be deliberate and appropriate to the level of expertise of the students. Asking pupils to regularly write entire essays when they start secondary school may not be the best approach: their lack of fluency in the various components that make up an essay may mean that they will struggle with such an extended task.

REAL-LIFE CASE STUDIES TAKEN FROM PEAK

Isaac Asimov, one of the most distinguished and prolific writers of science fiction, wrote almost 500 books in a career that spanned more than 40 years. A study (Ohlsson, 1992) explored Asimov's writing career in an attempt to draw inferences regarding the effects of practice. The study split his oeuvre into groups of 100 books. Although the books would obviously vary in length and complexity, the researchers assumed that this would roughly average out. Asimov completed his first 100 books in 237 months; his second 100 books in 113 months; his third 100 books in 69 months and his fourth 100 books in 42 months. His writing sped up significantly as his career progressed and it seems reasonable to attribute this improvement to practice and increasing expertise.

A second study (Raskin, 1936) found that scientists and authors produced their best work in their mid-30s, ten years or so after their first publications. In a study of poets (Wishbow, 1988), researchers found that over 80% of 66 poets that were listed in the Norton Anthology of Poetry were first published 10 years after starting reading and writing poetry. Both of these studies can also be seen as lending support to the idea that practice is beneficial.

DEFINING PRACTICE

We have already explored how practice can be guided, independent, massed, distributed and cumulative, but what else is required to ensure that practice is maximally effective? In his brilliant book, *Peak*, Anders Ericsson (2017), the world's leading expert on deliberate practice, explains that if practice is to be an effective means of developing expertise, it needs to be 'purposive' or ideally 'deliberate'. Let's have a look at each one in turn.

PURPOSIVE PRACTICE
WELL-DEFINED, SPECIFIC GOALS

Teachers should choose goals that are suited to their student's current level of expertise. If their pupils are struggling with transcription, then asking them to produce extended pieces of writing will not be the best instructional choice. It will be more useful to build their transcriptional fluency, perhaps through systematic spelling instruction, dictation activities or short, timed writing practice.

A pupil's level of writing expertise is unlikely to be the same across genres or different types of tasks. Expertise is often very narrow and highly domain specific. When pupils begin secondary school, they are often pretty good at writing stories, having learned and practised this text type a lot during primary school. Although they are adept at writing narratives, they are usually relative beginners or even complete novices at writing analytically. Because of this, it will probably not be a good idea to expect them to write essays that are of a comparable length to their creative pieces. Instead, instruction and practice should be focused at the sentence and paragraph level, building fluency with these components with the eventual aim of creating fluency in the wider, composite task of writing essays in response to texts.

PUTTING A BUNCH OF BABY STEPS TOGETHER TO REACH A LONGER TERM GOAL

Although the end goal may be the ability to write fluent and proficient extended compositions, the best way to achieve this is likely to involve practising the components that make up the whole performance (Binder, 1996).

Practising components, initially in restrictive activities, can help students become accurate and fluent before they are asked to use them in extended writing. This will often take much longer than you think and students will need frequent, distributed practice in order to become fluent. The time spent here is worth it though: extended writing is made up of sentences and proficient writers deliberately choose, combine and adapt specific constructions, resulting in well-written and well-argued final pieces. If the writing contains incoherent sentences, then it will be a badly written piece. If the sentences contain poorly spelled words or unclear vocabulary, then they will not make sense either. Each level depends on the strength of the level below (essay–paragraph–sentence–word) and each level will benefit from modelling and practice.

A common long-term goal in English lessons is for students to be able to write competent analytical essays in response to a text that they have read. This composite skill is made up of lots of components, each of which will benefit from isolated practice before being combined together. Here are some of the components:

EMBEDDING QUOTATIONS. This is the gateway to writing in response to texts and without this skill, students cannot respond effectively.

Some initial, simple structures to practice are

Agard writes 'blind me to my own identity', *meaning...*

Agard repeats 'dem tell me' *because...*

Boxer says 'I will work harder', *conveying*

Once students have mastered these, you can move onto more complex embedding structures. Modelling these orally, over and over again is a good approach, saying the punctuation out loud: *When the Landlady says QUOTE MARKS HOW DARK QUOTE MARKS COMMA she demonstrates her ignorance and prejudice.* In the early stages of practice, writing the evidence at the top of a page (so that everyone is embedding the same quotations) allows practice to be more efficient because it is then easier to give corrective feedback.

Chapter 11 will present and explain a multi-lesson instructional sequence for teaching embedding.

FINDING EVIDENCE. Like the live modelling of writing, students can also benefit from watching a teacher live model the process of finding evidence. Students often underline far too much, selecting multiple sentences when they really only need to explore a few words and modelling the concise selection of evidence can be really useful. This also allows further practice with embedding as the teacher can initially give oral examples of how to embed the evidence that they have chosen, before asking students to do it, applying the constructions that they have been taught.

FOCUS AND ATTENTION

If pupils aren't concentrating or paying attention, then it doesn't matter how good we think our lesson is, they won't get better at writing.

Students often seem enthralled with novelty, complaining that they have done something before and exclaiming 'not this again!' However, repetition should not be seen as something to be avoided. Effective practice often involves procedures and tasks that have been done many times by the teacher and the students, both being so familiar with the instructions that the teacher is able to devote maximal concentration to behaviour management, misconceptions and questioning, while the student can devote maximal attention to what it is they are learning.

FEEDBACK

In Peak (2017, p. 22), Ericsson points out that 'meaningful positive feedback is crucial for motivation...this can be internal feedback such as the satisfaction of seeing yourself improve at something, or external feedback provided by others'. To prevent errors from becoming ingrained, in the initial stages of instruction, corrective feedback should be immediate (Watkins and Slocum, 2003). Effective feedback requires the giver to have a well-developed mental representation of what is being performed. If a task is vague, then this can make things difficult. Feedback involves comparing these expert mental representations to the performance: the difference is what the student needs to do to improve (Kellogg and Whiteford, 2009).

GETTING OUT OF YOUR COMFORT ZONE

Purposive practice should involve a level of challenge that is just above pupils' current performance levels. It should be achievable yet challenging and this is often a hard balance to achieve. Rosenshine's principles of Instruction, would point to 80% as being an optimum success rate for pupils during guided practice activities: on average, pupils should be getting 80% of the answers correct in a lesson (Rosenshine, 2012). If it is too easy, pupils may lose interest; if it is too hard, pupils may give up. They need to see that if they devote sustained attention to the task, that the goal is achievable.

DELIBERATE PRACTICE

Deliberate practice requires that teachers 'set practice activities designed to help pupils improve'. In order to create such activities, the teacher will need to follow a number of guidelines:

TEACHERS MUST KNOW WHAT MAKES UP EXPERT WRITING

Deliberate practice is different from other forms of practice because it requires a fairly well established domain where 'the best performers have attained a level of performance that clearly sets them apart from people who are just entering the field' (Ericsson and Pool, 2017, p. 98). Writing seems to fit this description. Although there will be huge variations in style, tone, register and form across expert writing, even within a specific genre or text type, expert writers will likely have utilised similar cognitive processes in order to create their pieces. Deftly juggling mental representations that span author, text and prospective readers, they will have recursively planned, composed and reviewed their writing. These processes can be isolated and practised with students and these mental representations can be incrementally developed too, through extensive reading and studying models. Pupils should also be taught and asked to apply specific sentence structures or literary techniques.

How can this be achieved:

- Practice, practice, practice. Teachers should regularly be practising writing themselves by completing the same tasks that pupils are asked to do. Almost every time pupils write, I write as well.
- Reading, analysing and discussing student work with colleagues.

TEACHERS MUST UNDERSTAND THE RELATIONSHIP BETWEEN COMPONENTS AND WHOLES

Extended writing, like most other complex cognitive or physical skills, can be split up into different components, each of which can be taught and practised in isolation before being combined into increasingly complex wholes. There are many advantages to this approach and it is no surprise that drills and restrictive practice tasks are standard in sports training and music teaching. Drills allow initial massed practice so that pupils, through immediate corrective feedback, are able to perform accurately. These drills can then be distributed over time so that pupils retain the skill and, once the desired level of accuracy has been reached, pupils can begin to work on their fluency by attempting to complete trials within a specific time limit. If pupils become fluent in these components, they are far more likely to be able to use them in wider writing.

Practising sentence structures on their own, however, is unlikely to be very successful. Pupils need to eventually use these components in their wider writing and an effective instructional sequence will gradually shift from restrictive practice to wider application.

How can this be achieved:

- Components should be chosen and sequenced based on their utility-anaphora may well be more useful to pupils than anastrophe.
- Components should be chosen that are easily combined with others: specific high utility sentence structures are ideal here.
- Particular attention should be paid to the shift from drills to wider application so that pupils are able to apply what they have practised in extended writing. If not, pupils will not transfer their knowledge to wider writing. Transfer can be difficult to achieve, although one method of achieving it is to make pupils aware of the similarity between different contexts or tasks. This can be achieved through prompts, success criteria and asking pupils to underline the components that they have included in their writing.
- Ensure that there is a suitable balance between practising components and appropriate extended writing. Most of the time, classes should be doing both: drills to develop accuracy and fluency; extended writing to push pupils' thinking about the content as well as to combine and apply fluent components. If pupils only complete drills, this will only help them get better at drills and they may not transfer this knowledge to extended writing. If pupils only do extended writing, this is unlikely to accelerate their progress as much as balancing the two.

PRACTICE ON ALL THREE STAGES OF THE WRITING PROCESS

Although there are lots of models for describing writing, many split it into three main cognitive processes: planning, writing (often called 'translating' in research) and reviewing (Graham et al., 2018). As well as practising the components of writing-things like sentence forms, punctuation and paragraph construction – students will also need extensive and deliberate practice on each of these three processes, reducing the relative effort required for each (Kellogg et al., 2013).

Planning, writing and reviewing should not be seen as serial and separate stages of processing. Instead, all three are recursive and connected, interacting in complex patterns when we write. Even though planning is typically thought of as the first part of the writing process, writers plan throughout the entire process: as they write, they will be planning how to compose the next sentence or thinking about how what they are writing fits their initial whole text plan. Similarly, even though review is often thought of as the end of the writing process as students check their work for errors, suitability and coherence, in reality they will be constantly reviewing throughout the whole process. As they plan, they may be reviewing their planning choices; as they write, they will be reviewing the last few sentences in order to inform their next steps (Kellogg et al., 2013).

Even though the writing process involves all three stages (planning, writing and reviewing), students will benefit from deliberate, isolated practice with each stage. In order to write proficiently, each of the component processes must become relatively automatic and effortless, a state that can be achieved through practising each stage in isolation (Kellogg and Whiteford, 2009).

PLANNING EXTENDED WRITING

If students are writing a persuasive essay, one useful strategy is 'STOP' (Reid et al., 2013). Mnemonics can be really useful, reminding students to include all the necessary stages.

STOP:

Suspend Judgement: This encourages students to consider both sides to the issue and think of ideas for and against the topic.

Take A Side: Students should then choose whether they are for or against, based upon the ideas that they generated in the first stage of the planning process.

Organise My Ideas: Using the ideas that they generated in the first two stages, they should decide on how to sequence them in their writing. One way of doing this is by deciding which arguments are the strongest so that the essay can end with the most important point.

Plan More As I Write: This is a reminder to students to continue to revise, evaluate and plan once they have begun writing.

PLANNING STRATEGY 2: PERSONAL-GENERAL

When journalists write pieces about serious issues, they often begin with an emotive description of a person who is experiencing the problem, thereby turning the abstract into the concrete and personalising the story. After hooking the reader with an often poignant and vivid picture of the travails of an actual person, the next section then extrapolates to the general, outlining how the person's situation is commonplace and the issues that are faced are widespread. By linking the personal with the general, description with exposition and then concluding by returning once again to the individual described at the beginning, a writer is able to produce a pleasingly circular, well-constructed argument that has both pathos and logos.

Here's an outline of this approach:

Imagine you students are answering this question: *'Zoos are cruel' Write an article for a magazine arguing for or against this view.*

Section 1: Personal

Students describe a young person who is unimpressed with a zoo.

> As the sleet streaks across the November sky, the frail frame of a predatory cat shivers in a concrete enclosure, its pen a quagmire of mud, its face hidden beneath its sinewy legs. Peering over the unforgiving concrete wall, James struggles to see his favourite animal as it cowers in a muddy corner. In James' mind, the fastest cat in the world sprints across the savannah; in Chester zoo, a pathetic shivering feline crouches in a puddle. James feels sorry. Sorry for the cheetah; sorry for the other animals and sorry that his money has helped perpetuate this cruel and exploitative situation.

Section 2: General

This section sets out the problem.

> How is it that we are willing to tolerate the forced displacement and imprisonment of animals? How is it acceptable that we gain pleasure from visiting open air prisons? Does a 100 km/h cat belong in a 10 m squared enclosure? No. Does a giraffe, an animal used to an arid climate, belong in the grim British December? No! Animals suffer for our enjoyment. Animals are trapped for our pleasure. This has to stop. Yes, zoos are popular, but this should not make them acceptable and more importantly their very existence causes pain and trauma as animals are displaced, imprisoned and often neglected. Not only are zoo animals three times as likely to suffer illness, but they almost always live shorter lives as a result of their captivity.

Section 3: General

This section presents possible solutions to the problem and alternatives to the current situation.

> There is another way. Instead of zoos, governments should be supporting indigenous conservation. Instead of forcibly removing animals from their habitats, governments should protect them and help them to survive. If zoos were closed, money could be redirected to local conservation projects, not only providing jobs but also helping to conserve the beautiful countryside where these animals are found. Animals are not entertainment: they are sentient beings and we have a moral obligation to protect them, especially as most of the problems that they face are our creation. A cheetah belongs in the savannahs of Africa, not the puddles of northern England.

Section 4: Return to the Personal Story

This section could see a return to the person from the first section, explaining how their situation has actually changed as a result of heeding the recommendations made in Section 3. Alternatively, it could be written using hypotheticals and predictions, outlining how their situation *could* change if they had benefited from the solutions in Section 3.

As James relaxes on the sofa, his feet resting on a footstool, the dulcet tones of David Attenborough announce the beginning of his favourite programme: Africa. The opening sequence ends and a panoramic shot of the Namibian grasslands, taken from an aerial drone, reveals an expansive vista filled with space. A herd of wildebeest gather around a watering hole; three giraffes reach into the canopy of a slender tree. In the corner of the screen, partially hidden by elephant grass, a cheetah waits, its face a picture of concentration, its ears pinned back: alert aware and ready to attack. James smiles and feels happy: happy for the cheetah; happy for the other animals and happy that he is able to experience the full wonder of nature.

REVIEWING

If you ask students to check their writing when they have finished, can you be sure that they understand exactly what they are checking or what checking really means? It can be useful to be more prescriptive and explain exactly what they are supposed to check and the order in which they are supposed to approach their review. The 'SCAN' revision strategy is one useful approach (Reid et al., 2013):

SCAN:

STEP 1: Read Your Essay
STEP 2: Find the sentence that tells you what you believe…is it clear?
STEP 3: Add two more reasons why you can believe it
STEP 4: SCAN each sentence and ask yourself:

*Does it make **S**ense?* Will the reader understand it?
*Is it **C**onnected to my belief?* Does it directly support the development of my argument?
*Can I **A**dd more?* Do more details need to be added to improve it?
Students then **N**ote down any errors. Are there any errors that need correcting?

This approach encourages students to review what they have written in a more methodical fashion. They need to 'SCAN' each sentence that they have written to ensure that it is clear, useful, complete and error-free.

EXPECTATIONS AND MOTIVATION

All of the strategies above form a purposive or deliberate practice approach to writing. Splitting up a complex task into manageable and achievable practice activities, combined with a gradual increase in difficulty can be hugely motivating for students as they can experience regular and consistent success. The satisfaction of seeing themselves improve at something is a powerful motivational force: students change from thinking 'I can't write essays' to 'I am a successful writer'.

As well as the burgeoning intrinsic motivation that can develop from effective instruction, the teacher can also do a number of other things to ensure student work is of a good standard and that they continue to be motivated to work harder:

PRAISING GOOD WORK

Showing and deconstructing good student work under a visualiser or document camera can be really powerful in terms of motivation. Before showing it, the teacher can tell the students what they should be looking for-further reinforcing the success criteria and helping students see how these things look in final pieces. If there are lots of good bits in lots of student's books, you can draw a star next to the good bits and then make a note. The students can then be asked to read out that section when you give feedback. Tactically varying the chosen work is worthwhile here: there will always be a few students whose work is the best, but choosing a range of students (as long as it is not disingenuous) can be really motivating.

Praising how the student has achieved something is also important-some students may not realise what focused, hard work looks like; others can benefit from learning that some behaviours will have a negative effect on their performance.

> Look at this, Rachel has written 1.5 pages and this is because she focussed for the entire time-I rarely saw her face as she was concentrating on her work throughout. She didn't take a break after the introduction, nor did she spend any time looking out of the window. She also began straight away. Look-here is her booklet, it is filled with useful annotations and this meant that it was really easy for her to write as she has worked hard to build her knowledge of the text.

EXPECTATIONS

Set precise expectations as to what you expect. Do you want one page? Maybe two pages? If your instructional sequence has provided enough practice on the components, has had a gradual yet consistently achievable increase in difficulty and has asked students to slowly combine and apply the components then you can expect all students to meet your expectations. If students are able to write a page, then you need to insist on them doing so.

However, even if they have engaged in sufficient purposive practice, some students will still prefer to produce the bare minimum because they think that they can get away with it. This may be entirely rational: why work hard if you don't have to? Attaching a consequence to your expectations can help here as there are always some students who are only motivated by the desire to avoid this. However, assuming that your teaching has allowed for consistent student success, a student's motivation may well change from a desire to avoid a consequence to a desire to do the work. This doesn't mean that the consequence should be removed, only that it will slowly be no longer needed as the primary motivating factor.

A BRIEF RECAP...

So far, we have explored a number of different ideas as to how to choose the optimum approach to instruction. Table 9.1 gives a summary of what we have covered so far.

Table 9.1   Summary of what we have already covered

	Novice	Developing in expertise	Expert
Type of Instruction	Direct Instruction	Guided Problem Solving	Unguided Problem Solving
Stage of Instruction	Teacher Demonstrate	Guided Practice	Independent Practice
Type of Practice	Massed Practice	Massed/Distributed	Distributed
Type of Task	Restrictive Drills	Narrowed Context	Wider Application
Instructional Goal	Acquisition/ Accuracy Fluency/Retention	Accuracy/Fluency/ Retention	Fluency/Retention/ Generalisation
Cognitive Load Theory	Worked Examples	Completion Problems	Problems
Explicit Instruction Stage	I	We	You

SUMMARY

- Deliberate practice can help students build fluency by automatising components and skills. This can reduce the demands made on their attention, allowing them to concentrate on and succeed at extended writing.
- Effective practice tasks are unlikely to look like the final performance: restrictive drills that focus on individual components can help students perform better at complex tasks like extended writing.
- Deliberate practice requires specific goals that are combined together to reach a longer term goal.
- Students need to focus all of their attention on what they are practising: learning tasks should be procedurally simple.
- In order to sustain motivation, instant feedback should be given in the early stages of instruction.
- Deliberate practice should be achievable yet challenging, pushing students to get out of their comfort zones.

REFERENCES

Binder, C. (1996). Behavioural fluency: Evolution of a new paradigm. *The Behavior Analyst*, *19*(2), 163–197.

Ericsson, A., & Pool, R. (2017). Peak. Vintage.

Graham, S., Liu, X., Aitken, A., Ng, C., Bartlett, B., Harris, K. R., & Holzapfel, J. (2018). Effectiveness of literacy programs balancing reading and writing instruction: A meta-analysis. *Reading Research Quarterly*, *53*(3), 279–304.

Kellogg, R. T., & Whiteford, A. P. (2009). Training advanced writing skills: The case for deliberate practice. *Educational Psychologist*, *44*(4), 250–266.

Kellogg, R. T., Whiteford, A. P., Turner, C. E., Cahill, M., & Mertens, A. (2013). Working memory in written composition: An evaluation of the 1996 model. *Journal of Writing Research*, *5*(2), 159–190.

Ohlsson, S. (1992). The learning curve for writing books: Evidence from professor Asimov. *Psychological Science*, *3*(6), 380–382.

Raskin, E. (1936). Comparison of scientific and literary ability: A biographical study of eminent scientists and men of letters of the nineteenth century. *The Journal of Abnormal and Social Psychology*, *31*(1), 20–35.

Reid, R., Lienemann, T. O., & Hagaman, J. L. (2013). *Strategy instruction for students with learning disabilities* (2nd ed.). New York, NY: Guildford Press.

Rosenshine, R. (Spring 2012). The principles of instruction research-based strategies that all teachers should know. *American Educator*, *36*(1), 12–39.

Watkins, C. L., & Slocum, T. A. (Summer 2003). *The components of direct instruction in Journal of Direct Instruction* (p. 78). California State University, Stanislaus and Utah State University.

Wishbow, N. A. (1988). *Studies of creativity in poets*. Doctoral dissertation (*Vol. 51*, p. 0491A). Carnegie Mellon University Dissertation Abstracts International.

10

CREATING INSTRUCTIONAL SEQUENCES

In this chapter, we will explore

- The general principles that underpin successful instructional sequences
- A summary of the main ideas from previous chapters
- Two explained example instructional sequences

INTRODUCTION

Over the last nine chapters, some important theory and research has been outlined that can potentially increase the effectiveness and efficiency of your teaching. This chapter will demonstrate how many of these ideas can be synthesised in order to create multi-lesson instructional sequences.

INSTRUCTIONAL SEQUENCES

The approach explained here leans heavily on the approach used within Engelmann's Direct Instruction Programmes. There is, however, an important distinction to be made. DI programmes have been rigorously field tested to ensure that instruction is maximally efficient, while the sequences in this book have not been developed, refined or tested in such a methodical fashion. Although they have proved to be successful in classrooms, there are certainly many improvements that can be made to all of them in terms of clarity and efficiency. Additionally, there will be many other combinations of examples, alternative teacher instructions and possible routes that could be plotted from initial teaching to independent practice.

These example sequences are presented not as ready to use instructional sequences but instead to give you an idea of how to create similar sequences of your own. You will undoubtedly be teaching different content and may choose to teach different writing components. Also, you may find that your class needs a greater or lesser amount of practice.

GENERAL PRINCIPLES

EFFICIENCY

If we are to maximise efficiency in our instructional sequences – a key and important goal given that lesson time is finite – then we need to carefully consider two competing demands. Firstly, we should ensure that students experience a consistently high success rate: 80% for new material and even higher for material that is being practiced and firmed. Secondly, we should use backwards fading so that students are asked to write independently as quickly as possible. Turn back to Chapter 8 to remind yourself of the six shifts of task design within Direct Instruction: you will see these shifts in action in these sequences.

Table 10.1 gives a useful summary of the six shifts and many effective instructional sequences will follow a similar pattern:

Table 10.1   Summary of the six shifts of task design

Lesson	Instructional choice	Source of information	Context of practice	Type of practice	Feedback
1 **Initial teaching**	Worked examples with prompts	Teacher	Individual sentences	Massed	Immediate
2 **Initial teaching**	Worked examples and completion problems	Teacher with student help	Individual sentences	Massed	Immediate
3	Completion problems with most steps completed	Student with teacher help	Individual sentences	Massed	Immediate
4	Completion problems with some steps completed	Student with teacher help	Individual sentences	Massed	Immediate
5	Completion problems with one step completed	Student with teacher help	Individual sentences	Massed	Immediate
6	Independent practice	Student	Individual sentences	Distributed	Immediate
7	Independent practice	Student	Individual sentences	Distributed	Immediate
8	Prompted independent practice	Student	Include 'technique' as a success Criteria in a paragraph	Distributed	Delayed
9	Prompted independent practice	Student	Include 'technique' as a success Criteria in a paragraph	Distributed	Delayed
10	Independent practice	Student	Wider writing	Distributed	Delayed
Later lessons	Independent practice	Student	Wider Writing	Distributed	Delayed

How long students should spend on each instructional stage will be determined by the quality of the instructional sequence as well as the prior knowledge of the students. Feedback to the teacher is key here: if students are performing successfully on a stage, then you can make the transition to a lower level of support, increasing the number of steps that a student is expected to complete and removing models, prompts, and teacher assistance.

CLARITY AND PACE

The tasks should be delivered at a brisk pace and teachers will benefit from practicing their approach before using it in class. If instructions are given slowly or teachers make errors, then this can often result in students losing concentration or becoming confused.

HOW DO YOU OPTIMISE PRACTICE DRILLS?

This chapter will present instructional sequences for teaching participle phrases and noun appositives. In both example sequences, the subject matter of the examples is the content that is being taught so that as well as developing their writing skills, students will also be deepening their understanding of the content.

In *Teach Like a Champion*, Lemov (2010, p. 104) explains 'At Bats', the idea that 'succeeding once or twice at a skill won't bring mastery, give your students lots and lots of practice mastering knowledge or skills'. This is crucial. When students are asked to complete problems independently, they should practice extensively, ideally across many lessons and including 'multiple formats and with a significant number of plausible variations'. Here are some of the possible variations when teaching participle phrases or appositives.

1. Varying where the phrases are in a sentence (at the start, somewhere in the middle or at the end)
2. Varying the writing genre for the task (analytical, descriptive, rhetorical)
3. Varying the content (Macbeth, Ozymandias, The Crucible)
4. Adding quotations to the phrase
5. Varying the number of phrases in a sentence
6. Varying the length and level of detail within the phrase
7. When they have mastered all of the above, combining both phrases or integrating other sentence skills that you are teaching

Before we dive into some explained example sequences, let us recap the ideas that underpin them (see Table 10.2).

Table 10.2 Summary of main principles covered so far

Chapter	Principles	Implication/Application
1 What is learning?	If there is no change in long-term memory, nothing has been learned	Students need to remember what we teach them
	The start point of learning is often inflexible knowledge; the goal, however, is flexible knowledge	• Repetitive drills can be a useful start point for learning something new • Students need to be able to transfer what they have learned and apply it to new situations
2 and 3	Working memory is limited	• Split up complex tasks into components • Only introduce small amounts of new information at one time
	We rapidly forget what we learn	Distribute retrieval and practice to prevent forgetting
	Performance is not the same as learning	Fully independent student output produced much later than initial instruction should be used to infer learning
	Understanding is about making sense of information.	• Students need to engage in semantic processing and all 3 stages of SOI (select, organise and integrate) to 'understand' what they are learning. • Failure to engage in 1 or more of these stages will preclude understanding. • Teaching should support students to engage in sense making
4 Novices and experts	Learning is about building accurate and well organised mental models of information in our long-term memories and then practising applying these models.	• Initial instruction should begin with worked examples. These act as schema substitutes, building students' mental model of what they are learning • Initial instruction should contain worked example problem pairs. Students can use the examples as analogies to complete tasks • Initial instruction should contain completion problems. These can be important halfway points between building mental models and applying the models to successfully complete tasks.
	Novices learn differently to experts	• As students develop in expertise, they are expected to succeed with increasingly less support • Worked examples for novices; application tasks as they develop and refine their background knowledge and mental models
	Expertise can be perceived as a hierarchy	• Instructional choices should be suited to the stage of learning that a student is within • Initial instruction should build accuracy and fluency; later instruction should build retention, generalisation and adaptation
5 Vocabulary	Possessing a wide and accessible vocabulary can help students in English	• Lessons should involve a high volume of reading and ambitious vocabulary
6 Explicit instruction	Student success rates should be consistently high	Students should be taught all the information that they will need for success
	Instruction should seek to develop flexible knowledge that students can independently apply to new situations	• Students should be taught how to apply the information that they are taught • Students should apply what they are taught to increasingly wider contexts

(Continued)

Table 10.2 Summary of main principles covered so far *(Continued)*

Chapter	Principles	Implication/Application
7 Rosenshine	We rapidly forget what we learn	Instruction should involve regular review to prevent forgetting and to increase the ease of application
	Novice learners can find it hard to access prior learning or make connections	Instruction should activate prior knowledge
	Working memory is limited	New material should be presented in small steps with practice after each step
	Students need to think hard about the meaning of content	Teachers should ask lots of questions and check the responses of all students
	Learning is about building accurate and well organised mental models of information in our long-term memories and then practising applying these models.	Initial instruction should begin with worked examples. These act as schema substitutes, building students' mental model of what they are learning
	Proficiency requires practice	• Initial practice should be guided to develop accuracy and fluency • Independent practice is important for students to develop flexible, transferable knowledge
8 Engelmann	Student success rates should be consistently high	Students should be taught all the information that they will need for success
	When learning something new, the possibility of learning misconceptions is high	All details of instruction should be controlled to minimise the opportunity for misconceptions
	The goal of initial instruction is acquisition	• Initial instruction should span at least two or three lessons • Initial practice should be massed
	Concrete examples are often easier to learn from than abstract descriptions	Instruction should involve carefully sequenced examples and non-examples
	Feedback to the teacher is important for diagnosing student problems	Initial practice tasks should make student thinking apparent to teachers
	Demonstration should precede gradually more complex student application	• Instruction should follow the I-We-You model • Initial instruction should focus on simplified contexts • Prompts can help support students • Massed practice before distributed practice
9 Practice	A useful learning goal is automaticity so that performance is effortless	• Knowledge and skills should not go away • Curricula should ensure that components are combined and practised in increasingly complex ways
	Accuracy and fluency are useful initial learning goals	• Initial instruction should involve repetitive, guided, restrictive practice tasks • Initial instruction should involve instant corrective feedback, preventing errors from being retained
	Some knowledge and skills are more useful than others	High utility knowledge and skills should be practised, providing students with the greatest benefit and widest application

Here's the first example of an instructional sequence. It teaches participle phrases, high utility constructions that students can use across all three types of writing that are typically taught at secondary school: rhetoric, creative/descriptive and text response. Each numbered title is not meant to be an entire lesson: this approach presupposes that a lesson will contain many other tasks and activities. For each distinct part of the sequence, an explanation of the ideas that underpin it as well as guidance as to how to teach it is included.

PARTICIPLES SEQUENCE

For all of these sequences, the teacher and all students will need the same resource. The teacher displays their resource under a document camera that is projected onto a screen so that all students can see what the teacher is doing. If, however, you do not have this display technology, you could complete the sequences by giving clear instructions to students focused on the 'teacher demonstrate' and 'student test sequence' steps a–c.

Table 10.3 gives an overview of the first four lessons in the sequence.

Table 10.3   Lessons 1–4 overview

Lesson	Teacher demonstrate	Student test	Guided practice: completion problems	Guided practice: prompted practice	Independent practice
1	Present participles	Yes	Yes		
2	Present participles	Yes	Yes		
3	Present participles	Yes	Yes		
4	Present participles	Yes		Yes	

Initial teaching of this construction is spread across four lessons and in each one, students will engage in massed, restrictive practice. The first three lessons end with completion problems where students finish sentences. The goal here is acquisition and accuracy.

Participle phrases 1: teacher demonstrate

Participle phrases act like adjectives; they describe the subject of a sentence.

Teacher demonstrate

a. Underline the participle phrase/s
b. Circle the subject that the phrase/s describe
c. Draw an arrow from the phrase to the subject

1. Rudely asking 'ARE YOU LIGHT OR VERY DARK', the landlady demonstrates both her ignorance and her racial prejudice.
2. The landlady demonstrates both her ignorance and her racial prejudice, rudely asking 'ARE YOU LIGHT OR VERY DARK'.
3. The landlady, asking 'ARE YOU LIGHT OR VERY DARK', demonstrates both her ignorance and her racial prejudice.

(Continued)

4. He sank into the comfy chair, closing his eyes, preparing to finally get some well-earned rest.
5. Closing his eyes, preparing to finally get some well-earned rest, he sank into the comfy chair.

Table 10.4 Participle phrases 1: teacher demonstrate

WHAT?	• 1–5 are all examples of present participle phrases • Some are for descriptive writing; others are for analytical writing
HOW?	1. Class reads definition out loud 2. Teacher completes a–c in order for number 1 to exemplify the definition. Students look at the board and do the same on their sheet. 3. Teacher then asks *Who is 'rudely asking'* Class then chorally respond: *The Landlady* 4. Teacher then repeats step 2 and 3 for all other example sentences. (Asking *who is 'closing his eyes/preparing to finally get some well-earned rest'* for examples 4 and 5)
WHY?	• Arrows and labels make function and form of phrases clear to students • Choral response increases the likelihood that everyone thinks about the content • Choral response questioning reinforces the function of the participle phrases, asking students to focus on the connection between subject and phrase. • Examples are minimally different, demonstrating how phrases can be moved to different locations within sentences yet still have the same function • Skills and knowledge do not go away: the analytical sentences focus on taught content, providing further opportunities for students to think about and practice important content; in this example, embedded quotations were taught in a previous sequence: their inclusion here (in a more complex form as part of a participle phrase) is helping to broaden students' mental model of the possibilities for embedding. • Examples will be used as analogies for students in **'Participle Phrases 1 Student Test Sequence'**

The first four lessons will present a sufficiently wide range of examples of present participle sentences so that students are more likely to develop a useful and broad mental model of them. If there was only a narrow range of examples, students may develop an impoverished and unnecessarily restricted mental model of these constructions.

Figure 10.1 shows what the teacher should do:

Teacher demonstrate:

a) Underline the participle phrase/s

b) Circle the subject that the phrase/s describe

c) Draw an arrow from the phrase to the subject

PROMPTS

1) <u>Rudely asking 'ARE YOU LIGHT OR VERY DARK'</u>, (the landlady) demonstrates both her ignorance and her racial prejudice.

2) (The landlady) demonstrates both her ignorance and her racial prejudice, <u>rudely asking 'ARE YOU LIGHT OR VERY DARK.'</u>

Figure 10.1 Example of teacher annotation and labelling

Participle phrases 1: student test sequence

After the teacher has demonstrated these first examples, students need to complete the 'student test sequence', labelling these *different* sentences in exactly the same way that the teacher did:

a. Underline the participle phrase/s
b. Circle the subject that the phrase/s describe
c. Draw an arrow from the phrase to the subject

1. Raising her arm, Miriam tried to get the teacher's attention.
2. Miriam tried to get the teacher's attention, raising her arm.
3. Thinking back to last Christmas, Jenny remembered how nice it was to see her family all together.
4. Jenny, thinking back to last Christmas, remembered how nice it was to see her family all together.
5. Shouting loudly, waving her arms in the air, the woman tried to warn them of the danger.
6. Criticising the derogatory term 'half-caste', Agard wants the reader to appreciate that racial identity is complex and nuanced.
7. Nichols creates an image of monotony and boredom, ending the poem with 'Another London Day.'
8. Agard's poem, beginning with the phrase 'standing on one leg', ridicules the idea of being 'half-caste.'

Table 10.5 Participle phrases 1: student test sequence

WHAT?	• 1–8 are all *different* examples of participle phrases

HOW?	1. Students work through steps a–c for each example
	2. When all students have finished, feedback can be given chorally:
	    Teacher: *'In sentence 1, everyone, say the subject'*
	    Students: *'Miriam'*
	    Teacher: *'In sentence 1, everyone, say the participle phrase'.*
	    Students: *'Raising her arm'*
	    Teacher: *'In sentence 1, everyone, Who is raising her arm'?*
	    Students: *'Miriam'.*
	• If it is clear that students are making errors, the teacher should stop and correct them

WHY?	• Because it tests *different* examples, the student test sequence tests if students have acquired what they are being taught and that they are performing accurately. • Choral feedback is efficient and allows teachers to focus on accuracy, instantly correcting students who have made errors • Choral feedback further reinforces the function of participle phrases, asking students to focus on the connection between subject and phrase. • This is the first tiny step towards building flexible knowledge. As the instructional sequence continues, students will be expected to gradually complete more of the steps in creating these constructions

Participle phrases 1: completion problems

After the student test sequence, students need to finish completion problems

a. Before writing, students should complete some orally, making sure they SAY the punctuation.
b. Copy and complete these sentences in your books so that each has at least 1 present participle phrase:

1. ...., the teacher was proud of the student.
2. The teacher was proud of the student, ...
3. Ending the poem with 'Another London Day', Nichols...........................
4. Repeating 'Limbo', the poet could be highlighting...............................
5. Looking at the man in complete shock, she..............
6. The nurse, checking the patient's....................................., began to...........................

Table 10.6   Participle phrases 1: completion problems

WHAT?	• Students finish these sentences so that they make sense and are accurate. • Analytical sentences focus on previously taught content
HOW?	1. Before writing, the teacher can give some oral examples, saying the punctuation out loud to emphasise the importance of accuracy: *Reading the essay aloud to the class COMMA the teacher was proud of the student FULL STOP.* 2. Students can then give further oral examples, again, saying the punctuation out loud so the teacher can give instant corrective feedback. 3. Students then complete the sentences in their books. 4. The teacher can circulate, pointing out errors: this is guided practice and the goal here is accuracy. 5. When students finish, they can make specific checks to ensure accuracy: *does the participle phrase describe the subject? Are the commas in the right places?*
WHY?	• These are an important middle stage between studying models and independent practice, helping to ensure that students are able to apply what they have acquired. • Guided practice is essential before independent practice if success rates are to be consistently high.

Participle phrases 2: teacher demonstrate

Participle phrases act like adjectives; they describe the subject of a sentence.

Teacher demonstrate

a. Underline the participle phrase/s
b. Circle the subject that the phrase/s describe
c. Draw an arrow from the phrase to the subject

(Continued)

1. Claiming that 'rhetoric is the art of ruling the minds of men', Plato recognised the power of language and how it can be used to manipulate and control people.
2. Plato, claiming that 'rhetoric is the art of ruling the minds of men', recognised the power of language and how it can be used to manipulate and control people.
3. Plato recognised the power of language and how it can be used to manipulate and control people, claiming that 'rhetoric is the art of ruling the minds of men'.
4. Even though it was bitterly cold, he marched out of the door, gripping his bag tightly, lowering his head against the wind.
5. She sat quietly in the corner of the café, watching, waiting, hoping Selma wouldn't be late.
6. Happily standing on top of the climbing frame, grinning at the other children, Pete felt that he had finally overcome his fear of heights.

Table 10.7   Participle phrases 2: teacher demonstrate

WHAT?	• 1–6 are all further examples of present participle phrases • Examples are broader here, including one-word participle phrases, even though and phrases that start with an adverb
HOW?	• Same method as **Present Participle Phrases 1 Teacher Demonstrate**
WHY?	• Widening the range of examples helps to broaden and refine students' mental model of participle phrases and their uses • Examples will be used as analogies for students in **'Participle Phrases 2 Student Test Sequence'**

Participle phrases 2: student test sequence

a. Underline the participle phrase/s
b. Circle the subject that the phrase/s describe
c. Draw an arrow from the phrase to the subject

1. Exclaiming 'I have a dream', Martin Luther King wanted to show that America could be a country free from prejudice.
2. Describing how people had been 'seared in the flames of withering injustice', King draws attention to the pain caused by segregation and racial violence.
3. Martin Luther King, describing how people had been 'seared in the flames of withering injustice', draws attention to the pain caused by segregation and racial violence.
4. Speaking in front of a quarter of a million people, King gave an impassioned speech filled with vivid imagery and powerful rhetorical flourishes.
5. King, speaking in front of a quarter of a million people, gave an impassioned speech filled with vivid imagery and powerful rhetorical flourishes.
6. Opening the door slowly, she peered through the gap.

(Continued)

7. Proudly wearing the new jacket that her mother had bought for her birthday, Paula sat next to the window at the back of the bus.
8. Paula sat next to the window at the back of the bus, proudly wearing the new jacket that her mother had bought for her birthday.

Table 10.8   Participle phrases 2: student test sequence

WHAT?	• 1–8 are all *different* examples of present participle sentences
HOW?	• Same method as **Present Participles Student Test Sequence 1**
WHY?	• Like in **Participle Phrases Student Test Sequence 1**, the goal here is acquisition and accuracy.

Participle phrases 2: completion problems

a. Before writing, students should complete some orally, making sure they SAY the punctuation.
b. Copy and complete these sentences in your books so that each has at least 1 present participle phrase:

1. Even though it was pouring with rain, she.., wearing..........................., smiling like...
2. Repeating 'I have a dream', Martin Luther King wanted.......................
3. Apologising for............................., she rushed into the examination hall.
4. She stood on the tube platform, waving..
5. Dragging her heavy suitcase along the pavement, she..........................

Table 10.9   Participle phrases 2: completion problems

WHAT?	• Students finish these sentences so that they make sense and are accurate. • Analytical sentences focus on previously taught content
HOW?	Same method as **Participle Phrases 1 Completion Problems**
WHY?	• These are an important middle stage between studying models and independent practice, helping to ensure that students are able to apply what they have acquired. • Guided practice is essential before independent practice if success rates are to be consistently high.

Participle phrases 3: teacher demonstrate

Participle phrases act like adjectives; they describe the subject of a sentence.

(Continued)

Teacher demonstrate

a. Underline the participle phrase/s
b. Circle the subject that the phrase/s describe
c. Draw an arrow from the phrase to the subject

1. She entered the room slowly, nervously checking the faces of the people who were there; Christine knew this would be tough.
2. Using a metaphor, Agard describes Toussaint L'Ouverture as 'de beacon'.
3. The writer uses a series of harsh images, conveying a sense of horror and violence, making the reader feel unsettled.
4. Attempting to indoctrinate the animals, the pigs ask them to recite 'Four legs good, two legs bad'.
5. He says 'it was true', suggesting that he didn't expect her to be racist.
6. Shaking uncontrollably, the boy hid his face in his hands; he had been there for over an hour, rocking slowly in his chair.
7. She looked up at the arrivals board, quickly scanning the notices to find her train; after a panic stricken few second, she found it at the bottom of one of the boards.
8. Checking his watch, searching the crowd for her face, Ryan bit his lip as he realised that time was running out; she was meant to arrive in 10 minutes.

Table 10.10   Participle phrases 3: teacher demonstrate

WHAT?	• 1–8 are all further examples of present participle phrases • Examples are broader again, including semicolon sentences and sentences with multiple clauses
HOW?	• Same method as **Present Participle Phrases 1 Teacher Demonstrate**
WHY?	• Widening the range of examples helps to broaden and refine students' mental model of participle phrases and their uses • Examples will be used as analogies for students in **'Participle Phrases 3 Student Test Sequence'**

Participle phrases 3: student test sequence

a. Underline the participle phrase/s
b. Circle the subject that the phrase/s describe
c. Draw an arrow from the phrase to the subject

1. Soyinka exclaims 'it was true', suggesting that he was shocked by the landlady's prejudicial attitude.
2. The persona uses intelligent humour to mock the landlady, making her seem ignorant and ridiculous.
3. Laughing loudly, the girl couldn't control herself; she couldn't believe what had just happened.

(Continued)

4. The horse, flicking its tail across its back, seemed agitated and annoyed; as it stood next to the gate, it stomped its feet, sending little clouds of dust into the air.
5. Asking 'what business is it of mine', the persona seems indifferent to his neighbour's plight.
6. The last of the customers began to leave, carrying heavy shopping bags and heading for the station; Tia, struggling to hold her overflowing backpack, followed the crowd out of the marketplace.

Table 10.11   Participle phrases 3: student test sequence

WHAT?	• 1–6 are all *different* examples of present participle sentences
HOW?	• Same method as **Present Participles Student Test Sequence 1**
WHY?	• Like in **Participle Phrases Student Test Sequence 1**, the goal here is acquisition and accuracy.

Participle phrases 3: completion problems

a. Before writing, students should complete some orally, making sure they *say* the punctuation.
b. Copy and complete these sentences in your books so that each has at least one present participle phrase:

1. People had been queuing for hours, patiently waiting for.......................
2. Calling his soldiers 'dear friends', Henry wants to..........
3. Commanding his soldiers to 'stiffen the sinews', Henry tries to..........
4. Henry commands his soldiers to 'stiffen the sinews', conveying a sense of..........
5. She ate slowly,..

Table 10.12   Participle phrases 3: completion problems

WHAT?	• Students finish these sentences so that they make sense and are accurate. • Analytical sentences focus on previously taught content
HOW?	Same method as **Participle Phrases 1 Completion Problems**
WHY?	• These can be a useful middle stage between studying models and independent practice, helping to ensure that students are able to apply what they have acquired. • Guided practice is essential before independent practice if success rates are to be consistently high.

Participle phrases 4: teacher demonstrate

Participle phrases act like adjectives; they describe the subject of a sentence.

(Continued)

Teacher demonstrate

a. Underline the participle phrase/s
b. Circle the subject that the phrase/s describe
c. Draw an arrow from the phrase to the subject

1. Swerving through the traffic, narrowly missing a parked van, the car thundered down the street; a few seconds later, a police car turned the corner, speeding after the stolen vehicle.
2. The car thundered down the street, swerving through the traffic, narrowly missing a parked van; a few seconds later, speeding after the stolen vehicle, a police car turned the corner.
3. Imploring his men to 'imitate the action of the tiger', Henry alludes to the strength and fortitude they will need in order to gain victory.
4. Henry alludes to the strength and fortitude they will need in order to gain victory, imploring his men to 'imitate the action of the tiger'.
5. Henry asks his men to 'lend the eye a terrible aspect', conveying a sense of aggression and rage as if he wants them to steel themselves for the upcoming battle.
6. Commanding his troops to 'stiffen the sinews' and 'summon up the blood', Henry attempts to provoke a primal instinct towards violence in the men.

Table 10.13   Participle phrases 4: teacher demonstrate

WHAT?	• 1–6 are all further examples of present participle phrases
HOW?	• Same method as **Present Participle Phrases 1 Teacher Demonstrate**
WHY?	• Further examples to help broaden students' mental model of participle phrases • Examples will be used as analogies for students in **'Participle Phrases 4 Student Test Sequence'**

Participle phrases 4: student test sequence

a. Underline the participle phrase/s
b. Circle the subject that the phrase/s describe
c. Draw an arrow from the phrase to the subject

1. Opening his rousing speech by urging his men forward into a gap in the French fortifications, Henry tells them 'Once more unto the breach, dear friends.'
2. Henry tells them 'Once more unto the breach, dear friends', opening his rousing speech by urging his men forward into a gap in the French fortifications.
3. Watching his father's every move, the boy desperately wanted to help put up the tent; his father, clearly struggling with the poles, stopped to wipe the sweat off his brow, gritting his teeth in frustration.
4. The boy desperately wanted to help put up the tent, watching his father's every move; gritting his teeth in frustration, clearly struggling with the poles, his father stopped to wipe the sweat off his brow.

(Continued)

Table 10.14   Participle phrases 4: student test sequence

WHAT?	• 1–4 are all *different* examples of present participle sentences
HOW?	• Same method as **Present Participles Student Test Sequence 1**
WHY?	• Like in **Participle Phrases Student Test Sequence 1**, the goal here is acquisition and accuracy.

Participle phrases 4: prompted guided practice

Copy the italicised example sentence. Complete the others by adding a present participle phrase where the ^ is. Use different participle phrases for each sentence.

Example: The lion roared loudly ^.

The lion roared loudly, *opening its mouth and flashing its razor sharp teeth.*

1. The monster howled.^
2. The monster ^ howled.
3. ^ The monster howled.

Table 10.15   Participle phrases 4: prompted guided practice

WHAT?	• Students are prompted to add present participle phrase to sentences
HOW?	1. Students copy the italicised example sentence: this can be used as an analogy. 2. Students add in a participle phrase to each of 1–3, using a different phrase each time 3. The teacher can circulate, pointing out errors: this is also guided practice and the goal here is accuracy 4. When students finish, they can make specific checks to ensure accuracy: *does the participle phrase describe the subject? Are the commas in the right places?*
WHY?	• This guided practice demonstrates the application of backwards fading: these drills involve even less support than the completion problems as students need to do more of the thinking here. They need to generate ideas and ensure that their sentences are grammatically correct • Prompts (^) are a useful intermediary support strategy before fully independent practice

So far, in lessons 1–4, instruction has only focused on present participles. In lesson 5, past participles will be introduced. Initial teaching of these additional constructions will span three lessons so that students are more likely to develop a useful and broad mental model of them.

Tables 10.16 and 10.17 show an overview of the next few lessons.

Table 10.16 Overview of next lessons

Lesson	Teacher demonstrate	Student test	Guided practice: completion problem	Guided practice: prompted practice	Independent practice
5	Past participles	Yes	Yes		
6				Present participles	
7	Past participles	Yes	Yes		
8				Present participles	
9	Past participles	Yes	Yes		
10					Past/present participles
11					Past/present participles

Participle phrases 5: teacher demonstrate

Participle phrases act like adjectives; they describe the subject of a sentence.

Teacher demonstrate

1. Underline the participle phrase/s
2. Circle the subject that the phrase/s describe
3. Draw an arrow from the phrase to the subject

1. Glazed with barbecue sauce, the rack of ribs lay nestled next to a pile of sweet coleslaw.
2. Sumerian, thought to be the oldest written language, is around 5,000 years old.
3. Mandela, incarcerated from 1963 to 1990, dedicated his life to ending apartheid.
4. Admired for her bravery, respected for her moral stance, Rosa Parks was a key figure in the U.S. civil rights movement.

Table 10.17 Participle phrases 5: teacher demonstrate

WHAT?	• 1–4 are all examples of past participle phrases
HOW?	• Same method as **Present Participle Phrases 1 Teacher Demonstrate**
WHY?	• Introducing past participle phrases • Examples will be used as analogies for students in **'Participle Phrases 5 Student Test Sequence'**

Lessons 5–9 will now be presented without additional what/how/why explanation, and this is because the process will be the same as previous lessons. Readers should refer back to a previous teacher demonstrate, student test, guided practice: completion problem or guided practice: prompted practice for guidance.

Participle phrases 5: student test sequence

1. Underline the participle phrase/s
2. Circle the subject that the phrase/s describe
3. Draw an arrow from the phrase to the subject

(Continued)

1. Orwell, horrified by the cruelties of the Russian revolution, wrote Animal Farm to satirise authoritarian communism.
2. Thought to be the largest Empire in human history, the British Empire was in its zenith in the 1920s.
3. Ahura Mazda, worshipped by Zoroastrians, is a formless yet omnipresent deity.
4. La Paz, situated in the valley of the Andes, is the highest capital city in the world.
5. Committed to victory, Henry gives a rousing speech to his soldiers.

Participle phrases: 5 completion problems

a. Before writing, students should complete some orally, making sure they say the punctuation.
b. Copy and complete these sentences in your books so that each has at least one present participle phrase:

1. Situated in South London,..
2. The football World Cup, held every........................., is.....................
3. Shakespeare, born in.., is.......................
4. Awarded the Nobel Prize for Literature, Soyinka is...............................
5. Confused by..., Pete didn't know what to do.
6. Defeated by.., the team walked home silently, embarrassed about........

Participle phrases 6: prompted guided practice

Copy the italicised example sentence. Complete the others by adding a present participle phrase where the ^ is.

Use different participle phrases for each sentence.

Example: Henry calls his men 'you noblest English'^

Henry calls his men 'you noblest English', *giving the impression that he is proud of their bravery and honour.*

1. Henry calls his men 'dear friends'^
2. ^ Henry calls his men 'dear friends'.
3. Henry ^ calls his men 'dear friends'.

Participle phrases 7: teacher demonstrate

Participle phrases act like adjectives; they describe the subject of a sentence.

Teacher demonstrate

a. Underline the participle phrase/s
b. Circle the subject that the phrase/s describe
c. Draw an arrow from the phrase to the subject

1. Shocked by her ignorance, Soyinka exclaims 'it was real' as he realises that the UK is as racist as he had been told.
2. King Henry's speech, filled with rhetorical flourishes, is impassioned and rousing.
3. Sunk into the ground, surrounded by debris, a burnt out truck was the last reminder of the battle.
4. Absolutely drenched, the boys shivered as they waited for the bus.

Participle phrases 7: student test sequence

a. Underline the participle phrase/s
b. Circle the subject that the phrase/s describe
c. Draw an arrow from the phrase to the subject

1. Embarrassed by his sister's ridiculous behaviour, Elliot tried to hide at the back of the hall.
2. Elliot, embarrassed by his sister's ridiculous behaviour, tried to hide at the back of the hall.
3. Completely covered in graffiti, the sign could no longer be read properly.
4. Described as 'indifferent', the location could be seen as conveying a lack of compassion.

Participle phrases 7: completion problems

a. Before writing, students should complete some orally, making sure they *say* the punctuation.
b. Copy and complete these sentences in your books so that each has at least one present participle phrase:

1. Disappointed by.., she knew she had to do better next time.
2. Worried about..................................., Steve couldn't sleep properly.
3. After he had finished speaking, Shereen stared in utter disbelief, shocked by.....................................

(Continued)

4. Even though he knew he had little chance of winning, he bought a ticket anyway, convinced that......
5. Considered to be England's..., Shakespeare is studied and performed throughout the country.

Participle phrases 8: prompted guided practice

Complete sentences by adding two present participle phrases where the ^^ is.

Use different participle phrases for each sentence.

1. The old man slumped in the deckchair.^^
2. ^^The old man slumped in the deckchair.
3. The old man ^^ slumped in the deckchair.

Participle phrases 9: teacher demonstrate

Participle phrases act like adjectives; they describe the subject of a sentence.

Teacher demonstrate

a. Underline the participle phrase/s
b. Circle the subject that the phrase/s describe
c. Draw an arrow from the phrase to the subject

1. Sat at the front in order to get the best view, Anna couldn't wait for the game to begin.
2. Galangal, used in many Thai dishes, is an Asian plant of the ginger family.
3. Written by John Agard, Half Caste criticises and mocks the prejudicial opinions of those who use the phrase.
4. Ridiculed by the persona in the poem, the Landlady is ignorant and dismissive.
5. John fell to his knees, battered by the gale force wind.

Participle phrases 9: student test sequence

a. Underline the participle phrase/s
b. Circle the subject that the phrase/s describe
c. Draw an arrow from the phrase to the subject

1. Utterly exhausted, Ruby fell asleep as soon as her head hit the pillow.
2. The mirror, cracked from top to bottom, was now completely ruined; as he stared into it, Joe's face was obscured by a spider web of lines.

(Continued)

3. Printed on expensive paper, decorated with intricate designs, the wedding invitations were beautiful.
4. Neymar is the most expensive football player in the world, bought by PSG for almost £200 million.
5. Soaked from the rain, the dog shook himself dry as he entered the living room.

Participle phrases 9: completion problems

a. Before writing, students should complete some orally, making sure they say the punctuation.
b. Copy and complete these sentences in your books so that each has at least one present participle phrase:

1. Located in the Himalayas, Mt. Everest is.....................................
2. Enjoyed by children all around the world, Harry Potter is about......
3. The bible, originally written in Hebrew and Aramaic, is...........................
4. The Mona Lisa, painted by Leonardo Da Vinci, is...............................

INDEPENDENT PRACTICE

In this sequence, lesson 10 is the first time students are asked to practice independently. However, even at this stage, they are given a model to use as an analogy to help them complete their independent sentences, harnessing the alternation strategy from Chapter 4.

Participle phrases 10: independent practice

Write three participle phrase sentences (start/middle/end). Each sentence must be *different* and have a *different* participle phrase.

Example: Topic: A man running for a bus.

a. *Gripping his umbrella tightly*, Darren ran.
b. Darren, *waving his arm frantically in the air*, sped down the pavement towards the bus.
c. Darren knew he had to get that bus and ran as fast as he could, *dodging pedestrians and shouting for them to get out of the way.*

1. A football match
2. A busy market

Participle phrases 11: independent practice

Write three participle phrase sentences (start/middle/end). Each sentence must be *different* and have a *different* participle phrase.

Example: Topic: A protest.

a. *Shouting at the police*, a woman stood in the middle of the street holding a placard.
b. The police car, *surrounded by protesters*, was completely stuck.
c. The crowd chanted rhythmically, *holding signs above their heads.*

1. The school playground at break time
2. An angry dog

Lessons 12 and 13 ask students to generate and write sentences with no support whatsoever. These could be seen as the first real test of independent application of what has been taught. At this point, teachers could begin to consider student output as evidence of learning rather than performance.

Participle phrases 12: independent practice

Write three participle phrase sentences (start/middle/end) inspired by the picture.

Each sentence must be different and have a different participle phrase.

Participle phrases 13: independent practice

How is Boxer presented in this extract?

To see him toiling up the slope inch by inch, his breath coming fast, the tips of his hoofs clawing at the ground, and his great sides matted with sweat, filled everyone with admiration.

Write three *different* participle phrase sentences about Boxer, each containing a quotation.

Table 10.18   Participle phrases 12 and 13: independent practice

WHAT?	• Fully independent practice of descriptive/analytical sentences.
HOW?	• Teacher displays a picture for students to describe or provides short extract to respond to.
WHY?	• Without scaffolding, prompts or models to aid them, students will now have to create accurate constructions from memory in order to perform well. • This is the first real test that there has been *'a change in long-term memory'* and therefore that students have learned what we have taught them.

Now that you have seen an explained example sequence, if you turn back to the table of principles and implications at the start of this chapter (see Table 10.2), it should be clear how the sequence incorporates these ideas.

LATER LESSONS: WIDER APPLICATION

These 13 lessons are, however, just the beginning. Later lessons should ask students to continue practicing these sentence forms across many more lessons in increasingly wider contexts, moving from sentence drills to paragraphs and then finally as part of unsupported extended writing. In order to prevent these drills from resulting in 'splinter skills', success criteria or checklists should initially be used in wider application tasks as reminders for students to apply what they have learned to their extended writing (Archer and Hughes, 2011, p. 20).

EXAMPLE SEQUENCE 2: NOUN APPOSITIVES

Here is a second example of an instructional sequence. It teaches noun appositive phrases, another high utility construction that students can use across all types of writing that are typically taught at secondary school. The approach taken by both teachers and students would be very similar to the participle phrases sequence and the tasks move through the same five categories of activity: teacher demonstration, student test sequence, completion problems, prompted guided practice and independent practice. Table 10.19 gives an overview of each of these five stages:

Table 10.19 Summary of different stages in a sequence

Stage	Instructional goal	Elements that help ensure success
Teacher demonstrate	1. Build students' mental model of what they are learning 2. Acquisition	1. Examples should match the intended final application and a sufficiently broad range should be presented to students 2. Clear labelling and communication to prevent confusion and draw attention to function and links between components 3. Massed questioning (choral response)
Student test	Acquisition/accuracy	1. Massed practice and instant choral feedback
Guided practice: completion problems	Accuracy	1. Massed practice and specific feedback checks
Guided practice: prompted practice	Accuracy/fluency	1. Distributed practice
Independent practice	Fluency/retention/ generalisation	1. Distributed practice 2. Increasingly wider context of practice: sentences-paragraphs-extended writing 3. Sufficient variation in practice content to ensure flexible knowledge is built

Table 10.20 provides an overview of the appositives sequence.

Table 10.20 Overview of appositives sequence

Stage	Lesson number													
Stage	1	2	3	4	5	6	7	8	9	10	11	12	13	14
Teacher demonstrate	Yes	Yes												
Student test	Yes	Yes												
Guided practice: completion problems	Yes	Yes	Yes											
Guided practice: prompted practice					Yes	Yes	Yes	Yes	Yes					
Independent practice										Yes	Yes	Yes	Yes	Yes	Yes

Appositives 1: teacher demonstrate

1. The Romantics, a group of writers who shared a desire for liberty, wrote poems that denounced exploitation.
2. A group of writers who shared a desire for liberty, the Romantics wrote poems that denounced exploitation.
3. Blake was part of the Romantic movement, a group of writers who shared a desire for liberty.
4. Rousseau declared that 'Man is born free, and everywhere he is in chains', a statement that demonstrates his concern about societal oppression.
5. The landlady, a racist woman who can only ask 'HOW DARK?' is ignorant and prejudicial.
6. One of the most famous enlightenment figures, Rousseau declared that 'Man is born free, and everywhere he is in chains'.

This is what the teacher should do (Figure 10.2):

1) The Romantics, a group of writers who shared a desire for liberty, wrote poems that denounced exploitation.

2) A group of writers who shared a desire for liberty, the Romantics wrote poems that denounced exploitation.

3) Blake was part of the Romantic movement, a group of writers who shared a desire for liberty.

Figure 10.2 Examples of teacher labelling

Appositives 1: student test sequence

1. The Tyger, a poem that explores the idea of the sublime, was written by William Blake.
2. The landlady curtly asks 'how dark?' a question that shows her to be racist, prejudicial and deeply ignorant.
3. Toussaint Louverture, a slave leader described by Agard as 'de beacon', symbolises hope and courage.
4. A poem that explores the idea of the sublime, The Tyger is one of Blake's most famous works.
5. Many children worked long hours during the industrial revolution, a time when factories and machines replaced small scale manufacturing.
6. A defiant character who considered death to be a 'glory', Antigone refused to obey her tyrannical uncle.

Appositives 1: completion problems

a. Students to complete orally
b. Copy and complete these sentences in your books

1. The Romantics, poets who.., are often seen as revolutionaries and rebels.
2. A play that explores......................................., Antigone is a classic work of Greek tragedy.
3. John Agard is from Guyana, a country...
4. Agard denounces the phrase 'Half-Caste', a derogatory phrase that..........
5. An allegory of..................................., Animal Farm satirises tyranny and the abuse of power.
6. Creon, a tyrannical leader who..., is infuriated when Antigone disobeys his proclamation.

Appositives 2: teacher demonstrate

1. He looked at his watch, an antique time-piece that his grandfather had given him.
2. Before he died, Old Major gave a rousing speech, a polemic that blamed 'man' for the suffering on the farm.
3. King Henry calls his soldiers a 'band of brothers', a metaphor that demonstrates his commitment to his men.
4. A stubborn man who refuses to 'yield', Creon doesn't realise that he needs to be flexible.

Appositives 2: student test sequence

1. Polynices is described as being 'like an eagle screaming', a simile that makes him seem predatory and belligerent.
2. The Chimney Sweep, a poignant dramatic monologue, describes the suffering of a child labourer.
3. Napolean, a tyrant, terrorises the other animals with his attack dogs.

Appositives 2: completion problems

a. Students to complete orally
b. Copy and complete these sentences in your books

1. Lewisham, ...,
   is in South London.
2. Although I was exhausted by the end, I completed the marathon,..........
3. Napolean declares that 'all animals are equal, but some are more equal than others', a.............statement that.........
4. Soyinka, a......................................., was the first African to win the Nobel Prize for literature.
5. Abuja is the capital city of Nigeria, ...
6. When describing how he attacked Thebes, the chorus describe Polynices as having a 'vast maw gaping', a ..... that makes him seem....................

Appositives 3: completion problems

a. Students complete orally
b. Copy and complete these sentences in your books

1. Boxer repeats 'I will work harder', a statement that.......
2. The Tyger is described as 'burning bright', a metaphor that....
3. Agard refers to the people who educated him as 'Dem', a vernacular word that....
4. Soyinka writes 'Red booth. Red pillar box', a description that...

Appositives 4: prompted guided practice

Copy the example. Complete the others by adding in an appositive where the ^ is.

Example: Blake ^ denounces suffering and corruption in London, his indignant poem.

(Continued)

Blake, *a Romantic poet who stood up for the marginalized,* denounces suffering and corruption in London, his indignant poem.

1. Blake denounces suffering and corruption in London. ^
2. He walked towards the building. ^
3. The Landlady asks 'how dark?' ^
4. The chimney sweep is described as a 'little black thing' ^

Appositives 5: prompted guided practice

Copy the example. Complete the others by adding in an appositive where the ^ is.

Example: Island Man wakes up to 'dull Northern Circular roar' ^

Island Man wakes up to 'dull Northern Circular roar', *a metaphor that hints at the oppressive monotony of city life*

1. His head 'curled like a lamb's back' ^
2. In the dream sequence, the boys are 'naked and white'. ^
3. Tom sees 'coffins of black' ^
4. Chimney sweeps ^ worked in horrible and dangerous conditions.

Appositives 6: prompted guided practice

Copy the example. Complete the others by adding in an appositive where the ^ is.

Example: When she finally got home, her shoes ^ were covered in mud from the fields.

When she finally got home, her shoes, *brand new trainers that her mother had bought her,* were covered in mud from the fields.

1. He loved his new jacket ^
2. The chimney sweeps 'shine in the sun' ^
3. ^ Blake was horrified by the oppression of the poor.
4. ^ December had been colder than usual.

Appositives 7: prompted guided practice

Copy the example. Complete the others by adding in an appositive where the ^ is.

Example: Caesar is described as being 'like a colossus' ^

(Continued)

Caesar is described as being 'like a colossus', *a simile that not only conveys the extend of his power and authority but also demonstrates his arrogant, pompous and supercilious nature.*

1. Caesar is described as having 'huge legs'. ^
2. Brutus ^ led the conspiracy to assassinate Caesar.
3. Flavius exclaims 'let no images be hung with Caesar's trophies.' ^
4. Rome ^ is in central Italy.
5. ^ Russia spans eleven time zones and over 9,000 km.

Appositives 8: prompted guided practice

Copy the example. Complete the others by adding in an appositive where the ^ is.

Example: Concerned about Caesar's burgeoning power, Flavius asks 'who else would soar above the view of men and keep us all in servile fearfulness'. ^

Concerned about Caesar's burgeoning power, Flavius asks 'who else would soar above the view of men and keep us all in servile fearfulness', *a rhetorical question that points to Caesar's despotic tendencies.*

1. Shakespeare wrote 154 sonnets.^
2. Cassius wants Brutus to realise that Caesar ^ is no 'god'.
3. Attempting to persuade Brutus that Caesar is no 'god', Cassius explains that Caesar has a 'feeble temper' ^
4. The mountain ^ towered over them, making them feel insignificant and vulnerable.

Appositives 9: independent practice

Write three appositive sentences (start/middle/end) for each topic.

Example: Topic: London.

a. *The capital of England*, London is a bustling metropolis.
b. London, *a multicultural city*, is home to a diverse range of people.
c. London is a multicultural city, *a diverse place where many languages are spoken.*

1. Topic: Shakespeare.
2. Topic: Caesar

Appositives 10: independent practice

Write three appositive sentences (start/middle/end) for each topic.

Example: topic: climate change.

a. *The most pressing issue of our time*, climate change should be the priority of every government.
b. Coal and gas, *fossil fuels that pollute and cause climate change*, should be banned.
c. Governments need to act quickly regarding climate change, *the biggest risk that humanity has ever encountered*.

1. Topic: Smoking should be banned
2. Topic: Describe a children's birthday party

Appositives 11: independent practice

Write three appositive sentences (start/middle/end) for each topic.

1. Topic: The Romantics
2. Topic: Animal Farm

Appositives 12: independent practice

Write three appositive sentences (start/middle/end) for each topic.

1. Topic: Brutus
2. Topic: Describe a busy supermarket

Appositives 13: independent practice

Write three appositive sentences (start/middle/end) for each topic.

1. Topic: Caesar at the start of the play
2. Topic: Cassius at the start of the play

Appositives 14: independent practice

Write three appositive sentences (start/middle/end) for each topic.

1. Topic: describe two old people sitting in a park
2. Topic: religion is a good/bad thing

Making instructional sequences like this should also involve a process of constant evaluation: teachers should be paying close attention to whether students perform accurately at each stage. If, upon moving to completion problems, students commonly make errors, perhaps you need to spend longer on the teacher demonstrate stage. Similarly, if students struggle with independent practice, perhaps the sequence requires a greater amount of guided practice.

Although both of the example sequences focus on teaching sentence constructions, multi-lesson instructional sequences can also be used for teaching essay introductions and paragraph writing.

SUMMARY

- Instructional sequences that span multiple lessons can be an efficient method of teaching new writing skills.
- Although the goal of instructional sequences is always flexible knowledge that students are able to independently apply to the widest range of relevant contexts, initial instruction will be restrictive, repetitive and guided, allowing students to build accuracy and fluency.
- Effective sequences will result in consistently high success rates, moving students through the stages of the instructional hierarchy-beginning with acquisition, accuracy and fluency and moving towards generalisation and adaptation.

REFERENCES

Archer, A. L., & Hughes, C. H. (2011). *Explicit instruction: Effective and efficient teaching.* New York, NY: Guildford Press.

Lemov, D. (2010). *Teach like a champion.* San Francisco, CA: Jossey Bass.

11

ANALYTICAL COMPONENTS

In this chapter, we will explore

- Embedding evidence
- Tentative language
- Zooming in on words
- Multiple interpretations
- Combining Evidence and building arguments

INTRODUCTION

This chapter will explain how teaching specific components can help students to improve their analytical writing. It will explore 5 different, high-utility approaches that can be combined, developed and adapted in order to produce extended and sophisticated responses to texts.

ANALYTICAL WRITING: A BRIEF OVERVIEW

Writing analytically in response to texts is a complex skill which needs to be broken down, made explicit and demystified for students. When students write about texts, we usually want them to write about three main areas:

1. What the author is saying
2. How they are saying it
3. Why they are saying it

These three foci, often known as 'what/how/why' can be really useful to help students understand what they are supposed to write about in their essays. While what/how/why describes the typical content of analytical writing, we can teach specific analytical components that exemplify the form of the writing, helping students to express their ideas with precision and sophistication.

There are many different existing approaches to teaching analytical writing such as PEE/PEEL/PETAL. While these can be helpful for complete novices, reminding students to include evidence before explaining their selection, such frameworks often become stultifying and restrictive, resulting in clunky, predictable and overly formulaic paragraphs. Invariably, these approaches tend to advocate fixed orders, placing evidence in the middle, one of the problematic inferences being that each train of thought contains only one quotation: interesting analytical writing, however, does not follow a predictable, sequential order, nor does each point rely upon only one piece of evidence. A further problem with such approaches is that they can effectively prevent students from learning how to embed quotations, due to the unnatural scaffolding of sentence stems like 'My evidence for this is...'.

Here is an example of PEE, a common way to teach analytical writing:

Point: Romeo seems despondent and morose
Evidence: My evidence for this is 'artificial night'
Explanation: This tells me he is isolating himself and does not want to see anyone
    because Rosaline has rejected him.

I'm sure you would want your students to quickly reach a level of competence where they no longer need such a structure and as a result, they will then have to *unlearn* how to write within the confines of such a structure and move towards crafting more fluid and skilful analysis. As a result, teaching such an approach to students seems inefficient and limiting. Instead of focusing on an approach that is fixed at the paragraph level, we can teach individual analytical skills which students can combine in different ways *within* paragraphs. Such an approach provides students with a wider range of expression, allowing them to make choices as to the form, style and focus of their analysis and therefore resulting in far more sophisticated writing.

Here are the skills:

1. Embedding evidence
2. Tentative language
3. Zoom in
4. Multiple interpretations
5. Evidence in explanation

SKILL 1: EMBEDDING EVIDENCE

WHY TEACH IT?

Analytical writing usually involves using quotations from the text that is being analysed: students need to select an apt word or phrase, embed it into their own writing and then explore the what/how/why behind the words that they have chosen to focus on. If their long-term memories contain useful mental models of embedding, they will be able to retrieve and apply these when writing. If students can accurately and fluently (and therefore effortlessly) embed evidence into their writing, they will be able to devote more attention to developing their analysis instead of getting stuck as a result of their laborious transcription skills. Not only that, but essays with embedded evidence are often much easier to read, the fluid synthesis of evidence allowing for a greater range of analytical approaches as a result of fewer breaks, interruptions or clunky formatting. Because of this, teaching students to embed is really important and it is worth spending a lot of time on it when they begin to learn to write analytically.

WHAT TO TEACH?

As there are innumerable ways to embed evidence into writing, we should begin by teaching the simplest and highest utility approaches to students so they can quickly acquire and begin to apply them in their writing. Additionally, the constructions should be generalisable so that they can be applied and adapted to the widest possible range of relevant contexts. Instead of telling students to use repetitive and non-adaptable sentence stems like 'My evidence for this.../a quotation that supports this idea is...', we can create instructional sequences that teach to the general case. We don't want essays filled with the exact same sentence stem over and over again; we want students who have understood the deep structure of different approaches to embedding so that they can adapt them accordingly: we are aiming for flexible knowledge that they can transfer to different texts or writing tasks.

Table 11.1 shows some generalisable embedding structures that would be useful to teach to students when they begin writing analytically.

You will notice that several of these use present participle constructions. If you think back to Chapter 8 where we explored ideas from Direct Instruction, you will remember that two core elements of a well-designed curriculum is that 'skills and knowledge do not go away' (Engelmann, 2017, p. 14) and that we should teach 'generalisable strategies' (Watkins and Slocum, 2003). These embedding structures are generalisable as well as providing students with further practice using participle phrases, exactly like how the participle phrase instructional sequence in the previous chapter provided students with further practice in embedding.

Table 11.1   Embedding structures

Sub-category	Example
BASIC 1 **Subject+Verb+Quote** Character says... Writer says... It says...	• Agard writes 'blind me to my own identity', meaning... • Agard repeats 'dem tell me' because... • Boxer says, 'I will work harder', conveying his...
BASIC 2 **Subject+Verb+Quote** Further examples	• The poem ends with the line 'Another London day', giving an impression of... • Island man wakes up 'groggily' as if he is... • The landlady's accent is 'clinical'
Phrase/Word/Technique Zooming in/technique	• The phrase 'half-caste human being' suggests that Agard feels... • The word 'indifferent' makes the location seem... • The simile 'limbo like me' suggests that...
Passive	• The landlady is described as 'rancid', meaning... • He is confronted with 'ill-mannered silence' which seems... • The landlady is described as having 'good-breeding' as if... • The location is described as being 'indifferent', conveying a sense of...

HOW TO TEACH EMBEDDING

We want students to be able to effortlessly and automatically embed quotations in their wider writing. If we use a multi-lesson instructional sequence based upon similar principles to those in the last chapter, we can ensure that students develop accurate and flexible mental models that can be applied to a good range of texts.

Table 11.2 summarises what a useful embedding sequence may contain.

Table 11.2 Summary of different stages in a sequence

Stage	Instructional goal	Elements that help ensure success
Teacher demonstrate	1. Build students' mental model of what they are learning 2. Acquisition	1. Useful definition for students to use 2. Examples should match the intended later application and a sufficiently broad range should be presented to students 3. Non-examples are minimally different to examples and are labelled differently 4. Clear labelling and communication to prevent confusion and draw attention to function and links between components 5. Massed questioning (choral response)
Student test	Acquisition/accuracy	1. Massed practice and instant choral feedback
Guided practice: pre-selected quotations	Accuracy/retention	1. Evidence already chosen so students can focus on practicing skill of embedding 2. Spoken models given to further support students 3. Massed practice and specific feedback checks 4. Students have to choose which structures to apply to each quotation
Independent practice	Fluency/retention/ generalisation	1. Distributed Practice 2. Increasingly wider context of practice: sentences–paragraphs–extended writing 3. Sufficient variation in practice content to ensure flexible knowledge is built

Table 11.3 shows an overview of a possible sequence.

Table 11.3 Embedding sequence: a summary

Lesson	Teacher demonstrate	Student test	Guided practice: pre-selected quotations	Independent practice
1	Basic 1	Basic 1		
2	Basic 1	Basic 1		
3			Basic 1	
4	Basic 2 Phrase/Word/Technique	Basic 1 Basic 2 Phrase/Word/Technique		
5			Basic 1	
6	Basic 2 Phrase/Word/Technique	Basic 2 Phrase/Word/Technique		

Table 11.3   Embedding sequence: a summary *(Continued)*

Lesson	Teacher demonstrate	Student test	Guided practice: pre-selected quotations	Independent practice
7			Basic 2	
8	Passive	Basic 2 Phrase/Word/ Technique Passive		
9			Basic 1 Basic 2	
10	Passive	Basic 2 Phrase/Word/ Technique Passive		
11			Basic 1 Basic 2 Phrase/Word/ Technique	
12	Additional Examples of each sub-category	Basic 2 Phrase/Word/ Technique Passive		
13–19			Basic 1 Basic 2 Phrase/Word/ Technique Passive	

Like with the sequences in Chapter 10, each 'lesson' here is not an entire lesson. Each 'teacher demonstrate' task and 'student test' task may take 15 minutes or so and each 'guided practice' task may take around ten minutes.

You will notice that there is no independent practice in this initial sequence. Independent practice would follow these lessons and students should be expected (and initially reminded through specific success criteria or prompts) to apply these embedding constructions in extended writing.

Embedding 1: teacher demonstrate

If a quotation is embedded, the sentence makes sense.

1. Lewis writes 'you set aside race, class, age, language and nationality', meaning that he is proud of how people have united.
2. Lewis write 'you set aside race, class, age, language and nationality', meaning that he is proud of how people have united.
3. He 'had to see and feel it', meaning he wanted to be a part of the movement.
4. He 'to see and feel it', meaning he wanted to be a part of the movement.
5. 'Truth is still marching on', meaning that people are still fighting for their rights.

(Continued)

6. It says the 'truth is still marching on', meaning that people are still fighting for their rights.
7. Lewis 'fear constrained us like an imaginary prison', suggesting that even though he was free, he felt like he was trapped.
8. He says that 'fear constrained us like an imaginary prison', suggesting that even though he was free, he felt like he was trapped.
9. Repeat 'you must', suggesting that it is really important that people take action.
10. He repeats 'you must', suggesting that it is really important that people take action.

Table 11.4   Embedding 1: teacher demonstrate

WHAT?	• Examples of basic embedding structures • Minimally different non-examples of basic embedding structures • Non-examples that are sentences which start with a quotation (common error for novices)
HOW?	1. Class reads definition out loud 2. Teacher reads sentence 1, then says 'This quotation is embedded, how do I know? Because the sentence makes sense' 3. Teacher reads sentence 2, then says 'This quotation is *not* embedded, how do I know? Because the sentence *does not* make sense' 4. Teacher reads sentence 3, then says 'This quotation is embedded, how do I know?' Students then chorally respond with 'Because the sentence makes sense' 5. Teacher repeats step 4 for all other sentences
WHY?	• Clear instructions signal the difference between examples and non-examples • Choral response increases the likelihood that everyone thinks about the content • Non-examples are minimally different to examples, reinforcing the meaning of 'the sentence makes sense' part of the definition and helping students to build an accurate mental model of what is being taught • Skills and knowledge do not go away: the sentences focus on taught content, providing further opportunities for students to think about important content • Examples will be used as analogies for students in **'Embedding 1 Student Test Sequence'**

Embedding 1: Student test sequence

1. Lewis say 'ordinary people with extraordinary vision can redeem the soul of America', meaning that everyone can make a difference as long as they are determined.
2. He says 'it is your turn to let freedom ring', meaning he wants young people to stand up and make a difference.
3. He repeat 'you', suggest he is directly talking to the reader which makes it seem powerful and persuasive.

(Continued)

4. He wants 'respect for human dignity', meaning that everyone should be treated with compassion.
5. Lewis likes 'good trouble', meaning he thinks people should be prepared to disrupt and challenge those who exploit and oppress others.
6. He 'let the spirit of peace and the power of everlasting love be your guide', suggesting a sense of reverence and making his message seem even more important.
7. He 'Now it is your turn', meaning he wants people to stand up for their rights.
8. He repeats 'must', that it is crucial that people get involved and make a stand.
9. Lewis explains 'Democracy is not a state, it is an act', meaning that people need to do something if they are to defend their rights and make the world a better place.

Table 11.5 Embedding 1: student test sequence

WHAT?	• 1–9 are all *different* examples of the same sub-category (**Basic 1**) of embedding structures
HOW?	1. Students read sentences individually in silence. For each one, they add a tick if it is embedded or a cross if it is not embedded.
	2. When all students have finished, feedback can be given chorally:
	Teacher: 'Is sentence 1 embedded?' Students: 'No' Teacher: 'How do you know?' Students: 'Because the sentence doesn't make sense' Teacher: 'Who can correct sentence 1?' Teacher then selects a student to correct it Selected Student: 'It should be 'Lewis SAYS 'ordinary people. . .'
	3. This process should be repeated for each sentence.
	4. If the sentence is incorrect, all students should correct theirs, using the selected student's correction.
	5. There will often be more than one way to correct sentences.
	6. *If it is clear that students are making errors at any point, the teacher should stop and correct them.*
WHY?	• Because it tests *different* examples, the student test sequence tests if students have acquired what they are being taught and that they are performing accurately.
	• Choral feedback is efficient and allows teachers to focus on accuracy, instantly correcting students who have made errors.
	• Choral feedback further reinforces the meaning of 'the sentence makes sense' part of the definition, helping students to build an accurate mental model of what is being taught.

Lesson 2 would look very similar to lesson 1, albeit with different examples in order to broaden and refine students' mental model of these embedding structures. Let us now look at lesson 3:

Embedding 3: guided practice pre-selected quotations

Embed these quotations properly: for each one, you need to include at least one interpretation.

off to a lengthy absence

one neat sack for a stainless record

so long they don't take the yam from my savouring mouth

stuffed him

Table 11.6   Embedding 3: guided practice pre-selected quotations

WHAT?	• All four preselected quotations fit structures from **Basic 1** sub category

HOW?	1. Teacher should begin by giving lots of oral examples, saying the punctuation so that accuracy is reinforced:
	  a. The poet writes 'off to a lengthy absence', meaning that Danladi has been kidnapped by the soldiers.
	  b. The soldiers QUOTE MARKS stuffed him QUOTE MARKS into a jeep COMMA suggesting he was physically abused. It seems sinister and oppressive.
	2. Students can give some spoken examples too.
	3. Students should then embed each quotation into a sentence in their books, adding at least one interpretation to each one.
	4. The teacher can circulate, pointing out errors: this is guided practice and the goal here is accuracy.
	5. When students finish, they can make specific checks to ensure accuracy: 'are there quotation marks around the quotation? No sentence should begin with a quotation'.

WHY?	• Pre-Selecting quotations means students can focus on embedding. • Further spoken examples help support weaker students. • Guided practice is essential before independent practice if success rates are to be consistently high. • There are many ways to embed these quotations: even at this early stage, students are practising selecting the constructions that they will use.

If you look back to Table 11.3 that summarises this sequence, you will see that the content within 'Guided Practice: Pre-Selected Quotations' task gradually expands as the sequence continues. At the beginning, students are only selecting structures from one sub-category (Basic 1). As the sequence progresses, students are asked to choose and use embedding structures from an increasingly longer list of categories. The fact that students practice choosing is really important as this is one of the sub-skills within embedding: in later years, when students have developed in expertise, they will be able to effortlessly choose from a wide range of embedding structures when writing analytically. For them to do so, however, they need to build accurate and well organised mental models of what embedding can look like and multi-lesson instructional sequences are one way to efficiently do this.

Although there are many other possible ways to embed, Table 11.7 shows some other generalisable embedding structures, all of which could be taught through a similar method:

Table 11.7 Further examples of embedding structures

Sub-category	Example
2 Objects	• He calls the people who taught him 'dem' because... • He describes Toussaint as 'de Beacon', meaning • He describes the people who taught him as 'dem', conveying his
2 Verb chain	• Antigone *thinks* that Creon *is* a 'fool' because... • Agard *says* that his education *affected* his 'identity' because... • Agard *explains* that his teachers *told* him 'bout Dick Whittington', hinting at...
Explain first	• The poet has experienced racism before, so he says 'I hate a wasted journey' • The landlady seems prejudicial because she asks 'HOW DARK?' • The landlady thinks that Soyinka is unintelligent, but she asks 'ARE YOU LIGHT OR VERY DARK', demonstrating...
Despite	• Despite her 'pressurised good-breeding', she seems...
Phrase level embedding	• Exclaiming 'I could not say Amen', Macbeth seems... • A 'practical man of business', Birling seems to... • Lord Capulet is furious and domineering, enraged by Juliet's 'chop logic' as she attempts to defy his commands.

SKILL 2: TENTATIVE LANGUAGE

WHY TEACH IT?

Studying literature at a sophisticated level requires a reader to recognise that there is a plurality of acceptable interpretations available. Literary analysis often has a tentative and exploratory tone: interpretations are inherently subjective and tentative language implicitly demonstrates that a line of argument is one of many and certainly not definitive.

WHAT TO TEACH?

Although there are many ways to create a tentative tone, here are some useful structures to teach:

1. Perhaps
2. It is as if/as if
3. It could hint at/hinting at
4. Seems
5. It could suggest/suggesting
6. ... gives the impression/giving the impression
7. ... appears to be

HOW TO TEACH TENTATIVE LANGUAGE?

EARLY INSTRUCTION

a. **Initial examples**

Students should regularly read models that contain the structures they will be expected to use: these could be in model paragraphs or example sentences in vocabulary tables as explained in Chapter 5. Teachers can begin by high-lighting and drawing attention to tentative language within these worked examples.

Write model sentences that contain tentative language; ask students to copy and label.

- Henry commands his men to 'imitate the actions of the tiger'. *It's as if* he wants them to be vicious, aggressive and brutal.
- Henry commands his men to 'imitate the actions of the tiger'. *Perhaps* he is asking them to be predatory and violent.
- Henry commands his men to 'imitate the actions of the tiger' which *could suggest* that he wants them to be dominant in battle like a predator.

b. **Spoken practice**

Ask them to complete sentences *orally*, using the same structures that you used in the models above. Keeping the same sentence structure here is crucial, allowing students to use them as analogies.

- Henry asks his men to 'disguise fair nature with hard-favour'd rage'.

c. **Distributed retrieval practice**

Student could also be asked to complete retrieval practice of the specific tentative constructions, perhaps giving them clues to aid recall:

1. Pe..................
2. It is ....
3. It c............. h.......... at
4. s...........ms
5. It c........................... suggest
6. give the im........................
7. ap.............. to be

d. **Editing paragraphs**

Write a short paragraph with *no tentative* language. Under the visualiser, change the first few sentences to *tentative* and then ask them to do ones that are italicised.

Henry gives a rousing speech to his men, commanding them to 'stiffen the sinews'. ~~He wants them~~ **It is as if he wants them** to toughen up and steel themselves for battle. He orders them to 'summon up the blood' ~~which means~~ **which could suggest** he wants them to be impassioned and prepared. He knows that the odds are against them and that the battle will be arduous and dangerous. He commands them to 'set the teeth'. *This means that* he wants them to look menacing and threatening. *This is because* he wants them to terrify the enemy.

WIDER APPLICATION

- At first, include 'tentative language' as a success criteria in their paragraphs. Eventually, take this success criteria out.
- Similarly, include 'tentative language' as a specific check when they read through their work; again, remove this check when it is no longer needed.

SKILL 3: ZOOM IN

WHY TEACH IT?

Literary analysis requires students to respond to both the bigger picture and the finer details within a text: sophisticated analytical writing will contain a well-balanced mixture of the wider overarching ideas-perhaps thematic concerns or authorial intention – and a 'fine-grained' analysis of salient textual evidence. If students are able to identify and interpret a significant word, phrase or technique, then this skill can help to develop the precision of their writing. Although more general textual references can also be effective, zooming in on a noteworthy word or two helps students to be specific, ensuring that their interpretations are firmly based upon evidence from the text.

With regular practice in zooming in, students become more economical and efficient with how they use their quotations as they are conditioned into moving beyond merely making a cursory remark and then hastily moving on to the next piece of evidence, and instead ensuring that they analyse each significant word or phrase in turn.

WHAT TO TEACH?

In the initial stages of instruction, students could be taught to respond to a piece of evidence and then zoom in on one or two significant words or phrases within it. Here is an example:

Creon angrily commands 'never let some woman triumph over us' showing his fury towards Antigone because of her defiance. *The phrase 'some woman'* conveys his scathing and dismissive attitude towards his niece.

HOW TO TEACH ZOOM IN

Show a model to the class:

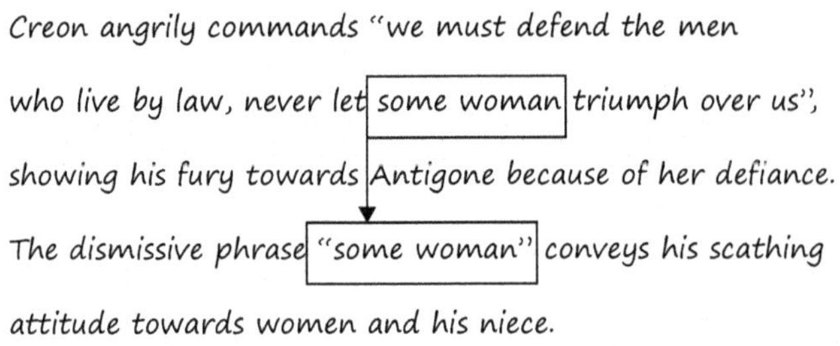

Creon angrily commands "we must defend the men

who live by law, never let some woman triumph over us",

showing his fury towards Antigone because of her defiance.

The dismissive phrase "some woman" conveys his scathing

attitude towards women and his niece.

Figure 11.1   Example of a model

The teacher can then label the example, ensuring that there is a prompt that links the zoomed in part to the original quotation. The teacher can then ask questions about it:

- Why have I used the word 'command' here?
- What does 'phrase' mean? (Low attainers may need further practice on the difference between 'word' and 'phrase' and this can be taught through a series of examples and a test sequence much like the one described below in LESSON 1: Step Four.)
- What have I zoomed in on? How do you know?

LESSON 1: STEP TWO

Present a second, minimally different example under the visualiser (Figure 11.2).

If you think back to Chapter 8, the intention here is to ensure that all irrelevant aspects of the example are held constant. By carefully manipulating only the relevant aspects – in this case the part of the evidence that is being zoomed in upon – students are less likely to become confused. This second example deliberately zooms in on a word rather than a phrase: students should be presented with examples that cover the full range of the concept that is being taught and with 'Zoom In', students need to be able to zoom in on phrases as well as words.

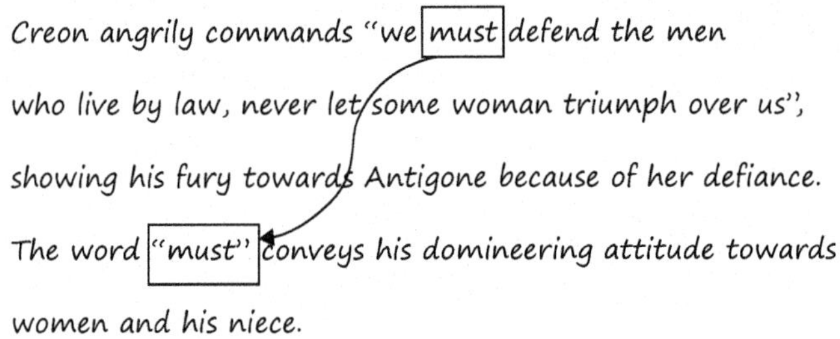

Creon angrily commands "we must defend the men

who live by law, never let some woman triumph over us",

showing his fury towards Antigone because of her defiance.

The word "must" conveys his domineering attitude towards

women and his niece.

Figure 11.2   A different example

The teacher can then ask questions about the second example:

- 'What does 'obstinate' mean?' This is a retrieval practice question
- 'What have I zoomed in on? How do you know?'

LESSON 1: STEP THREE

Present a third, minimally different example under the visualiser (Figure 11.3).

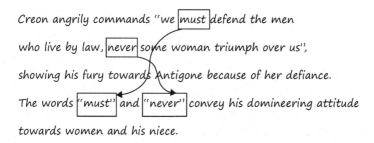

Creon angrily commands "we must defend the men
who live by law, never some woman triumph over us",
showing his fury towards Antigone because of her defiance.
The words "must" and "never" convey his domineering attitude
towards women and his niece.

Figure 11.3   Example of zooming in

This third example contains two separate examples of zooming in, demonstrating how students can combine evidence in their responses. Looking for patterns and links between language and pieces of evidence – the two examples here both conveying a sense of resolve and certainty – is a key skill when analysing a text.

The teacher can then ask questions about the third example:

- 'What does 'domineering' mean?' This is a retrieval practice question
- 'What have I zoomed in on? How do you know?'
- 'How are 'must' and 'never' similar?'

Presenting three minimally different examples allows students to begin to see the breadth of the skill of 'zooming in'. While there are certainly other variants of this concept, the range presented here gives a good starting point.

LESSON 1: STEP FOUR

NON-EXAMPLES. As we saw in Chapter 8, when teaching through examples, it is often necessary to demonstrate the limits of the concept by presenting non-examples that are minimally different. One possible misconception for very low attaining students is that they will make poor choices as to which words or phrases to zoom in upon. Staying with the same example paragraph, the teacher can then present a sequence of examples and non-examples.

Creon angrily commands 'We must defend *the* men who live by law, never let some woman triumph over us.'

Teacher: 'Can I Zoom in on this word? No. How do I know? Because there is *nothing interesting* to say about it.'

Creon angrily commands 'We must defend the men who live by law, never let some woman *triumph over* us.'

Teacher: 'Can I Zoom in on this phrase? Yes. How do I know? Because I *can* say something interesting about it.'

The teacher should stress the italicised words here to make clear the difference between the Yes and No response.

Creon angrily commands 'We must defend the men *who* live by law, never let some woman triumph over us.'

Teacher: 'Your turn: Can I Zoom in on this word?'

Students: 'No.'

Teacher: 'How do I know?'

Students: 'Because there is *nothing interesting* to say about it.'

Creon angrily commands 'We must defend the men who live *by* law, never let some woman triumph over us.'

Teacher: 'Your turn: Can I Zoom in on this word?'

Students: 'No.'

Teacher: 'How do I know?'

Students: 'Because there is *nothing interesting* to say about it.'

Creon angrily commands 'We must *defend the men* who live by law, never let some woman triumph over us.'

Teacher: 'Your turn: Can I Zoom in on this phrase?'

Students: 'Yes.'

Teacher: 'How do I know?'

Students: 'Because I *can* say something interesting about it.'

Creon angrily commands 'We must defend the men *who live* by law, never let some woman triumph over us.'

Teacher: 'Your turn: Can I Zoom in on this phrase?'

Students: 'No.'

Teacher: 'How do I know?'

Students: 'Because there is nothing interesting to say about it.'

I have deliberately chosen reasonably clear cut cases here as the intention is to get students to recognise that they need to choose interesting words or phrases that are worthy of analysis. There are obviously going to be words that *may* be worthy of analysis, but I am focusing on the easiest discriminations first. Two of the over-arching theoretical ideas from Direct Instruction support this decision: firstly, we should teach easy skills before harder ones, and secondly, consistent instances should be taught before exceptions.

LESSONS 2, 3, 4

In these next few lessons, the teacher should follow a very similar process to lesson one except with a different set of examples for each lesson. While these examples should focus on the same specific types of 'zoom in' (a word/a phrase/two separate words that are to be combined to strengthen a line of argument), they should have a different content focus each lesson. They could focus on a different character, be from a different part of the text or even come from a different text altogether. If we are to teach to the general case, ensuring that students learn a skill that can be generalised, we need to present a sufficient range of examples. If we only present a limited range of examples, the danger is that students will incorrectly infer that the concept is limited to the instances that they have experienced.

While the examples in lesson one had a prompt arrow linking the zoomed in word or phrase with the quotation that it came from, this prompt could now be removed.

LESSON 5 STEP 1

While earlier lessons involved the teacher presenting examples to the students, these lessons should see students completing examples that have been started by the teacher.

The teacher can begin by writing a sentence with an embedded quotation:

Tiresias explains that 'stubbornness brands you for stupidity-pride is a crime' because he wants Creon to recognize he is at fault.

The teacher can then give students further practice on choosing words worthy of analysis.

TEACHER PRESENTATION. Tiresias explains that 'stubbornness brands you *for* stupidity-pride is a crime' because he wants Creon to recognise he is at fault.

Teacher: 'Can I Zoom in on this word? No. How do I know? Because there is *nothing interesting* to say about it.'

STUDENT TEST SEQUENCE. Like in lesson one, student responses should ideally be choral, allowing students to maximise the amount of practice that they complete.

Tiresias explains that 'stubbornness *brands* you for stupidity-pride is a crime' because he wants Creon to recognise he is at fault.

Teacher: 'Your Turn: Can I Zoom in on this word?'
Students: 'Yes.'
Teacher: 'How do I know?'

Students: 'Because I can say something interesting about it.'
Teacher: 'What can you say that is interesting?'

The teacher can then use this final question as an opportunity for individual students to give interpretations and analysis. The teacher should insist that a student expresses their ideas using the same language that they will be expected to use in their writing as well as *narrating* the punctuation: this maximises student practice whilst allowing the teacher to make precise and swift corrections with regards to accuracy.

Example student response: The word *quotation marks* brands *quotation marks* has connotations of pain as if Creon's decision is causing him to suffer.

After listening to the oral example, students can write their own, zooming in on the same word. Because of the restrictive nature of the task – all students will produce something very similar – feedback can be precise. The teacher can either use their own model or another student's work to give feedback, asking students to compare what they have produced with the model in order to check the accuracy of their constructions.

LESSON 5 STEP 2

The teacher can then present a series of additional examples, covering a broad range of structures and containing opportunities to practice all forms of zooming in (one word/one phrase/two separate words to be combined). While earlier instructional sequences had prompts and opportunities to practice choosing an interesting word, this and later practice sequences should see students making choices themselves in the absence of visual prompts, fading support so that students gradually learn to complete the skill independently.

Here are two possible examples:

Tiresias warns Creon that 'Great hatred rises against you – cities in tumult' in order to make Creon aware of the ramifications of his obstinacy.

Creon is 'poised once more on the razor edge of fate' because of the difficult decision he has to make.

Students could then be asked to copy each example and add in a second sentence that zooms in on a word or phrase. These are completion problems as students are only being asked to complete some of the steps.

LATER LESSONS

This skill could then be integrated with other skills and students could be asked to complete further practice activities similar to those described in Chapter 7.

Once students have become accurate and fluent, 'Zoom in' should be included as a success criteria in increasingly wider writing, beginning with isolated paragraph practice. Eventually, this prompt should be removed.

GENERAL POINTS

- Do not expect them to use 'Zoom In' in a paragraph or more extended writing until they are able to do it accurately and independently at a sentence level.
- Success rate should be continually high at each stage (70%–80% correct for all students).
- If it is lower, maybe you need to provide more scaffolding, give more examples or more back a stage on the I-WE-YOU continuum.

SKILL 4: MULTIPLE INTERPRETATIONS

WHY TEACH IT?

Developing more than one interpretation about a specific textual reference or piece of evidence demonstrates a critical perspective: in depth analysis considers and explores multiple viewpoints, building an argument and resulting in detailed, exploratory responses.

WHAT TO TEACH?

Perhaps the simplest way that students can produce multiple interpretations is by producing analysis that has consecutive interpretations within it. Novice students often produce writing that offers only one interpretation for each textual reference and the initial job of the teacher may be to prompt them to produce additional ideas for each piece of evidence, helping students to make their writing more developed and ensuring that each textual reference is examined and discussed in sufficient detail.

HOW TO TEACH MULTIPLE INTERPRETATIONS

The teacher writes something like this:

> Candy tells George that Curley's wife 'got the eye' because he thinks that she is promiscuous. His comment could also demonstrate his misogyny because he sees women as a threat and something to distrust.

The teacher can then present a second example (a completion problem) with prompts about what to include

Candy calls Curley's wife 'a tart' because...

- Include *flirtatious*
- Include *derogatory*
- Include *patriarchy*

The bullet pointed prompts can help students to understand what their next steps are and the worked example can be used by students as an analogy so that they understand what is required.

Once students become proficient at changing the prompts into short pieces of analytical writing, the teacher can then ask the students to generate ideas themselves.

After students are able to create analysis that contains a number of successive interpretations, they can be taught to apply some specific sentence structures like these:

- Not only.........but
- Even though/Despite

Teaching the 'not only...but' construction allows students to refine their ability to express complimentary perspectives when responding to texts. Additionally, this construction lends itself well to rhetorical or transactional writing.

LESSON 1: STAGE 1

Teacher writes an example (The 'I' Stage):

> Macbeth says 'let not light see my black and deep desires'. *Not only* has he decided to commit a heinous crime, *but* he has also decided to hide it.

The teacher can then label the example, drawing attention to the 'not only...but' construction. It is important to draw attention to the reversal of the subject and auxiliary verb here which has the form of a question (Not only *has he* decided).

Here are some possible questions that the teacher could ask about the worked example:

- Read out the first interpretation
- Read out the second one
- Which words from the quotation are explained by the first interpretation?
- What does the word 'deep' mean? What are the connotations of the word 'black' here?
- Which words from the quotation are explained by the second interpretation?

The teacher could then ask students to precisely copy the example into their books. Students will then be able to use this initial worked example as an analogy when completing the next stage.

LESSON 1: STAGE 2

The teacher writes half an answer. This is a completion problem:

> Lady Macbeth says that Macbeth 'is to full o'the'milk of human kindness'. Not only

The teacher should write until 'not only' and then stop. Stopping just before the reversal of the subject and auxiliary (Not only *does this*...) is important as it allows students to practice this potentially confusing aspect of the construction when they give oral responses, which, unlike written responses, can be immediately corrected if necessary. Students can be asked for ideas and interpretations and the teacher can then ask a range of students to orally complete the half written example. With really weak classes, the teacher may want to give a number of oral examples themselves before asking for student responses. After a number of students have orally completed the completion problem, all students can be asked to complete it in writing. The teacher can then circulate, offering support to those who need it and to look for a perfect piece of work to show under the visualiser. This can then be used to give feedback to all students: 'this example has a reversed verb form, check that yours does. This example has a comma before "but", check that yours does'. If it is clear that the success rate is really high, then students can be asked to do independent massed practice.

LESSON 1: STAGE 3

INDEPENDENT MASSED PRACTICE. In the initial stages of massed practice, students can be given 'problems' with prompts, ensuring that they know what to write about. Yes, student responses here will be very similar, but the purpose of these initial restrictive practice activities is to practice the form of the 'Not only… but' construction. In the absence of prompts, many students may stumble over their lack of ideas, precluding them from ever practising the desired construction. Later practice activities in later lessons would see these prompts removed.

Lady Macbeth says 'come you spirits unsex me here.'
Include

• Male power
• Witches

With this initial prompted practice activity, the teacher should give an oral example that demonstrates how to turn the notes ('strength of man'/'witches') into proper analytical sentences:

LM says 'come you spirits unsex me here'. Not only does she want the strength of a man because she lives in a patriarchal society and was expected to be subservient, but she also uses the language of the witches, making her seem sinister.

The teacher can then ask for students to give oral responses. The notes ('strength of man'/'witches') are deliberately short so that there are a number of ways to complete the activity. If the notes were more detailed, there would be fewer possible responses and students would do less cognitive processing when converting them into proper analysis.

After this initial walk through, students could then be asked to complete a number of similar activities themselves:

Duncan says 'this castle hath a pleasant seat'.

Include:

- Dramatic irony
- Vulnerable/oblivious

Lady Macbeth wants Macbeth to 'look like the innocent flower but be the serpent underneath'

Include:

- 'Stars hide your fires let not light see my black and deep desires'
- Ready for regicide

Again, feedback can be given through showing a perfect student response and giving comments like:

- My/Student X's work starts with a Capital...check that yours does
- My work has quotation marks around the evidence..............check that yours does
- My sentence makes sense... check that yours does
- My interpretations fit the evidence and comment on it... check that yours does.
- My 'Not only... but' has a comma before 'but'... check that yours does
- My sentence ends with a full stop...check that yours does.

Giving feedback like this is much more efficient than written marking. It is also immediate, thereby preventing errors from being learnt and misconception going unchallenged.

LESSONS 2, 3 AND 4

Students should be given more practice using models that contain the steps needed, like in 'Lesson 1 Stage 3'.

LESSONS 5, 6 AND 7

The utility of the 'Not only...But' construction can be broadened to include examples that fit 'rhetoric' and other texts. These examples should also demonstrate that the expression can be used without evidence or textual references. We should present the widest range of possible examples to students so that their understanding of what is being taught is made as broad as possible. Limited examples will result in limited understanding.

The teacher should present a broader range of examples, perhaps like these:

- Not only is regicide a heinous crime, it was sacrilegious too, offending God Himself.
- Not only did Priestley believe that the upper classes were selfish, but he also wanted society to change and become more equal.

- Not only was King James interested in the supernatural, but he also wrote a book about witches called 'Demonology'.
- Not only do school uniforms look terrible, but they stifle our individuality.

Using the examples above as analogies, students can then complete examples like these:

- Not only does Sheila regret her actions, but...
- As a lower class woman, not only is Eva destitute, but she...
- Not only does Lady Macbeth subvert the conventions of femininity, but she...
- Not only do phones provide a faster way to study, but...

LESSONS 8, 9 AND 10

While lessons 1–4 involved students using prompts to help them know what to write about, at this point these prompts can be removed.

While lessons 5–7 involved students completing 'not only...but' sentences that can be applied in persuasive writing, in these later lessons, they can be given broad topic headings instead. The teacher can then ask them to produce two or three 'not only...but' constructions for each one.

Example:

Topic 1: Parents are overprotective

Not only do parents patronise teenagers by refusing to allow them sufficient freedom, but this results in resentment, causing teenagers to rebel further.

LATER LESSONS

Ask them to include 'Not only...But' in their wider writing.

GENERAL POINTS

- Do not expect them to use 'Not only...But' in paragraphs or more extended writing until they are able to do it accurately and independently at a sentence level.
- Success rate should be continually high at each stage (70%–80% correct for all students).
- If it is lower: maybe you need to provide more scaffolding, give more examples or move back a stage on the I-WE-YOU continuum.

SKILL 5: COMBINING EVIDENCE

Proficient analytical writing involves multiple pieces of evidence where arguments are sustained and developed through the addition of further textual references. Sometimes this development can take the form of several references in support of one idea; sometimes it can involve a number of sequential references that contribute to and develop a line of argument; alternatively, subsequent pieces of evidence can be judiciously added in order to subtly demonstrate that the ideas within the argument are closely matched to the text itself.

WHAT TO TEACH?

Here are some examples with commentary:

1. An example of multiple bits of evidence that contribute to a single point:

   > Priestley uses dramatic irony to undermine Birling's close minded views on the world through phrases such as 'the Germans don't want war' and referring to the titanic as 'unsinkable.'

   In this example, the use of two quotations potentially provides a more substantiated argument. It also demonstrates that the writer is able to notice patterns – in this case both Birling's habit of pompous pontification as well as Priestley's frequent usage of dramatic irony. The ability to collate and combine evidence is dependent on two variables: the amount of text that you are using as your evidence base as well as the depth of knowledge that you have of the text. If you set aside the relative complexity of the language contained within a text – Shakespeare is almost always going to be harder than Priestley for students – it is often harder to collate evidence from across an entire text than it is from two sentences, one speech or one page. The former requires knowledge of far more content. The narrower the source, the easier it is to see patterns; the wider the source, the harder it is to do so.

2. An example of multiple bits of evidence that sustain an argument: each piece complements the one that precedes it, building and developing an argument across a paragraph.

   > Tempted by the witches prophecy, Macbeth seems torn and conflicted by their words, exclaiming 'cannot be ill, cannot be good'. It is as if he desires the throne but recognises that to achieve it, he would need to commit the worst crime imaginable: regicide. When he says 'whose murder yet is but fantastical', the word 'yet' foreshadows the upcoming crime. Macbeth has very quickly moved from being intrigued by the witches' language to a position of certainty where Duncan's murder seems inevitable. Perhaps Shakespeare is exploring the power of greed and how hubris can quickly dominate a character's judgement.

   In this example, the writer is using pieces of evidence sequentially, each building upon the previous and each contributing to the same chain of argument. In this case, the writer is analysing Macbeth's initial reactions to the witches equivocal language and commenting upon the malign influence of hubris.

3. Evidence in explanation:

   > Birling is an Upper Class man who revels at the idea of 'lower costs and higher prices', a selfish notion that conveys Priestley's argument that the rich exploited the lower classes and treated them as *cheap labour.*

He has passed the point of turning back and is in 'blood stepped in so far' that his reign causes Scotland to suffer *'under a hand accursed'*.

Enfield, like all the upper class men, is singularly focused on his own reputation; he avoids discussion and does not pry into the lives of others because 'asking a question is like starting a stone', a statement that conveys his fear of gossip and his desire to avoid *'disgrace'*.

In these three examples, the final italicised quotation is an example of 'evidence in explanation'. This approach to using evidence is slightly different as, instead of helping to substantiate or develop and argument, it is being used to justify an argument. When using evidence in this way, the quotation will often come at the end of a line of reasoning, demonstrating that the ideas and interpretations are closely matched to the text itself. If a line of reasoning ends with a quotation – or has one embedded within its final conjecture – then it reads as if the ideas are defensible, lending them a certain credence and making them easier for a reader to accept (Table 11.8).

Table 11.8 Evidence uses

Type of evidence use	Form	Purpose
1. Multiple quotations in support of one single point	Ev+Ev+Ev=idea	To substantiate
2. Sequential quotations in a chain of argument	Ev+Idea+Ev+Idea=Big Idea	To substantiate AND to sustain or develop
3. Evidence in explanation	Ev+Idea=Ev	To justify

Successful analytical writing treads a narrow line between the need for perceptive and interesting interpretation – essentially the input of the reader – and the need to ensure that these interpretations are based upon textual evidence. If it sways too far from the text, then it can become baseless, absurd or even just plain wrong; if it is swamped with excessive quotations, then analysis and interpretation find no room to breathe. A successful essay will achieve this fine balance. It will – to use the language of mark schemes – contain the 'judicious use of precise references to support interpretation' and hopefully will avoid the repetitive chaining of PEEL paragraphs where the monotony of the restrictive and clunky structure diminishes the overall quality of the writing. In the absence of a PEEL type structure, students are freer to use evidence more flexibly and creatively.

HOW TO TEACH IT?

If you are teaching students to combine evidence, an effective way is to write live in front of the class, so that you are able to make your thought processes and choices explicit to the students. If you turn back to Chapter 7, the section on modelling explains the importance of 'Model and Describe' (Lemov et al., 2012) and a similar approach would be ideal here too.

SUMMARY

- Paragraph centred approaches to analytical writing that have a fixed order can result in predictable, formulaic writing. Once students become more proficient, these methods can impede their ability to progress further.
- Teaching specific components that students develop, adapt and combine in different ways can help them develop the sophistication of their analytical writing.
- Instructional sequences that span many lessons are an efficient way to teach students such components.

REFERENCES

Engelmann, S. (2017). *Successful and confident students with direct instruction*. Eugene, OR: NIFDI Press.

Lemov, D., Woolway, E., & Yezzi, K. (2012). *Practice perfect*. San Francisco, CA: Jossey Bass.

Watkins, C. L., & Slocum, T. A. (Summer 2003). *The components of direct instruction in Journal of Direct Instruction* (p. 78). California State University, Stanislaus and Utah State University.

INDEX